The Dove Shall Fly

A Texas Revolution Trilogy

sequel to *Those Bones at Goliad*

Judith Austin Mills

"A sprawling novel focuses on the burgeoning revolution in 19th-century Texas

The characters explore questions of Manifest Destiny and slavery as they contend with war and shifting alliances, keeping the narrative grounded in history while addressing topics relevant to contemporary readers... deftly written and well researched...

...a substantial piece of thoughtful historical fiction."
—*Kirkus Reviews*

Other books by Judith Austin Mills
- *How Far Tomorrow: Remembering the Georgia Battalion in Texas* (Plain View Press, 2011)
- *Accidental Joy: a streak of poetry* (Plain View Press, 2014)
- *Those Bones at Goliad: a Texas Revolution Novel* (Plain View Press, 2015)

The Dove Shall Fly

A Texas Revolution Trilogy

Sequel to *Those Bones at Goliad*

Judith Austin Mills

Plain View Press, LLC   www.plainviewpress.net
1101 W 34th Street, Suite 404 Austin, TX 78705

Copyright © 2018 Judith Austin Mills. All rights reserved under International and Pan-American Copyright Conventions. No part of this book may be reproduced or distributed in any form or by any means, or stored in a data base or retrieval system, without written permission from the author. All rights, including electronic, are reserved by the author and publisher.

ISBN: 978-1-63210-036-8
Library of Congress Control Number: 2018939775

Cover art: *Primal Rhapsody* by Gary Pahl
Maps of Texas and Southern Region by Karen Boudreaux
Cover design by Pam Knight

Note: This book is a work of fiction. While people and events connected to the Texas Revolution and broader history were researched for reasonable accuracy, all characters are fleshed out according to the author's imagination. For authenticity, many names and dates included are those about which historians mostly agree. The author claims no special knowledge of any portrayed individual's heart or everyday actions.

for
First Sergeant Francis Marion Hunt of Georgia
and his cousin Joseph Stovall
whose Texas Revolution service inspired this undertaking

and for
James Peter Trezevant,
a Georgia Battalion survivor,
who reached Houston's army in the days before San Jacinto
and rose to brevet major by the end of 1836

Acknowledgments

Since starting my first Texas Revolution novel in 2010, I've been indebted to archivists who keep historical records easy to access online. After finishing How Far Tomorrow and Those Bones at Goliad, I looked for new links one day and was astounded to find a beautifully researched and presented site on another volunteer in the Georgia Battalion. This third novel would never have been undertaken had not descendants of James Peter Trezevant remembered their own valiant ancestor. Direct relative Robert W. Trezevant, with input from Richard Allen of the extended family, maintains a superb website on J.P.Trezevant, who rose from private to brevet major in 1836. The extraordinary account of his service in the independence fight captivated me immediately.

While thanking Trezevants for documenting their ancestor's role, I should state that my understanding of Colonel Juan Seguin is grounded in that native Texan's autobiography. Taking the time to recall his participation the 1836 revolution, he provided readers over 180 years later with thorough details and a unique voice.

Special thanks to Eddie M. Garcia, Community Services Director of Pflugerville, Texas. His information about a search along the Brazos River for cannon shot discarded by Santa Anna shaped my view of the Mexican general's confidence before San Jacinto.

I also want to credit a nineteenth-century doctor whose poem gave me the title for this third novel. Only weeks after the Goliad executions in 1836, "Texas and Liberty" appeared in the Augusta Sentinel. Dr. Thomas Holly Shivers' refrain, "The dove shall fly to thee" must have comforted many bereaved battalion families. The wording has stayed with me during this nine-year undertaking.

For this cover, I am indebted to long-time friend and artist Gary Pahl. My thanks again to Texas artist Karen Boudreaux for use of her artwork in my first two covers and for her hand-drawn maps.

Finally, Plain View Press deserves my gratitude. Following the loss in 2010 of PVP's originator, Pam Knight took on all press commitments, and she has been the most supportive and dedicated publisher any writer could wish for. I'd be remiss in not thanking family and friends for their encouragement, especially my mother and husband and the members of Shoal Creek Writers.

When James Peter Trezevant returned to the United States as a brevet major after the Texas Revolution, his mother asked the twenty-one-year-old to have his portrait painted in his uniform. A New Orleans artist produced this miniature in 1837. In later years, JPT's sister Charlotte passed it to his widow in Louisiana. The painting is now housed in the Louisiana State Museum in New Orleans.

Contents

Acknowledgments		6
Truth in the Telling		11

In This Forgotten Spot   13

Chapter 1	Scattered Angels	15
Chapter 2	Long Lullaby	28
Chapter 3	Tendrils	43
Chapter 4	A Day of Reversals	54
Chapter 5	The Approach of Thunder	67
Chapter 6	What's in a Name?	80
Chapter 7	Along Comes Chaos	99
Chapter 8	Farewell, Light Heart	116
Chapter 9	No Way But Forward	137
Chapter 10	The Shortest Dreams of Mercy	151
Chapter 11	Riding the Aftermath	155

The Hum of Elegies   163

Chapter 12	A Hard Path Home	165
Chapter 13	Long Shadows	182
Chapter 14	Remains of a Battalion	199
Chapter 15	Word of Mouth	217

Celestial Fire   233

Chapter 16	Past Meets Prologue—New Orleans, 1839	235
Chapter 17	To See What He Could See—Near Seguin, 1856	249
Chapter 18	Again at a Riverbank—Austin, Texas, 1869	268
Chapter 19	Blessing in a Bottle—Yucatan, 1726	286

Afterword	293
Sources	297
About the Author	299

Map of Texas, 1836

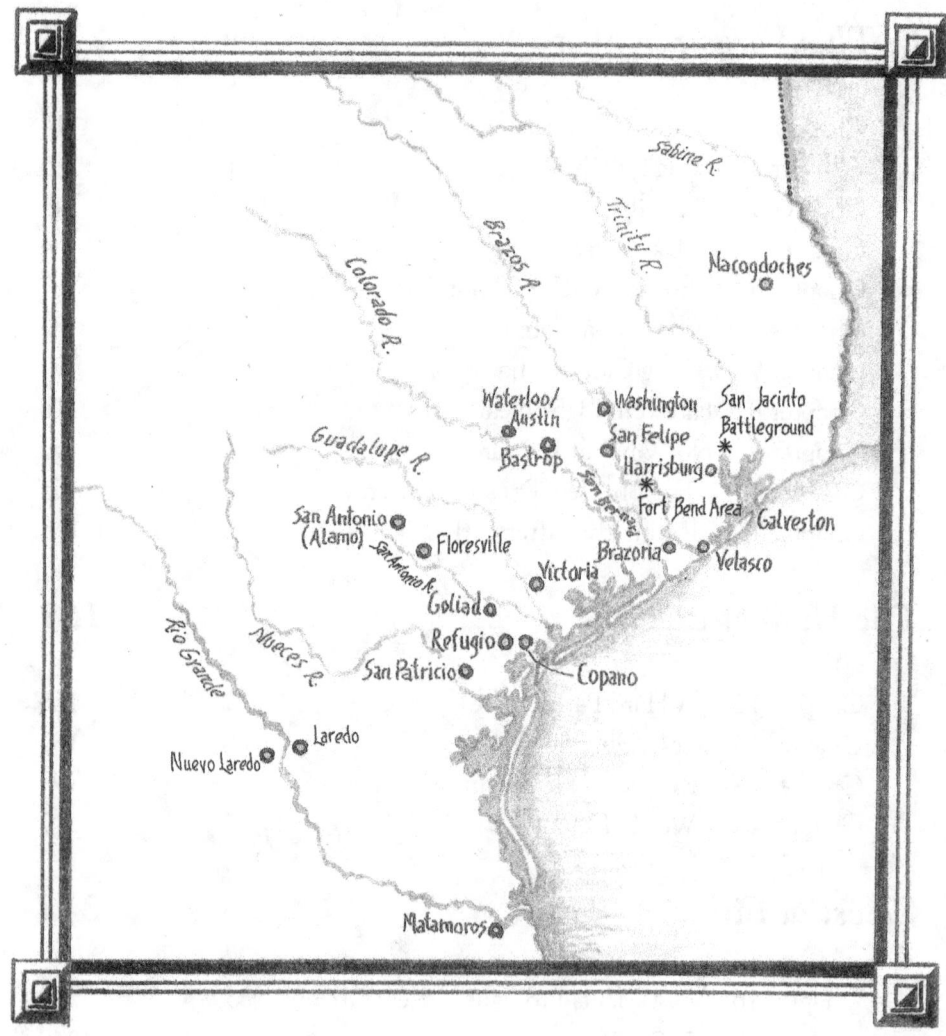

Truth in the Telling

Five weeks after the Alamo's fall, thousands of panicked settlers rushed to the Brazos River to evade Santa Anna. Women and children and elders discarded cumbersome belongings, though some marshalled their slaves. Husbands and older sons with General Houston edged toward battle or retreat.

Only a fortnight earlier, over three hundred and forty American recruits were executed at Goliad

This is in tribute to two independence fighters whose service won them little or no fame. This is also the story of a woman whose color made liberty more elusive. However they piece together their memoirs, their dark days near San Jacinto's battlefield stay central.

Map of Southern U.S. Region, 1835

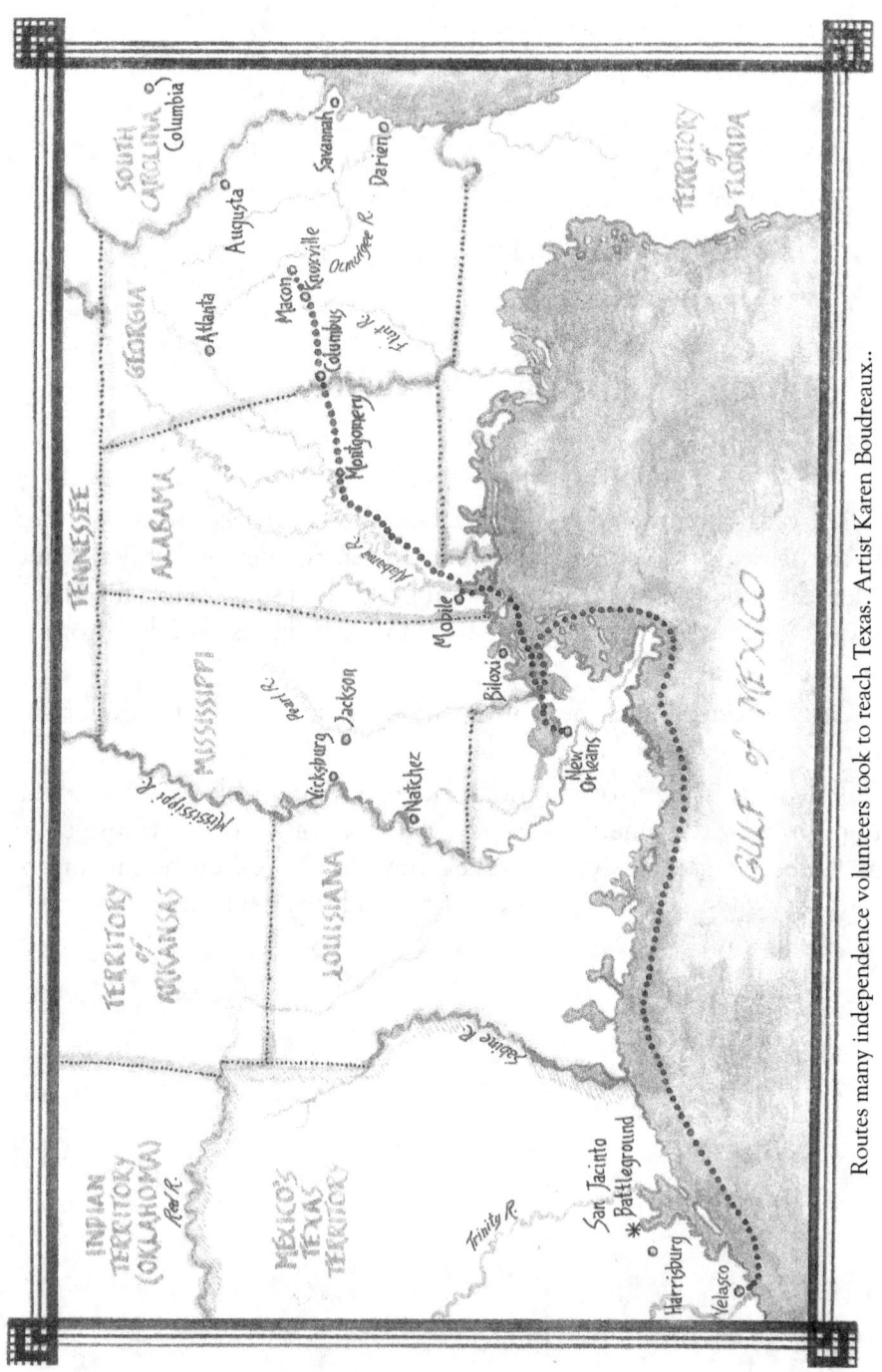

Routes many independence volunteers took to reach Texas. Artist Karen Boudreaux.

In This Forgotten Spot

Chapter 1   Scattered Angels

Yarico thought the clamor was subsiding. She could tell the rush of the wild river from the noisy throng at the bend a mile away. The other sound, she realized, was only her ragged heartbeat. There was no separating the smell of damp earth and horse dung from the pungent odor of her own body. Within arm's reach, Adeline and Aunt Maggie slept as if dead. Nearby lay the surviving Wainwrights. Downpours along the escape trail had washed distinguishing color from their clothing, but the stink of fear adhered.

Just south on the opposite bank of the Brazos, they had all witnessed crowds charging wildly at two ferries. If Santa Anna remained heartless after the slaughter at the Alamo and at Goliad, he might brutalize a thousand wailing children led by females and old men. But as far as the Harper women and Mrs. Wainwright knew, the Mexican general had yet not caught up with any panicked colonists. Only a dull groan came now from downriver. Most at the Fort Bend landings must have struggled on across, as Yarico and the six with her had managed after backtracking upstream.

The river itself quieted some in the hour after both families reached the eastern shore. A tangle of branches stanching the torrent earlier made crossing on horseback possible, but afterward something as big as a wagon pounded its way through. The angry river came crashing along behind. No one with Yarico heard if splintering boards or screams followed. Now, the water flowed more solemnly, and the rumble of any approaching army would warn them. The horses tethered to a nearby desert willow stood sentry, too spent to take an interest in April grass.

Only the third sound tormented the Harper woman as she kept watch. Her own pulse made her put her hands to her ears.

Immediately, she slumped down onto her side with her dank shawl as blanket and pillow. She felt consciousness dropping into a dark well, but the voice of responsibility nagged. She reassured herself that the girl and her aunt still curled against each other. They lay mostly hidden among a grove of mesquite. The other children and their mother still wrapped themselves together. None in the group had strength to trek farther inland.

Dread nudged Yarico back into wakefulness and when she suddenly sat up, the tan horse jerked its head in her direction. Even if the two families outran the revolution, it would be miles and years before any of them stopped dreaming of tiny Wendell, the Wainwright infant buried on the edge of the northern trail. Instinctively the woman on watch clenched her fists and dug her fingernails into the palms of her hands to keep from drifting off again.

"Is it time…time to…has something…" Adeline was mumbling, but she never opened her eyes.

"Shhh, nothing happened…everyone's all right. You go on and sleep now. Shhh, we'll just stay here a while."

Upon reaching the shore earlier, the thirteen-year-old let herself sob, and Yarico, too, had surrendered to emotion. This time, she steered her thoughts away from their sorry state and from the baby whose suffering was over. War took no more heed of normal fare than a mad bull took of a picket fence. A baby, after its last breath, could be laid to rest in mud. A black woman, who had known only domestic life in Georgia before the journey to Texas, could take on safeguarding six white folks.

It was Yarico who'd readied a musket against marauders a fortnight ago, with the Wainwrights as well as Adeline and Aunt Maggie obeying her quiet commands. No one suspected the paper hidden away in her boot and the signature saying she was nobody's property. Never mind that Santa Anna, for his own purposes, had abolished slavery in Mexico months before. Yarico knew now that she could steady a firearm to defend the other two Harper women no matter what document or flag was waved overhead.

"So," she murmured to herself. She lifted her hands to her ears a moment longer. "In the beginning, this right here is what freedom feels like."

Her next thought centered on a more urgent necessity. Hunger would soon rouse the others from their stupor. Some fistfuls of dried peas remained wrapped in a kerchief at Yarico's waist. She judged it safe to soak the peas in river water. They might be tender enough by nightfall to chew, with a portion left for the next morning. Tomorrow, the seven traveling together would trudge on in the direction of the Louisiana border.

When she stood up, she remembered that her feet had gone numb. Her knees felt ready to slip askew. As she waited for a dark dizziness to pass, words came to mind, but her lips lost their connection to her brain.

So, at first, this right here is what dying feels like.

A terrible possibility occurred to her, that she and Adeline might be the lone survivors of the river crossing. When vertigo faded, she bent over Mrs. Wainwright's children to check for life signs. Susannah's chest rose and fell. The mother's younger two sucked their thumbs. When Yarico moved nearer Little Abel, she was surprised that the noise he made did not stir the others. During the ride across the Brazos, he and Cassandra had each worn an empty pail as a hat, leaving arms free to hug the adult holding the reins. Easing the tin-ware up from the ground, the alert woman tried not to let the handles click. She was encouraged when her feet obeyed and moved silently. Surely there wouldn't be a Mexican army shouting threats from across the water when she reached the bank.

With the rain letting up, no further surge of floodwater was likely, but halfway back to the swollen river, an entirely unexpected sight brought her to a halt. A large oleander bush flourished in the repetitive landscape. Yarico thought its dense red blooms might be a vision from the first home she remembered, Savannah, where specimens were shipped in to adorn the coastal setting. She at first thought desperation might be warping her senses. A decaying cabin timber embedded in the clay nearby, however, suggested the flowering shrub had been brought to this site years ago to grace a solitary dwelling. Who would have transported the exotic species to Texas territory, she wondered—a family from New Orleans or from as far away as Florida? She shook off the rest of the mystery about the survival of red blossoms. She dislodged from her mind the disappearance of the first newcomers who'd tended their hopes in this spot.

Yarico felt such a distinctive landmark on the way back should prevent her getting lost and separated from her own people. She found it hard, though, to tamp down worry.

"Any slave between here and Macon summons this much pluck without blinking," she chided herself. *Look at the work before you. See you've got no choice. Make every movement a prayer.* She smiled to think how her charge, Adeline, used to pull on her boots before dawn back near Macon and trot up the hill behind their vegetable patch to witness first sunlight. "Jesus help me do right by Delphine's only daughter."

When Yarico reached the riverbank, her feet stopped and she imagined the water rebuking her for such loyalty. In the middle of frantic exodus, what fool taken for a slave would not hunt for the opportunity to run off? The lone woman held her shoulders stiffly and answered without speaking.

Who else in this wide world loves me but Delphine's child?

From the brushy bank, she looked up and down the swollen Brazos. Before making it to Texas, her only river experience was the trip up the Ocmulgee with Delphine Harper and Mr. Harper. The weeklong venture on flatboats from Savannah to Darien to Macon was enough to make the dark-skinned traveler shake her head about any such travel in the future. Raised as a sister rather than a servant, Yarico would have guessed the bride's aversion to boats.

"I've seen enough water to last a life time."

"Then we wasted time packing our cups and glasses," Daniel Harper teased his new wife. The three sat on a cotton bale near their sleeping tent, and the afternoon sky drew their attention from the current for a while. Thinking about the ordeal from Yarico's perspective, Delphine tugged the edge of her companion's cape so she could whisper.

"Your first people must have had fortitude we can't imagine."

"I expect they knew complaints went ignored." Few Georgia citizens would have waited for a black woman to finish her thoughts. "Any so weak they died crossing the ocean got thrown overboard, I don't doubt."

"Delphine says your ancestors most likely came from royalty." The two women looked at each other.

"The gospel according to Madame Martin!" Delphine and Yarico spoke almost in unison and smiled in spite of the somber topic. Mr. Harper was used to their shared amusement. He had no inclination to stifle his wife's early memories.

"I was likely kin to a freeman well-known in Saint Domingue," Yarico went on. "Revered more as a god than royalty by those in worst bondage."

Delphine reached to pat the younger woman at her side. Her husband took an interest in history and ancestry. She patted his hand, too, before explaining more.

"It's likely General Toussaint Louverture was Yarico's grandfather," she whispered. "Or great-uncle." This was fact according to the widow Martin, who'd fled turmoil in the French islands with the infant trusted to her care. An informed Southerner, Mr. Harper certainly knew of Haiti's black general who had led his people in revolt. He was surprised that his wife and her companion had been able to keep that secret even from him.

Their conversation, however, was bordering on the very reason the trio needed to flee Savannah. Their object was to remove themselves a safe distance from family involved with the slave market there. Some Pagnol relatives were no more sympathetic to Yarico's elevated status in the family than Harpers were. The whole city, if not the entire Southern coast, was roiled by fear of uprisings on plantations. An elder uncle disapproved vehemently of Yarico's preferential treatment.

"Shame on you for the female domestic you allow your wife to keep close like family…already with an education fit for Napoleon's empress…" The Harper uncle glared over the rims of his glasses. "That's what gave that black devil in French territory the gall to rise up in Saint Domingue. Against his former master who trusted him with learning in the first place! That black devil Louverture!"

A handful of people in Savannah knew of the little slave girl the Pagnols had inherited. Though there was some compassion among friends for the couple whose only daughter would have been lonely otherwise, none knew the other child Yarico could read in two languages by the time she was six. Before Delphine was brought into the parlor occasionally to demonstrate those same skills for guests, she was reminded how to field questions about her companion.

"If they ask about Yarico, just say *she's passable help in the kitchen.*"

The lone woman stood now at the edge of the Brazos and tried to remember how Delphine's giggle would cut off when she was too tickled to catch her breath.

"I turned out passable and then some with a needle and thread," she spoke aloud to the river, "but Delphie used to say I was no more gifted in the kitchen than a fence post."

Well, she went on thinking, *we Harper women have managed to provide our own edibles so far.* But she predicted that soaked peas wouldn't much assuage anyone's hunger. She let flit through her mind the crumb cake that Rodina Kolar had fixed for trail neighbors weeks ago in the primitive, northern encampment. Yarico steered herself away, however, from further recollections of civility or generosity. The Alamo and Goliad had dashed all hope of a relatively bloodless revolution. With menfolk heading off to join Sam Houston's army, advancing Mexican forces left settler families no choice afterward but desperate flight.

No drifting forward or into the past, she thought. *Fill these pails with water right quick, you, and get back to your people.*

As she neared the brush at the river's edge, the image of a sinking raft came to her nevertheless. They'd witnessed a dozen chained slaves go down in the rushing torrent. *Where were the bodies now?* she had to ask herself. *Downstream only another two miles? Making a thud against one another in the silt at the coast? Already out into the yawning gulf? Edging already upon the widely sown Antilles? Washing ashore in Haiti?*

"Let me just fill these pails," Yarico spoke to the Brazos. "I'll just dip these pails and be on my way."

She had spotted a curve in the shoreline where water appeared no more than knee-deep. She stepped through a swath of blue wildflowers and pockets of pink blossoms before easing down close to a clear eddy. Pebbles glistened on the riverbed. A flat rock the size of a spinning wheel looked a safe spot to set her boots and stockings, as well as the first pail of water while she dipped for the second. Her mind cleared somewhat as she undertook the task.

"Let me just fill my other pail." Yarico tried to lash her thoughts to the present, to the scene immediately before her. The water flowed gently into the second pail as she lowered it, but it was not easy for her to disconnect this mundane chore from the catastrophe earlier, where the wild river was complicit. Adeline had needed to jerk her elbow to make her turn away from the sinking raft of chained black people. On a lonely survival errand now, Yarico fought again to wrest her thoughts from those so cruelly drowned.

The two little girls in the Pagnol house had shared a love for poetry as they learned to read, and she imagined it was Delphine's voice speaking fresh lines to her and making her skin tingle.

> *Forsake your fear, my sister from the shore*
> *Of Saint Domingue. Your freedom loves you more.*

Yarico's feet, though they rested on smooth pebbles, had sunk a few inches into the riverbed. When she shifted position in the mud to get firmer footing, her heel brushed against something behind her, something more solid than wet-grass. Her first fear was that one of her boots must have fallen in and become waterlogged. But, no, both boots were on the stone where she'd set them. Gingerly raising her pail, she wondered if the object brushing her ankle could be a sizeable fish, though a live fish would have darted away at contact.

She turned slowly in an effort to halt another episode of dizziness. She rotated her body toward the shore, so that she could glance down.

The Dove Shall Fly

Before stepping to solid ground, she could identify the thing bobbing against her lower leg. When Yarico steadied the pail, she looked at the surface of the water and saw now what appeared to be a brown glove, too altered in shape by soaking to ever dry to a state of usefulness. It was only a ruined glove. People fleeing from the north Brazos colony, San Felipe, had flung possessions along the trail—cradles, trunks, heavy coats, heirloom bedding—whatever would lighten the load on horses and mules. Here, a ruined glove had made it into the current and across nearly to the other shore.

Back at the flat rock, Yarico was grateful that her knees could still bend sharply enough for her to sit and shove her feet into her boots. She was relieved about the clear water in both pails and the efficiency with which she had completed her errand. Adeline and Aunt Maggie were most likely still sleeping. The Wainwrights were surely as she had left them.

Instinct made her look in the direction of the bloated glove that had been partly visible at the river's surface. Its fingers, almost black from soaking, curled downward nearly submerged. Exposed now was more of the broad part meant to cover a hand. And then, at further inspection it seemed a wrist was exposed. In one horrifying second, Yarico saw that an arm was still attached to that wrist and hand! It was a dark and swollen limb, torn from a shoulder that wafted in the wet-grass just below the water's surface!

She partly stifled a scream as she recoiled, but as she ran, she lost most of the water she'd collected. She grabbed both pail handles with one hand, so that she could lift her skirt hem above the flowering perennials on the upper bank. If her brain had detached from her lips earlier, she suddenly felt her whole body operated at a singular distance from her intellect. *Make every movement a prayer*, some voice of reason cautioned her. But her boots kept thrashing through the brushy bank upriver. Her feet were still numb, while a voice inside her head chided her, *Look at the work before you! See you've got no choice!*

Her people needed her. Adeline and the girl's aunt and the Wainwright family needed to eat. They all needed water.

When she went to the edge of the Brazos again, Yarico tried to keep her mind on the simplicity of the task. With her boots still on, she crouched at a particularly shallow eddy and allowed each pail to fill. She shook her head at the pounding in her ears and shrugged off the faint stench of rust or blood. Her boots appeared to still have some sense.

They seemed determined to keep snug contact with her feet, and her feet stayed attached to her ankles. This, and the fairly clear water sloshing in the pails, was all she allowed herself to acknowledge.

She knew she had fled upstream from her first attempt to collect water, but before backtracking, she walked inland far enough that she could no longer see the river. She didn't think she could bear to catch sight of the floating arm again. She didn't want to imagine how near or far a mangled torso might be. After moving a hundred paces in the same direction the current flowed, Yarico stood facing east to visualize the way back. With any luck, she would spot a solitary oleander up ahead to the right. The distinct bush would reassure her that her people rested not too many more steps beyond.

The ground was even where she walked, and as she saw only a trickle jostling out from the pails, she could not help noticing again the profusion of wildflowers carpeting the fields off shore. After just one day without any rain, the stalks of red paintbrush righted themselves. Yellow tick-weed amassed in contrast. Pink blossoms mounded down closer to the ground, and long-stemmed white florets swayed in the breeze. Dandelion greens were edible, Yarico reminded herself, but she kept searching for the oleander with its first red blooms. She had previously recognized the shrub by its foliage, though she knew from having lived in Savannah it could also flower in pink or white—poison in any hue. A hackberry thicket to her left came into view, but beyond that, she spied the familiar blood-red bush with its mass of slender and deadly leaves.

"There you are," she said aloud, greeting the solitary shrub ahead. Relief swept through Yarico. Her arms and legs tingled, and she allowed herself to set the pails down to rest for just a minute before taking on the remainder of her round-trip. She rested her hands on her hips and wondered whether her traveling companions had missed her, or had even yet awakened. She wanted to bless the oleander for washing away the image of a ghastly glove. Was she letting herself smile for the first time in days and days? Again she spoke, "There you are."

"*Buenas tardes.*" A pistol glinted in the hand of a black-haired man stepping from the hackberry thicket. "Señorita West? Is it to me you speak?"

Yarico's smile faded instantly, but her hands froze near her apron band, and she might have looked like a cemetery statue to the soldier judging her intent. It was not difficult for her to remain mute.

"We heard some noise…from the river," the man said. He spoke with a strong Spanish accent. Underneath a fraying poncho, the red chest-panel of a Mexican uniform was visible. "No army, we did not think. But on this side of the river, you gave us worry, so—" The officer replaced the silver pistol into its holster, but when Yarico also noticed that the tooled leather strap across his chest secured a rifle or musket on his back, she felt dizziness land upon her scalp and settle in.

She shook her head in an attempt to erase the lightheadedness.

"You are not Miss West?" He seemed puzzled by her inability to speak. "*Ingles* is your language, no?" The sun directly overhead made it too warm for a poncho, and he pulled it off, slinging it over his arm while he searched for another way to put a question to the strange woman. From sweat and road grime, his blue jacket sleeves had darkened to black. "*Hablas español? Deutsch?*"

A voice in Yarico's head was telling her to say "*Ja, ja Deutsch.*" A Texas volunteer riding counter to the exodus of settlers some days earlier had reported a strange fact about Goliad. A trickle of survivors from the day of execution there swore it was true. Only a handful, one man here and another just in time from another line, had been pulled because their last name was German, because they could say "*Nein*" or "*Ja*" or "*Danke.*"

But reason was backing away from Yarico's mind. As a final command, it ordered her not to look in the direction of the oleander. A dark dizziness was overtaking her whole body, while she willed herself not to look with any alarm at the landmark bush. She sank to the damp ground, and her body folded like an old quilt. Her head landed near a tuft of pink. Sliding away from consciousness, she moved her fingers toward the petals but they were losing their color. She wanted to concentrate on them, so as not to give away the location of Delphine's beloved girl Adeline. When a heavy lid closed off every light, a faint aroma of primrose lingered and then—nothing.

As Yarico came to, the soldier with striking black hair nodded soberly to her from the other side of a small fire. The dull striped blanket he was hugging now concealed his uniform, and his attention soon returned to a third person, a young man or boy yet, lighter skinned and with matted locks that touched the shoulders of his frayed civilian jacket. His crumpled hat brim cast a shadow over his forehead and brow. From where Yarico lay, she could not tell if the younger man's eyes were blue, muted by distress, or if they were naturally gray. Heat from the fire must have distorted her vision, because his eyes looked unnaturally wide and deep, as if they had beheld too much strife to bear or seen injuries that would never heal. The fellow looked so bedraggled that Yarico thought he might have been pulled from the river not far from the bloated glove. Trying to wrest her thoughts from the image, she shuddered at the trail soot caked under her own fingernails.

"Like this," the officer said to him. The soldier in charge flexed his hands in the direction of the fire. "When your fingers remember how to work, your voice will do the same." Then he studied Yarico again as she struggled to sit up. "This woman is not the spy with information on Santa Anna."

Yarico had no idea how she had been transported to their campsite, though her aching arms suggested she'd been dragged. One of her cooking pails was positioned over the skimpy fire, but no steam rose yet, so she guessed she had not been unconscious too long. It was impossible to determine whether Adeline and Aunt Maggie, or any Wainwright, knew where she'd gone. The captive woman feared they would call her name and give themselves away.

"Soon, this makes coffee. Will you drink some?" the armed man asked her. He spoke slowly to mitigate his accent. His tone conveyed civility in spite of exhaustion. Something in his dark eyes told her that command came to him naturally. "It will look like coffee, but we have only the same grounds for three days."

Yarico did not answer. Any person of color knew when to switch off the talking and offer no proof of comprehension to people who counted themselves in charge. She sensed, though, that the other man was just as spare with words. Though the soldier kept turning to him and encouraging him to warm his hands, the younger man—maybe an American with no more history in Texas than the Harper women had—stayed silent but alert. As if reading her thoughts, the officer turned again to her and nodded. She wasn't surprised when his voice rose above the crackle of the fire.

"I am Captain Juan Seguin, señorita." The second man slightly moved his head as confirmation. She had heard the Seguin name before, but she couldn't suppress her worry that strange voices would arouse her traveling companions. She sensed that her lips were about to form words despite her apprehension.

"*Je parle...français,*" she said. "*Zuh* water," she continued in her French accent, "it will take a long boil." Both men made sounds of assent or relief, perhaps, that she could speak. A small flame of empathy glimmered. Yarico's thoughts ran on as she weighed her new predicament against the overriding catastrophe of the last fortnight. *Such sorrowful specimens. Humanity flung along the banks of the Brazos—these two, darling Adeline, and the people with us. Are a thousand more strewn out past the ferries downstream? Who has seen anything but clumps of injured angels in days and weeks?*

"I know…some French," the quiet youth said. The officer, keeping his gaze on the fire, only blinked. But something like encouragement lit his expression.

"Private Trezevant fights for Texas, like me. Santa Anna will say *pirate*, not *private*. He travels with me to find Houston's men, *mademoiselle*. That is all the French I speak, yet it was the language of my great-grandfather. Or the one before him."

"*C'est un soldat*…a soldier for Texas? For *le général*, Monsieur Houston?"

"My *compadre* has no uniform." The officer understood her doubt. "Our rebellion has no money and no time for choosing colors. No fortune of the good kind since possessing the Alamo. And then later, only tragedy at the same San Antonio mission." He struck her as a man who wore authority easily but was not given to conceit. He needed a moment to take control of his emotions, and the private looked her way.

"*J'étais*..I was…with Ward's battalion…*avec* Fannin." The gaunt man was speaking as much to himself as anyone else. His eyes went distant, Yarico noticed. *Other worldly* was the phrase she would have used to describe his countenance. Seguin, meanwhile, seemed to be weighing his next words carefully.

"If your people over there, the women and the children…" He gestured toward the bush with red blossoms. "If your people have dried beans to share," the soldier went on calmly, "we'd say *muchas gracias* for what they give us." He patted the striped blanket at his chest, and Yarico knew that the shiny pistol was still holstered underneath. "The girl with the musket, she does not want to listen to me, perhaps. She takes aim from the strange bush with flowers like blood. Can you say to her we are with the Texians? Can you say we go to meet General Houston, not to fight him?" The younger soldier was slowly grasping their new danger.

"The girl?"

"Si, amigo. Do not move, *por favor*. The musket is for me, I think, but if you stay as you sit—"

"*La fille,*" the bedraggled fellow said to Yarico. He was pointing at the bush and waiting for the woman to respond.

"*La fille.* The girl?"

"*Oui, elle,*" he answered. "*Dites-lui…*" Yarico appreciated his struggle for the next French wording. She might have guessed that the two fighters were in dire need of another horse. She had no way of knowing they lagged only slightly behind other Tejanos and three more Goliad survivors, who were already sharing saddles and riding to the north where Houston's forces had amassed. The private eventually gestured to the officer and then himself, "*Pas dangereux.* We are not *les enemies.*" Captain Seguin appeared pleased that some energy and words were coming back to the younger man.

"You, mademoiselle, you *comprendes,* I think, that we are not the enemy." He and Yarico both glanced in the direction of the oleander. "If Santa Anna finds me, he will nail me to an oak tree," he said as if to himself. "You must tell the girl that we are not the enemy. We are not dangerous."

"*Pas dangereux,*" she repeated. She kept to French as she would have secured a veil. She sensed, though, that the captain was about to make a less comforting request. Her apprehension returned, and she felt a leak dampen her underclothes.

"Now, *por favor,* tell them," the Tejano officer said to the young soldier, "This woman or the girl may choose which horse. I counted three. I am hoping they will give us that one the color of dust. But we must take a horse before the sun moves twice toward *buenas noches.* You and I, amigo, should go east soon riding at a fast walk. Houston will need some good men with horses. Tell her you can make good use of the animal they choose. It is for the revolution."

"*Notre cheval?*" Yarico asked, though she had understood quite well. She knew that even three horses were not enough to ensure the escape of the Harpers and the Wainwrights. Adeline, whose first monthly bleeding had come that very morning, would need to get off her feet and ride as often as possible. It would be a terrible risk, under any circumstances, to shed an asset as fundamental as a transport animal. A wave of dread and guilt hit Yarico. If she had only made less noise at the river. If she had only dipped her pails first at a placid eddy. These two were not Santa Anna spies, she was sure, but danger could disguise itself as it had with marauders some weeks ago. An encounter looking like a welcome at first could still usher in doom. A knot formed again in the woman's stomach, and her head began to pound.

"Only one horse. For the Alamo," Seguin said to her. "For Goliad."

"*Tout va bien,* Adeline!" Yarico called out. "I'm all right!" She felt consciousness drifting downriver, nevertheless. She fought to stay sitting upright, but the scent of primroses and urine was suddenly back. "They are not…the enemy," she said again before her thoughts swept out past the silt on the gulf shore, before they drifted out into the open waves and washed in with the breakers at old Saint Domingue.

Chapter 2   Long Lullaby

"*Non, chérie, pas les enemis.*" Madame Pagnol's husband had assured her of this many times that evening. The carriage they'd hired continued jostling over the rocky trail winding out of Haiti's southern region toward the newly conquered North. But the woman with a toddler at her side and a baby at her breast was troubled about the shifting stories her husband told road patrols. She had never heard him lie before. The last road officer to lift a torch and peer into the transport had been almost friendly about so many colors in one family. In a pocket ledger, he made brief notes—*one older blond man, one plump mulatto female, a somewhat fair child easily their own, a darker infant suckling.*

"*Bon soir, les voisins.*" Officials in their part of the island often greeted people as "neighbors."

The woman traveling slipped her hand into her husband's. They had been warned, though, not to disclose any detail about their destination. Who could tell if a stranger held secret allegiance to the island's northern sector? Only last week, an encounter with military scouts, hospitable at first, had turned deadly for a mixed couple risking the better road inland. Yellow hair could ignite raw hatred in some. The proudly independent nation of color had devolved into a realm of rebellion, deceit, and bloody reversals. The turmoil was too much for the pharmacist and his young family. A schooner was waiting offshore of Saint Marc to take a small group away from Haiti altogether.

"*Bon soir,*" Monsieur Pagnol responded. He reached past an envelope inside his vest for an identity document. "*Merci dieu* we have a torch man riding ahead to show the way. We are going but a little farther. The wave of new fever cases in Port-au-Prince is alarming. A cousin sent for us to share the family retreat until the danger passes."

The officer immediately put a handkerchief up to his face and waved the carriage on. The couple did not speak until the only light came from a flame their road guide carried near his saddle horn. Her husband's lie

The Dove Shall Fly

made her shudder. Years before, when the kind pharmacist converted to Catholicism in order to win her hand, she had cautioned him.

"God will know if your change of faith is a lie, Nicholas." Now on the primitive road tracing the coastline, Monsieur Pagnol sensed her particular anxiety.

"Oh, Desirée, *calme-toi*. Heaven will forgive a man taking every step to protect his family."

"Could you not tell them an important truth, that your profession is medical, that safe passage for *les médecins* has long been the custom in the north as well as our south."

"Up in Cap François, Henri Christophe may have already declared himself king. His triumph in the north gives him many castles for a festive coronation. Safe passage is his to decree on a whim."

"If only France had never taken away our **général**, our Toussaint—"

"Le général is perhaps who first imbued our island with a yearning for royal tradition. Henri Christophe has now risen to power by one newly popular custom—hanging white soldiers from lamp posts." This tone of cynicism was also unlike her husband. The necessity of flight, of subterfuge, had bent them both somewhat out of character. They felt ill.

"But it was Toussaint's own niece who said to me…" Madame Pagnol struggled to keep her voice from breaking down. "When Lisette gave to me her little Josephine, she said that Henri, as a king might decree… could soon declare his share of Haiti safe for any white man marrying a woman of dark skin."

"It will never be the *mélange* of color we have in the south. And who knows how long before Henri Christophe's soldiers take Port-au-Prince and put all our part of the island under his command? Neighbors will suspect and murder neighbors. Henri will not likely seek agreement with any man of my color, or approval of absolute rule. From him, I anticipate no countryman's *s'il vous plaît*."

"But she was so certain, that we can bring the little darling back, that we can bring our hero's grand-niece home again when the welcome decree of King Henri goes out—"

"Do not forget the welcome Toussaint himself got from the French captain Le Clerc." Rebellion, deceit, and deadly reversals—no one in old Saint Domingue was ignorant of the treachery used to lure General Louverture and his immediate family into a ship bound back across the Atlantic to a French prison. The horrible truth had sunk in slowly, that

Haiti's hero of independence languished and then perished impossibly far from home.

"To think there is still such peril for any left in the general's family... to think a baby could be in danger. Yet, it is the sister of Toussaint Louverture, Lisette's own mother, who will not cease her call for vengeance. Who knows if other rebels betrayed him, as she says?" It was impossible to comprehend every upheaval in their homeland. The woman looked down at the infant who peacefully nursed. "And now those she accuses threaten any of Toussaint's people left in all of Haiti? Even...*les innocents?*" She stroked the baby's smooth brow. "And yet, I cannot wish any child a life parted from its natural mother and father."

Her husband had decided not to speak of a recent rumor on the outskirts of Port-au-Prince that Lisette and Louverture's sister had already gone missing. Instead, he blurted the unthinkable.

"Better, *mon amour*, than trying to wash a worse picture from your memory—the head of our child or this Louverture baby on a pike." The apologetic pat the man gave his wife now meant that it was time to stop talking entirely. Another road patrol was up ahead. With any luck it would be an escort to the hidden cove where a schooner waited to embark in the cover of night. "It is time, I think, for you to go by your father's name, perhaps to think of a name for the baby that will agitate no one." He shook his head about the docile infant. "What was their thinking, to name her after Napoleon's wife?" The mother, with milk ready to nurse an infant not her own, began buttoning the front of her blouse. Her fingers trembled.

"So little but named for an empress, and we who were married in a Catholic ceremony...two as one in the eyes of God..."

"The Almighty is surely as sad about the deadly curse on our country as we are," Nicholas Pagnol said to her gently. "I will say you are Madame Martin, my domestic, if the ship crew asks. Their daughter Claire, some months shy of her third birthday, had hints of her father's blond hair. She smiled back at him. "We will say you are caring for my child," he went on, giving the woman's shoulder an affectionate squeeze, "and your own new baby." She knew he was right, but she could not look his way for fear of breaking into sobs.

"Is it riders from the ship, *mon cher?*" She was leaning against him, peering in the direction of the road guards conversing up ahead.

"*Pas les enemies,*" her husband reassured her. He sounded tired, and she promised herself to appear more optimistic, for his sake, about the voyage to a cluster of islands off the coast of Georgia. She would have to assume a fraudulent identity, but white men there were in no danger about how they incorporated domestic help inside their family home. They could live discreetly. There, they could survive.

○

"Madame, do you bring enough fresh water?"

"With this arm around the baby, I only have one free for a jug handle." She was with the children while her husband made official payment in the captain's berth. The stocky young sailor checking the supplies of voyagers was as dark as the newborn she cared for. His respectful inquiry made her yearn for the hometown they'd left. True, some lighter skinned citizens—even those with African ancestry— took on an air of superiority as egregious as any Dutch slave trader's. But disrespect between the shades of brown in Port-au-Prince was widely considered uncouth. Who knew if she would ever be called *madame* on the island belonging to Georgia? If her husband's hospitable cousin still operated an indigo exchange there, perhaps. *Desirée Pagnol* she was in the sight of God—but she was tutoring herself to answer as *Madame Martin*.

She put all trust in her husband. He had looked pale going down below to the captain's desk. Perhaps he'd been chasing from his mind the image of pikes and the inert heads of children. Not realizing the sailor still stood close by, the mother shuddered to see her two-year-old smiling up at him. With his broad forehead and tame eyebrows, he looked more kin to the newborn than she did.

"*Normalement*, it takes as little as four days, with friendly winds and a calm sea." The dark man in uniform looked up at the first stars as if he could read how the voyage from Saint Domingue to the island Tybee, near Savannah, would go. "Another time it took fourteen." He kept to himself recent reports of a white family that had left a note in their dinghy at the end of two weeks. They had spotted a shore and were going to try to swim for the coast, using a bundle of cork mats to help them float. They had never been seen again.

"The food supplies worry me, madame. But water will be of greatest necessity."

He and the captain had already sized up the family's overall chances— too pale and blond for Haiti's changes, too dark for American attitudes. They would call the man's wife *Madame Martin*, if that was what the decent man wished. Both seafarers agreed that the pharmacist was too old for strenuous escape on the open ocean. If God regularly stepped in and gave umbrage to good men, well, the Almighty would surely spare such a gentleman, even with skin and hair so absent of color. But where in the roiling world, they had shrugged, could one point to divine intervention as common?

"You will be wanting food by the time you make the Georgia islands," the concerned sailor said again. "But want of water, madame, can drive the strongest person mad." He was repeating himself but the agreeable baby enchanted him. The infant's eyes had opened wide in the direction of his voice, though he supposed the newborn could not see much clearly even in daylight. How could the *café-au-lait* mother and her light-haired husband produce a child with almost ebony skin? If the infant were not her own, he thought as in prayer, shouldn't heaven step in and preserve such compassion? Perhaps it is only the moonlight on the blond *monsieur*, making his skin look so pale.

Two days into their sea travel, it was clear that the pharmacist Nicholas Pagnol was ill. Désirée made a pallet with her travel satchel for the infant, but whenever she dabbed at her husband's feverish brow with a handkerchief, their toddler daughter whimpered as if she were the one fighting away chills and nausea. Twice, when the infant needed to nurse, the considerate sailor walked Claire, around the deck. The family had already been ousted from the sleeping berths below, crowded with nervous expatriates. Her wide hips, though, made sitting on either level bearable. Madame Martin composed herself as a loyal domestic might. She suppressed the full emotion of a distraught wife.

"Tomorrow, we will sleep below again, out of this wind. The fresh air is good for your lungs…*monsieur*."

Even the infant stared unblinking in her direction as if she knew the comforting words to be a fiction. She nodded to the baby, then looked away and tried to remember a doxology worthy of the beautiful, sinking sun. On a ship deck no greater than the length of four sugar cane wagons, a passenger could take in sunrise or sunset from the same resting spot. When the sailor guided Claire back to the family's pallet, the child nestled her head at her mother's side. The sick man was roused and, as he looked about to speak, the wife suffered her own abdominal pang.

"Take the children below. It is their turn out of the wind."

"I cannot leave—"

"I shall lean on these rum barrels…if I feel the urge to sit. They won't budge. I will sleep here with no bother to others." A look of pleading from their daughter indicated the tiny child had understood. "It'll be a relief for the wee ones to take a respite below."

"You will keep our water jug close by," Désirée said. Only her husband had put his lips to the blue earthenware. She worried that the friendly shipmate might be within earshot, so she whispered. "We have been offered other water, *mon cher*, as we need. The captain assures me. You will keep the blue jug with you." The anxious captain had also told her to keep watch on the *monsieur* for signs of black spit or a festering rash.

"*Oui…non…oui*, don't drink after me. If I am not better tomorrow—"

"Of course, you will be better, *monsieur*."

"Perhaps God in heaven did not like the lie I told about new fever in Port-au-Prince."

"But you told the truth of a good-hearted cousin," she countered. She lowered her voice even more. "What you do to protect your family, mon Monsieur Pagnol, the merciful Almighty knows *très bien*."

She settled a crocheted bedspread over the drowsy man. Without contrasting color, the ecru coverlet matched the pallor of the sick man. Then, she and the children went below to a cramped room where a handful of other passengers slumped and shifted on shallow sleeping planks. Rough curtains rendered only three ledges somewhat private. The captain's office was no more than one corner made less grim by a flickering lantern. Her search for any open floor space was met by forced coughs and grimaces. In the uncertain light, she could see that four people with brown skin had settled across from the curtained compartments, and that the three white men guarding those pallets hugged their weapons. When the toddler and the infant in the arms of *Madame Martin* remained quiet, a dark fellow stood up near a stack of trunks and indicated that the space he'd left was theirs.

By a third night out from Haiti, the wife of Nicholas Pagnol was accustomed to the sudden silencing of sea gulls. She found their noisy return at first light reassuring. So many birds knew of a shore nearby, a safe beach with rocks or dunes for sleeping through the night. As the baby and child drifted into slumber, she shook her head about how little she herself knew of life on the shore or at sea. Yes, she might tell anyone asking in this new country, America, she was born on the island Saint Domingue, now called Haiti. She did not think of herself as a child of the seashore, however, any more than she thought of herself as a descendant of Africans. Her parents had lived at the edge of mountains surrounding Port-au-Prince—such inviting green in those forested hills, where her father found birds of remarkable color to bring to the market. Her mother dyed hemp rope in every hue and made baskets to sell alongside the beautiful birds. Her childhood had been washed with beauty and joy.

"Green and brown speckled," her papa used to say about the eyes of his Désirée. "My birds are singing to your eyes. They have seen nothing as beautiful as your eyes, except for their own eggs!"

Madame Martin slept soundly dreaming of her papa's voice and birdsong, of bright colors and green mountains she would likely never see again.

When she opened her speckled eyes, the friendly sailor was bending to offer a glass canteen, like so many seen in shops at the port near her husband's apothecary. Such articles from Europe were common in Haiti's towns now—perfume bottles, candelabras, combs, shoe buckles. Monsieur Pagnol had bought a crate full of water flasks just like the one the shipmate held out. His clients included many who credited their good health to the pharmacist's mixture of minerals and spring water from the mountains. The sailor bending at her side could look nothing like her husband's cousin, the one that might guide them to a safe and discreet shelter on Tybee. The deck hand was brown and stocky like the people on her mother's side, though, and she would have asked him about his own family if they had met at a bird market on any square in Port-au-Prince. But she had another question for him in the stuffy hull of the schooner headed north, because she was confused. She could not easily explain the crocheted bedspread draped over the sailor's shoulder or the envelope he grasped.

"Has my...Has Monsieur Pagnol's fever broken this morning?"

Instead of answering her, he picked up Claire who was reaching out his way. The child slid one arm around his back and hugged his chest with the other. It was clear that the toddler wanted to go on another walking round. It was clear that the child, with hair favoring her father's and skin like her mother, expected nothing from the wide world but beauty and joy.

"Madame...Martin," the sailor began.

"Has his fever—"

"Monsieur Pagnol, madame—"

The Dove Shall Fly

"Is he suffering a rash? Or has he—"

"I am so sorry, madame." The fellow was now smiling down at the infant, perhaps reluctant to face either the older child or the woman. "Madame… Monsieur Pagnol cannot be found."

In the first two hours without *monsieur*, Madame Martin circuited the ship deck and the berth below countless times. Too plump for so much walking with the infant, she would return breathless to the half dozen rum barrels where her husband had said he could lean and rest. There, she stood, transfixed by the anonymous waves beyond. Making progress northward, the ship passed one tiny island after another on either side. When no bobbing barrel appeared in the distance, when no flailing arms signaled the direction a rescue rowboat might go, she took to following the ship rails and began her circuit again. On the captain's request, the sailor offered her another flask filled with fresh water.

"The baby, she still has hunger, *non?*" He would lead Claire on a toddling excursion, while Désirée sat in a stupor cradling the infant. The next two hours and the next two hours unrolled in the same way, and the seafarer, who had been put in charge of the distressed trio, eventually brought a stool on deck to set down near them.

"This little girl is eating without distress, and saying words, madame."

"Bon…bon." Madame Martin heard her own voice, but her syllables sounded thick and bitter like what might come from the bottom of a rum barrel. All the oceans in the world could not dilute her despair. It would take a miraculous bolt from the blue sky, like the one that had struck when she first met Nicholas—only such a bolt could transport her from her grief. The envelope had held a page with the address of an attorney practicing on Tybee. Her stomach would not allow her to imagine explaining tiny Josephine to a stranger. But the sailor sitting with the family was not to blame. He seemed a charitable fellow. "What is your name, monsieur?"

"*Je m'appelle* Jean-Luc Lebrun."

"You are kind, Monsieur Lebrun." When she looked up at him, she was surprised by the intensity with which he studied her.

"My own mother was always kind, and *mon père* as well. To live as they did was a blessing, you see." The infant Josephine had turned her head again toward his voice. "But I am not the hero that your…that Monsieur Pagnol was for all aboard."

"He must have fallen. He must have leaned at the railing, and—"

"It was the first mate on watch last night. It was he who saw…your monsieur." Désirée was afraid to hear what the friendly sailor might go on telling her. "At first, he only stood up, and my *camarade* thought the gentleman's illness was passing. At first, your monsieur was holding close the pretty bedspread and the envelope. Then, he let fall *ces possessions*… to where he had been lying."

"I cannot bear to hear—"

"It was an act of only *le* héro, madame. He did not want the entire ship to die of fever."

"He must have fallen—"

"Monsieur put one leg over the railing," the sailor made himself finish, "*et puis*…and then the other…he lifted himself over." The woman was shaking her head. "He took a bloody handkerchief with him. The gentleman was our *héro*. This is what we all say to you, madame."

Still, the mother answering to the name Madame Martin could not help searching the shoreline called Florida as the schooner moved farther in the direction of Savannah's islands. Even if grief had not squelched her sensibilities, she would have been struck dumb by the thought of so vast a continent. The far-off gleaming sand to the west was only a shred of a beginning. Once they reached Georgia's coast, they had all been informed, the land would go in the direction of the sunset for miles that were no more easily counted than bright dots in the firmament. Where those miles ended, another ocean rose and fell for an even greater distance. All the widow from Port-au-Prince could imagine was a vast stretch of water with no final border at all. Far from sight now, a sea rose without impediment, like the heaven she believed her dear Nicholas to have made his home.

From an impossible distance, she squinted to see where the surf crashed along the Floridas, to see whether a dinghy might hold a passenger with blond hair. Had she sighted such an individual, she made herself admit, the captain would have been loath to put ashore to investigate. The peninsula was teeming with native peoples unfriendly to strangers black or white.

"Let the Spanish and the British try their mettle against the fierce natives. It is not the destiny of Haiti to settle disputes of the greater world." The captain was making one of his few rounds. He spoke in a brogue Désirée had heard before. "Let America try to uproot the heathens. They are mostly hidden, those savages, back from the where the breakers crash." His spit, she noticed, was not black. "They'd as soon boil us all in a stew pot as look upon us."

After another day at sea, the schooner from Haiti pulled up to the inward shore of Tybee. Passengers from below encroached on the working space of deck crew. The sailor, still acting as the family's chaperone, did not budge.

"Have you ever seen such a lighthouse, madame?" It was a landmark that took everyone's breath away. He smiled at her and the children as she shook her head. She felt detached from the others, from her own actions and words. Yet she knew she must practice some conversation before daring to plead with the lawyer whom her husband had expected to see.

"I am glad to be arriving at an island of some kind." Jean-Luc waited for her to speak more. "A whole continent is too much land for me. The three mountains on our side of Port-au-Prince, that was all the land I could understand."

"I think our families must have crossed paths many times," the attentive shipmate said. He was holding Claire, and he pointed out the lighthouse to the animated child. Suddenly, he began telling Madame Martin about a sweetheart at the Haitian port, who wanted this to be his last run to anywhere near an American state. "No matter the changes in our part of the island," he said cheerfully, "it was truly *familiale* where we grew up, *non?*"

"*Mais oui.*" The mother with an infant and a toddler was left mostly speechless by the lighthouse and had possibly lost her hearing as well. But he went on, because he felt an urgent need to say out loud that, yes, this was his last trip in secret from his homeland coast to the risky shores up north.

"The coming changes, under Henri, or any king or emperor of Haiti, they will not, I think, be changes putting people of my color into chains." He'd been imagining his sweetheart's relief upon his return. He would propose a wedding date this time. "*Ma chérie* was witness to much slaughter during the uprisings, terrible violence done to any slaveholders no matter if *laissez-faire* or brutal."

"Yes, my…Monsieur Pagnol did not wish for his daughter to witness such violence—"

"If an accusation of betrayal took hold," he went on in a whisper, "sometimes those with skin as black as General Toussaint's were attacked…"

"No more rational than Paris during the Revolution," monsieur used to say. They both looked at the helpless infant. Pulling into a port off the coast of the United States, she could not say whether her numbness came from relief or growing terror. Her husband's list of cautions and reliable names began to blur. "It is difficult to know the safe direction."

"On Tybee, it is not difficult," Jean-Luc replied. "I stay close to the ship. It is good you possess Monsieur Pagnol's envelope. Tybee is no place for a stranger of our skin to arrive without papers."

The captain of the schooner could not be called cordial, but he was insistent about escorting Madame Martin and the two in her care to the business avenue one block back from the wharf. He was just as adamant about his crew remaining on board—even the only other sailor like him, as white as any plantation owner.

"I presume you know to let me do the talking, ma'am."

"The letter from…Monsieur Pagnol states our case." He did not turn to look back at her, where she kept pace. The baby slept in a shawl she'd secured across her chest. She hugged Claire to her hip.

"Best not to let on that you can read." He took a pipe from his mouth in order to lower his voice. "And I'd best cease calling you *ma'am*. We're not in Port-au-Prince or Veracruz…Or, God knows, Aberdeen—bless 'er. Here, people even part ways brown better know who they belong to or be ready to state who bestowed the bliss of manumission." He pointed, indicating they were headed to the one story brick building at the end of a short avenue.

"You are from Scotland, monsieur?"

"Best not to let on you've studied any maps either."

"It is only that Nicholas Pagnol spoke of his Huguenot people. Long ago, some who did not come to the Americas escaped to Scotland instead."

At a door with peeling green paint, the captain stopped to take off his hat. Anyone observing could have mistaken his gesture of respect to be in preparation for greeting Mr. Ledbetter, the main attorney at the practice.

"I'm heartily sorry about Monsieur Pagnol." The ship owner scratched his head and his thick red beard. "If we none of us come down with the fever, we owe it to his taking matters in his own hands. But inside, you'll need to let me do the talking—"

"I haven't slept," Désirée suddenly confessed. For days, she had been too distraught to speak more than two words at a time. Now, language came tumbling out. "I'm in fear for the newborn, especially," she said. "Her mother was promised she'd be brought here, safe from political murder at home. But the infant can't be left without someone to nurse her."

The captain put his pipe back between his teeth and began rubbing grit from one boot toe and then the other on a pant leg.

"Mr. Ledbetter is a decent sort, as far as I can tell. I had to get my first mate out of the drunkard cell a few months back." He shifted his weight again and shoved one hand into a pocket. "But the man never took a wife. He's a bachelor. So, in his office, I wouldn't bring up the care of babies, I'd just—"

"I shall stay silent, monsieur, unless he poses a question."

The sailor, Jean-Luc, had been so helpful before and after the catastrophe. And then the captain, whose name she still failed to catch during introductions with the lawyer, showed himself remarkably protective. Desirée could not have hoped, though, for Tybee's primary attorney to be of service beyond what he had been paid to oversee. But Mr. Ledbetter was in fact as respectful and humane as the others. All three of these strangers had shown some of her husband's attributes, and yet sitting in the lawyer's office with two defenseless children in her care, the widowed mother suffered sharply from Nicholas Pagnol's absence.

She kept her wits as the captain bid *adieu*. The graying attorney stood so erect that he appeared tall, and he retained perfect posture when he sat. As he read aloud her husband's introduction document, however, Désirée gave in to her grief. Both Claire and tiny Josephine began to bawl. Neither the helpful sailor nor his captain would have predicted the lawyer's tolerance for such an emotional outpouring. They'd have both marveled to see the older man hand the stranded woman his own handkerchief. He gave Claire a crystal paper weight to hold and turn, and he spoke to the child in a way that soothed her, before turning to deliver news that could only make the mother, Madame Martin, fall into greater despair.

The cousin to whom Nicholas Pagnol had written three months earlier had moved some weeks ago to Savannah due to a medical emergency. Mr. Ledbetter went on to express his regrets that an official report had been delivered to his office only the day before. Hugues Pagnol had expired with a will intact, a statement assigning all proceeds after the sale of his indigo exchange to his younger brother, also of Savannah.

"He made a note denying any benefit to an older brother, however." Mr. Ledbetter shook his head before going on. "Any lawyer will tell you that saints and villains sometimes carry the same family name." He was letting himself digress as he assessed the woman's reaction to her predicament.

"This cousin Hugues had assured Nicholas there was need for apothecary expertise on Tybee."

"He would have made a secure living, no doubt."

"But now…but now…"

But now Désirée Pagnol found herself on a plantation island off the shore of the slave-state Georgia. Her husband's cash had been spent to procure safe travel for their family and the infant grand-niece of Toussaint Louverture. It seemed a hideous shift in circumstance that a dark-skinned infant could be safer where slavery went unchallenged than at home with her Haitian mother, that a mixed child with bright glints in her hair could be safer on old Saint Domingue than in a country whose birthright was freedom.

"No one will bother the infant while you tend to her needs, not while you're under my care and authority," Mr. Ledbetter assured her. "But there will be curiosity and…crass speculation about the fairer girl." The two adults watched her turn the chunk of crystal so that it caught lamplight. "I'm ashamed to say that in New Orleans, some are purchased as young as she…and trained for years to think of a gentleman's pleasure as their livelihood. Stealing a child like this one is not beyond the worst sort, and—" Even before the lawyer could collect himself to finish his statement, Madame Martin was picturing how she would plead with Jean-Luc Lebrun to take Claire back to Haiti for safekeeping. "Her hair alone might make the most unsavory sort react as if he'd seen a parcel of gold."

The schooner no bigger than four sugar cane wagons was originally set for its return trip in forty-eight hours. A message runner, however, brought a note to Mr. Ledbetter who immediately sent the tall youth off

The Dove Shall Fly

to show the same folded page to the captain. The stranded mother had been dozing fretfully on a settee as faded as the peeling door.

An informant was warning the attorney that vigilantes were gathering and would soon demand—*a full accounting of each colored person disembarking from the latest Haitian ship. If there were more loose immigrants roaming—and making their way to the office of a lawyer experienced in drawing up manumission papers—there was no telling how that might stir rebellion on the island's plantations.*

"Are you a cook of any kind, Madame Martin?" The lawyer watched the runner reach the end of the street. He was estimating how rapidly the schooner captain would fix sails and edge away from Tybee's main wharf.

"Monsieur Pagnol never complained."

"I'll testify that the young man who just left is trust-worthy, and I'm reminded just now that his legs are getting long. He's grown up in my employment. I should add to his weekly pay and relieve him of his chores in my kitchen space here."

"I'm sorry I've brought new worry to your office, monsieur. You have your own decisions to struggle with."

"Are you determined to stay by the infant's side?"

"*Chère petite* Josephine. She would not be surviving long without me, *non?*"

"You'd be accosted, I'm afraid, if you tried to take Claire back to the schooner yourself." The older child half wakened. When her eyes grew solemn, Mr. Ledbetter handed her the pretty paper weight. "You'd best tell me about Jean-Luc Lebrun again. Describe him. If the captain's crew is on the wharf untying ropes for the next few minutes—"

"He has a sweetheart in Port-au-Prince. She'll be waiting." The mother cradled Lisette's infant and pointed to a blanket she thought ought to travel back with her own daughter. She described the friendly shipmate—dark, stocky, a broad forehead. An ache in her throat kept her from telling the lawyer that the child would probably reach out if she saw the sailor.

"You'll be safe here," Mr. Ledbetter said. He was leading the little girl to the door.

"I saw a burlap sack out on your stoop. A jar of green paint was set down inside." As she spoke, Madame Martin felt a new numbness filling her body and mind, like the cold water a drowning man has no strength to keep from his lungs.

"Come along, Claire," the lawyer said. "Let's see some stars. Do you want to peek from inside a warm sack?" When he put his hand on the doorknob, the woman from Haiti was already unbuttoning her blouse. She was trying to read hope in the infant's untroubled brow. The lawyer's voice was kind, but nothing like the voice she was missing so much. "Let's see some stars, shall we? Perhaps your friend on the boat knows a long lullaby."

Chapter 3   Tendrils

"Your name is Adeline, señorita? Adeline, yes?" Captain Juan Seguin stood, holding his hands up so that the girl with the musket could see them, but he was shaking his head as a signal to the American soldier by the campfire that now was no time for him to struggle into action. "Your *amiga*, she is fainting again, you understand?" He kept his hands aloft until he edged around the fire to where Yarico had slumped over.

"Don't you touch her," the girl said, stepping out from the oleander. Seguin was surprised that she'd been holding the weapon aloft so long. With those damp braids and muddy skirt hem, she looked like a child. She could not have been much over twelve.

"One hand, only to see if she can take some coffee."

"Don't think I won't fire!"

The Tejano officer smiled in spite of his worry that her aim could be quite good. He was thinking she might shoot as well as his daughter Antonia, who could hug a cocked rifle and aim before she learned to read. He might lose an arm or the thick hair he took pride in if he grew careless with his words. Slowly, he bent over and nudged the woman's shoulder with his fingertips before addressing the girl again.

"Señorita Adeline, let the American bring her a sip of coffee."

"You all right, Yarico? Are you hurt?"

Adeline's voice caused the woman to sit up so suddenly that the officer took a quick step back. They waited for her to answer, but she appeared able only to wave weakly at the oleander bush and fend off another spell of dizziness. Then a movement from across the campfire drew their attention. Talk lapsed as the emaciated fellow warming his hands attempted to stand and maintain his own balance.

Juan Seguin had kept company with him and three other Fannin privates for a day and a half. The captain and his men encountered the desperate band wandering far from Goliad environs and making their way toward Sam Houston's last line. They were Georgia Battalion boys, and they'd all looked mostly used up, except for the youngest, a Private Hardaway of Macon. He and the other two had gone ahead as best they could with Seguin's patrol unit to intercept the main independence army. But the weary soldier with him now—Trezevant—needed a few hours respite.

The officer could not abide the thought of leaving him behind, but he also knew that two men on one horse would provide an easy target for Santa Anna. Perhaps, the captain thought, it was the mismatched footwear that had drained the recruit of his remaining strength—or what Hardaway had told them. The weakened private had been out riding scout around Refugio when the other battalion volunteers took a last meal inside the church there. The Tejano officer believed a reasonably fresh horse would lend a little life to the spent man. Sam Houston would need some kind of cavalry, however rag-tag.

Yarico and the girl and Captain Seguin were all dazed by what the fighter in tatters now managed. Upon holding himself steady, he reached out to the pan where boiled coffee grounds had been cooling. He took a tin cup he'd secured in his belt and adeptly poured so as to miss the handle. A sketch would have portrayed him as half dead—matted brown hair, haunted eyes, clothes grown into or worn off his body—but he poured a cup of coffee and set the tin pot on a trivet of sticks before stepping around to where Yarico watched. She held out her hand. It could have struck the others, too, that the soldier's brow and expression were as angelic as when they were first created. Even what the devil had done with his body and clothing could not alter the soldier's soulful countenance.

"*Merci*," the recovering woman said to him. She knew that the girl in her care had moved out from the shelter of the oleander. The captain was gradually lowering his other arm. The coffee did not taste like much, but it was warm. "I'm all right, Adeline."

"This is *bueno*, Trezevant," the officer said. "It is good you can stand and work your legs. Your feet have been a worry for me since our paths crossed."

Yarico and both men looked down at his footwear, one boot and one shoe. Each was caked with dried mud. The young man then shuffled back to the other side of the fire, where he seemed unsure of his next move. "Take a short walk if you can manage, why don't you?" Seguin gestured in the direction opposite the exotic shrub and the clump of mesquite. "Take a few steps, *amigo*, and inspect the flowers. The fat yellow ones have leaves we can eat, but do not bend to pick them. If you fall over, I cannot drag you back here to our fire. In a *momento,* I will come after you to see if you find some greens. When your legs stop shaking, it means we can move on *pronto.*"

The Tejano was nodding to him and then to Yarico.

"Just stay there, Adeline," she called. "My head went light, but now... *tout va bien.* I'm all right." She took more sips from the metal cup and then indicated to the officer that she was ready to accept his help in getting to her feet.

"Muy bien," he said, seeing her remain upright. He did not appear in a rush to talk until the youthful soldier was gone from sight. Yarico knew what his next words to her would entail.

"About the one horse—"

"The tan one."

"Si, señorita. The private is not much help to our army with the legs he has, and those feet. Only days ago, I sent one of my men to Galveston with two other poor Americans. It is in God's hands if either is alive by the time they reach a hospital. What Santa Anna's general did to the prisoners at Goliad, I cannot speak, but these Fannin men knew even greater suffering perhaps before the executions. So pitiful to hear how the Refugio battle not far from there ended and the nightmare attempt to escape—"

"I don't think that Adeline..." Yarico cut in. "I don't think the girl with the musket can tolerate any more news about Goliad."

"No, of course."

"Her aunt and I, we are all from Georgia. Some of those boys were neighbors."

"I see. It is pitiful."

"Mon dieu, if it's the last thing I do, I'll help her make it back across the Louisiana border." Then Yarico was sorry she had spoken as if the contest between Sam Houston's followers and the seasoned Mexican army were already a forgone conclusion. Yet she doubted that enough independence fighters from Galveston or anywhere else could charge in and help General Houston turn the tide. "If all the colonists get driven out of Texas..." Her French vocabulary fell away as she felt it urgent to make herself understood.

"Then we have agreement, Seguin said. "I was going to ask you, *por favor,* not to let this Fannin soldier talk with the musket girl and the other women, or the children you travel with." He looked off in the direction that Private Trezevant had walked, but something told Yarico the officer was marshalling his own emotions. "It is a comfort after many weeks, you must believe, to have civilized talk with a woman. But only a few sips, if you take my meaning. It is *no bueno* for a man on the march to relax in conversation, the kind that reminds him of his family and his home. Civilized talk, señorita, is *no bueno* before men gallop or stagger into the shock of a thousand muskets."

When Adeline and Yarico returned to the willows where their horses were tied, Mrs. Wainwright and her three children sat huddled together. Awakened by the sound of a man's voice and unfamiliar accent, they were terrified. Margaret Linder, though, smiled up at them where she knelt folding two handkerchiefs. Not true kin to the Harpers, she'd been embraced for years as a guardian aunt would be. The contents of a purse were spread out on her shawl. She was not in full possession of her mind.

Aunt Maggie had only partly perceived their danger since the Harper rig was turned away from Gonzales weeks earlier. She had not been in sound mental state since logic suggested to everyone else that her nephew was among those lost at the Alamo. Though young, he had surely been with the Gonzales men riding to join Travis at San Antonio days before everyone at the threatened mission was lost. This fact and others had been kept from the older Harper woman—that the town several miles east of San Antonio had then been razed by Houston himself to keep supplies from Mexico's armies, that four hundred volunteers under Colonel Fannin had been executed three weeks later at Goliad. She could only fret over the fate of her Texas nephew.

"If we meet up with my Matthew after the next river crossing," Aunt Maggie said, "I want my belongings presentable." Her companions smiled at her with concern. "Oh, I know you're thinking we don't possess much after discarding everything at the far shore. But a lady has to take care even if she's down to her last hankie." She beamed up at them. "And I still have two!"

Adeline urged Yarico to do the explaining. Annabel Wainwright and her children needed soothing. The family was calmed to learn that there were only two men a short walk away, soldiers on Sam Houston's side—*our men*. These stragglers were in a hurry to catch up with the independence army. When the two got on the move again, *shortly*, they would leave their campfire ablaze so the Harpers and Wainwrights could properly cook their peas. The soldiers still had some dried beef in their saddle pack, fortunately, and since they felt sure about finding Houston's commissary line in a day or so, they wanted to share their solid food. The officer and the private seemed gentlemen, from what Yarico could tell, and the two were determined to join what would surely be the final stand against Santa Anna. They didn't appear to shrink from the possibility of dying, but they wanted the colonists of Texas Territory to know that it was the chance of true freedom making that risk worth it.

Only gradually did Yarico work in some detail—how the independence soldiers needed one of the women's horses. She waited to mention that the soldier in charge might easily be taken for an enemy at first, but it was clear that he'd lately served with Travis at the Alamo, was trusted by General Houston, and had pledged to fight for Texas liberty on the final battlefield.

"Don't forget Big Abel and Ned are riding along with Houston, too." Anabel Wainwright spoke to her daughters and one young son. She was reassuring herself as well. "Like as not the two soldiers yonder will be saying howdy to your daddy and brother before we're blessed with the occasion our own selves."

"We would be taking turns in the saddle and on foot anyway." As Adeline chimed in, the wispy mother nodded as if she had already visualized how the Harpers and her brood would manage trekking on toward the border.

"It's your family's spare horse and your decision, but I won't argue against giving Houston better odds at walloping Santy Anny's butchers." She was so slight in stature that anyone might have wondered how she'd managed to bring five babies into the world. She was as tough as she was petite, though, and she'd regained her salty demeanor only days after her own newborn was buried. "If you all are givin' over your spare ride, I'd incline toward swapping saddles beforehand with the one on our horse. We can make do with a pack critter's tack, but such won't hold a soldier that's tryin' to tamp down powder. Best give the poorly private something where he can keep steady. We want him taking down rows of Spanish heathens, don't we?"

"Captain Seguin speaks mostly Spanish," Yarico quietly reminded them.

Mrs. Wainwright rose to her feet and shook her skirt without responding. It was not usual fare for a domestic to modify a statement made by a white woman. But the mother felt bound to indulge such overstepping until they all made the Louisiana border. It was the Harpers' Yarico, after all, who had recently defended both families against a pair of heartless thieves who disarmed folks with lies in perfect English. Recalling her indebtedness, Anabel Wainwright was moved suddenly to make another generous offer.

"These here are Big Abel's better boots. I've been wearing them since last spring when we dragged our wagon out from river mud shy of San Felipe." She looked at them again, perhaps already sorry she'd begun voicing the offer. "I've got four socks in layers, so's to make them fit. I'll switch out with the private over that-a-way if he can get his feet into these here."

"He looked as if solid boots would help his balance," Adeline said.

"As soon as we cross into Louisiana, I'll hunt down a pair of dancing shoes for myself." Mrs. Wainwright had more to say and grew serious again. "I know God can't be taking time to work out every deal with our likes. But I'll count on your witness that I gave up a good saddle and a pair of boots to the revolution. I'll count on your prayin', added to mine, that my husband and Ned come out alive from any last entanglement." She put her arm around Little Abel. "When I first see your daddy and brother again, I'll skip from one full moon to the next, with or without shoes!"

The distance between the mesquite grove and the improbable oleander, about thirty feet, functioned as a welcome barrier. The group of women and children were better off not hearing more about the ill-fated Georgia Battalion, and the two soldiers would have been unnerved by their tender-hearted response. *The Harper domestic kept as family*—as Mrs. Wainwright referred to her—was surprised that Adeline did not ask more questions about the American soldier. He might have served alongside their Macon neighbors. As Yarico led the saddled tan horse across to the campfire area where Captain Seguin and the younger man waited, the girl following finally spoke up.

"I can't keep from wondering...how, if the soldier in tatters escaped just before the Goliad horror..."

"It will all take a long time for full accounting." They slowed their walk, although the horse seemed fairly rested and required little tugging. Adeline nodded soberly.

"Not having full facts is its own suffering. That's all I had in mind. Like how the Wainwrights will ever find each other after all this ends.

The Dove Shall Fly

Even though we know we're all faring now as well as any, it could be that their papa and their older boy worry the worst has happened to the entire family. If they make it back to that upper bend of the river and no one's there, they might assume…"

"Fear is hard put to rest, you're right. But there's no help in taking the worst to heart, not until it's known for sure." They both could see the officer gesture for the weakened private to remain by the fire, and the girl ceased moving in their direction.

"I ought to go back and help comfort Mrs. Wainwright and the children. The captain seems more at ease talking to you." Yarico was amazed at how much mature consideration the thirteen-year-old had taken on in the crisis, but then Adeline brightened suddenly, like the child who used to run uphill at dawn. "Captain Seguin, and before him Walk Far…" The Harper girl couldn't help smiling. "If Aunt Maggie were herself, she'd tease you no end about catching the eye of such wanderers."

Yarico knew her eyes were glistening as she and Juan Seguin completed their transactions. If they had let themselves chuckle about Adeline's quip, they'd have needed to work all the harder to hold back tears. Who knew whether the tan horse and the spent young man and the captain himself were mere hours away from brutal finality? Who knew whether the next river crossing that the Harpers and the Wainwrights attempted would bring catastrophe? Who knew if three more Santa Anna generals would surround soldiers and civilians alike before nightfall, putting an end to hope and breath itself.

"You will be crossing two more rivers, Señorita Yarico." The captain had just showed her where some cooked dandelion greens were left for them on the trivet. "The Trinity is sometimes not as flooded as the Brazos in this time of year. Then, when you come to the second big river, you are surely safe. The other side is Louisiana. But I do not think Mexico has plans to chase down any who flee beyond that first river you come to. Surely even Santa Anna will let you and every other family run out of the country to the east. This is what I am thinking."

"He'll be on the lookout for Sam Houston's army," she said, "for you all, I expect."

He turned away from her to secure buckles on the saddle just handed over, but Yarico was watching the young man greet and talk to the rested mount. She liked the way he placed his hand gently near its nostrils, how he stroked the animal on its forehead. She knew that the officer had been right, and that the battalion soldier was finding his voice much more easily as he got acquainted with the tan horse than he would have trying to find answers for a Georgia girl's questions.

The exchange of footwear proved to be more time-consuming, and the Tejano had to help Private Trezevant remove his misshapen boot and shoe. The younger man let Seguin wrestle a Wainwright sock onto one foot and then the other. While the men tended to this chore, Yarico used the officer's hatchet and a rock to chop pieces of dried beef from a solid portion he kept in his saddle bag. She doubted that Houston's commissary transports would be well stocked, and she tried to reduce her estimate of what the two families rushing away from danger would need.

The Harpers and the Wainwrights could allow themselves a night to rest, the captain had advised her. Yarico convinced herself that a thinnest sliver of beef alongside of a dollop of greens and black-eyed peas would make a fine meal for that evening. She would instruct the others to keep an eye out for dandelions the next day as they trudged. The main wedge of cured meat, she would keep secret in her apron pocket until the next campfire, perhaps until they crossed the Trinity. There, a fish might be trapped. She shuddered, though, remembering how the Tonkawa man Walk Far had killed and skinned two rattlesnakes for roasting. It was savory eating that she had no skills or nerve to provide.

When Captain Juan Seguin suggested to the private that he needed to test the horse and saddle, as well as his steadiness, the rescued battalion fellow did not need much help mounting. The officer only held the reins until Trezevant could take them. The young man had started to breathe with energy. He had managed to put a boot toe in the stirrup and hoist himself up.

"Just let him walk," the captain advised.

"I grew up around horses."

"You are natural cavalry, I see. This is what my mind thinks."

Even Yarico observed a connection between the rider and his mount. She felt a jolt of hope that a hundred such men on horseback just might prevail in an attack. The officer was nodding as the young American patted the animal's shoulder.

"Just walk him a short distance. But, tell me what is your first name, Trezevant." The officer was more heartened than he could let on. "If you break your neck in three minutes, I will have to write down a formal report."

"James."

The Dove Shall Fly

"This is our last time speaking as *amigos*, I hope you understand." The officer could not conceal his relief that the soldier looked recovered enough to ride. "I don't want to know what your friends call you, but your legs look strong. You are meant for cavalry, and this makes me happy."

"Yes sir," the battalion man said. "I feel much better up here." He spoke a soft command and angled the reins. The Harpers' horse stepped out in the direction of the flowering fields. "My friends call me *Jamie*," he said to the captain. "That's what horses would call me if they could talk."

"Do not make me write an accident report about your neck, Private James Trezevant." The officer waited before speaking to Yarico. As before, he wanted the youthful soldier to move out of earshot. "The greens will have power on his bowels in a few minutes. This too is something a soldier must take care of well before battle. If the American can slide off his horse to relieve his pain…if he can then climb back on with no one to help, he will be ready to ride with me." There was no lightheartedness in his musings.

"What if the young man can't pull himself onto the horse a second time?"

"There will be others with General Houston who can." He looked at the woman with worry she took to be fatherly. "I must take the horse, regardless. If the private cannot fight, perhaps he will be able to travel with you."

Several minutes passed without further conversation. Yarico wanted to step out in the direction the private had ridden. No less than Adeline, she would have wanted to ask the youth if he'd served with a Francis Gideon and Joseph Tidwell or one of the Hunts from Macon. She wanted to ask if he had heard Captain William Ward or Lieutenant Hugh McLeod make inspiring speeches there. Impulsively, Yarico would have asked him how he had liked New Orleans when the companies under Ward practiced maneuvers during their wait for supplies. She had the sudden urge to rush after the battalion soldier and ask him if a flag with a single blue star had flown for a time over Goliad. Adeline had sent a letter to the coastal town Velasco, and she wanted to inquire whether the child's greeting might have reached the Macon boys before they marched inland.

Yarico Harper wanted to move briskly out into the field where the Georgia Battalion survivor could be struggling to get back onto his horse. *Did he remember hearing from some of the fellows that a family of women was traveling along with them? They had done some mending of socks—had he heard?* She would have been happy to get on her hands and knees and allow him to step upon her back to reach the saddle once more.

"I hope I don't collapse again," she murmured.

"You needed rest. You did not fall because of fear." Seguin was nodding and then shaking his head. "Once, when I came back to San Antonio after many months away on duty, Juanito, my little son, wanted to run across the plaza to where my company was riding in. But, instead, he sank down onto the first plaza stones, the ones across from our entry, and he cried many tears. Fear was the opposite of what he felt, yet he was ashamed. Next time you fall to the ground, señorita, may God permit it is from tears of happiness."

After a stretch of silence, Yarico thought it acceptable to broach a mystery from their initial encounter.

"Captain Seguin," she started. "When I was coming back from the river with my pails of water, you thought I might be someone else."

"We have been on the lookout for—"

"*Emily West.* That's the name you said."

"We came upon one of Houston's scouts riding post. He had a message about woman who might learn of Santa Anna's movements, his position. She has a mind to help us. The writing said to look for a black woman, with her own freedom papers from a home she left in the North of America." The captain was settling his poncho back over his uniform, though he had removed a red overlay in expectation of encountering Houston's army before any Mexican lines. "Like me, she is said to move among the enemy with some ease and little notice. Well," he corrected himself, "perhaps more notice than I command. They say she is beautiful, señorita."

Yarico wondered if every black person not working a Texas cotton field or drowning in one of its swollen rivers had a freedom letter hidden down in a boot. She marveled that a free woman from up north felt no restraint about producing her document or reserve about offering her help in the independence cause.

"If I meet up with Miss West, I will pass on the compliment and thank her for her bravery."

"Here is something brave, Miss Yarico." Captain Juan Seguin was looking out where wildflowers spilled bright color. He'd spotted the young soldier from Fannin's army astride the tan horse again. Steadier mounted than on his feet, the youth looked revitalized—fit for riding on. "Too late to keep from Private Trezevant the scene in his mind of pitiful killing at Refugio. And, then—José, Maria—what he knows of Goliad! As for the escape from Victoria, even I prefer not to imagine their weeks in the creek mud, nothing to eat. For one river crossing, he and his comrades could only cling to floating bales of hay." The captain coughed and turned away for a moment. "And yet he is on your horse again, his horse now, and he comes back with this knowledge…that we must ride into worse battle."

Yarico was blinking and trying to swallow. She needed to leave the campfire to these men, leave them alone to check their gear and ride off.

"Here is something brave," the officer said again.

Chapter 4   A Day of Reversals

"Jamie!" He heard his name called from the summer house porch, but he was inclined to stay out of view. The ten-year-old on horseback recognized his cousin Barbara's voice. He assumed the summons came at his mother's request. He and Deefy, however, had already made two leaps each over a fallen sycamore in the middle of a field, and Jamie's riding companion was preparing to spur a chestnut gelding for another run at it.

"James Peter Trezevant!" His mother must have reached a rare level of exasperation if she'd asked her niece to use all three names. Still, he didn't feel too ashamed about evading a reminder to take a bath. The family's Uncle Henry wasn't due in from Darien until late afternoon. As a signal to take the leap again, Jamie waved his arms at the other boy, a black youth with no power of hearing whatsoever but who possessed remarkable riding abilities.

"You first?" Deefy motioned. He could see that something had distracted his competitor. Jamie shook his head and pointed in the direction of the Trezevant house. He made a talking gesture with his hands, which he then placed over his ears. The deaf boy's laugh was high-pitched and contagious, and Jamie began to question whether their final run at the hurdle could possibly be their best efforts.

Then a dramatic wave drew Jamie's attention. Deefy took off his shirt and wrapped it into a turban. After making a sweeping motion to suggest the leap itself, he raised both hands above his head to indicate he would try to stay on his horse this time without hanging onto the saddle horn or even leaning over the animal's neck. Before looking for his companion's approval, he directed his horse to the edge of woods that rimmed the field. At direct angles to the fallen trunk, Deefy studied his approach for a few seconds. Only the Trezevant boy could hear the rising hum of bees and horse flies in the July heat.

Both riders were smiling, though Jamie tried to suppress his own inner voice of caution. He certainly didn't want anything else in his friend's head to get broken, but he also dreaded identification as the lesser equestrian. A spectacular success would leave no question about the friendly duel. There was also no chance that Jamie would change his own tactics next time. He had every certainty of laying himself flat along his horse's back and neck as it lifted all hooves from the ground and sailed over the dead tree.

What James Peter Trezevant beheld momentarily made him wish he'd ridden to the summer house and insisted that the entire family rush up the rise past the narrow thicket to the open field. The feat he witnessed stamped itself into his memory. Deefy studied the challenge a few seconds longer than usual. Then he took the horse into a stunning charge. The youngster's arms went straight over his head at the height of the animal's arc, and Jamie barely breathed for a full minute afterward. Except for vision, he felt his own senses drop away, but he was thankful he'd lent the cook's son his old boots for their morning ride. Usually, Deefy set out barefoot.

Jamie readied for his turn astride "Contentment," a high-strung horse he'd named after his uncle's plantation. Communicating in a code of syllables and strokes, he tried to prepare the animal for its third and final leap. He knew it was no easier to keep apprehension secret from a horse than from a dog, and he wondered what his mount inferred from a flurry of pats along the neck. The sunshine had grown intense by late morning, but Jamie realized the animal's pungent sweat could also be signaling its doubt about another jump. He was determined, though, to end the contest with a respectable leap superior to his previous efforts.

Contentment was thinking along other lines.

The horse responded to initial commands and set off at a determined gallop, but as the rider dug in his heels before the hurdle, the animal veered off in the direction of the farthest tree-line. Slick soles on Jamie's dress boots diminished his control in the saddle, and Deefy watched in dismay as rider and mount flew into the thicket.

The boy wearing a turban set off after the runaway horse and followed a gash of broken twigs and pliable limbs stripped of their leaves. Within a mass of juniper saplings, Jamie lay in a still heap, one sleeve torn from his shirt and dangling from a bent hackberry branch. Deefy jumped down and eased his friend's eyelids back, desperate to verify that the boy's pupils were not fixed. Prickly twigs stuck in Jamie's thick, curly hair, and his face had gone from pale to colorless. Rolling him gently onto his less abused side, Deefy held the ten-year-old's wrist and detected a regular heartbeat. His own head and chest pounded, and he couldn't decide whether to stay next to the accident victim or race back to the family's home for help.

The deaf boy's plaintive moans of distress caused blackbirds to suddenly burst from a treetop. Seeing their panicked flight, he feared a bear might be wandering close by. He grabbed a broken branch to fend off an attack and frantically patted Jamie on the cheek with his other hand.

"Any sign of my elusive second son?" Mrs. Trezevant stepped from the back porch into a room buzzing with food preparation. In spite of missing the momentous Fourth of July celebration in town, she had no regrets about stationing the family in the open country outside Darien for the summer months.

Barbara was caught up watching Callie drizzle icing on shortbread. Others labored at less delicate tasks. She finally shook her head and murmured *no*.

"I suppose he'll be out of sorts all week about not being witness to the parade."

"Your cousin Charles won't miss one detail in telling us how it all went."

"Hearing of an exciting event from an older brother, Aunt Margaret, that may be worse than no balm of any kind." They were both smiling, but talk trailed off. One older brother was the only sibling Barbara had left after a deadly fever took her mother and the younger ones a few years earlier. There could be no salve for such a loss. A widow herself, she counted herself fortunate to fill some of the void in her brother's family.

"I'll surely rejoice to see Henry again. And Jamie will hang on every word your papa tells of the merriment." She could see that the welcome dinner was progressing as needed. "To think the country is already having its fiftieth birthday, with all the greater sense of triumph after turning England back at New Orleans this last time."

"Whatever made it all come down to war again?" Barbara was close to seventeen, but she still let her finger touch where Callie's frosting oozed onto the baking tin. "Then, it didn't take but a handful of summers for the countries to reunite as allies."

"Well, let's be grateful for how fast friendship recovers, even if we aren't able to explain the—" Margaret Trezevant had just noticed a blank spot near the largest kitchen window draped in cheesecloth. She was searching the other corners of the room. "Have Jamie's dress boots been moved? I had Liza set them out for Benjamin. Is he already polishing them?"

"No ma'am," Callie said. She rested her wooden spoon in the bowl before explaining. "Earlier this morning, I saw Jamie ride out with Deefy. They went up the hill like they've done before. I didn't wonder had he asked you. But I did notice he'd put on his dress boots, ma'am. And it looked like young Jamie had my boy wearing those field boots today."

"Jamie changed into his dress boots for riding?"

"I'm sorry, ma'am. I didn't think of waving to Deefy before they went off. When he rides to let the horses stretch their legs, he'd just as soon put bare toes to the stirrup. I'm sure he didn't pester Jamie for the boots. My son knows better than to try on shoes that aren't his—"

"Callie, I'm not the least put out with Deefy. He's the only one as charmed by the stables as my son is. Jamie is in good company." Since moving from her brother's plantation, she was pleased to arrange suitable work for Callie's only child as well as her brother Benjamin. The widow wouldn't abide the wanton splitting up of slave families. If a deaf child couldn't keep in the care of a loving mother, she didn't want to be the one standing before God to explain why not. "It's only your boy keeping Jamie's mind from the festivities he missed in Darien this week."

"I'm surprised Papa wanted to mingle with such crowds," Barbara added, biting her lip. "He promised to avoid the peak events." She and her aunt shared an aversion to throngs that might invite pestilence. "I'll be so thankful when he and Charles come up that road. Shall I call Jamie again?"

"Oh, let's let him finish a morning ride with Deefy. He'll miss his first turn at a bath, though. Liza's already poured hot water. After he sees what Charlotte and George do with soap bars, he'll likely be more prompt next time. Of course, Elizabeth will insist on washing up first in a pristine tub. That girl has become rather finicky about her privacy and—"

"Mrs. Trezevant!"

She and her niece jerked in the direction Callie was pointing. From the ridge, the high strung horse Contentment came into better view, rider-less and trotting toward the summer house feed troughs. The kitchen was beset with shrieks, but Jamie's mother called for help clearly enough that Benjamin came running from the vegetable garden where he'd been shucking corn. He was more expert at grooming the family's horses than riding them, but he still was able in seconds to approach the loose animal, jump astride, and race in the direction the two boys had gone.

Mrs. Trezevant's kitchen help and her niece quivered in dismay as she led them in prayer. Then the women all poured onto the porch and took on both flights of wooden steps to the ground below. Her husband's death at age twenty-nine, the loss of her brother's wife and five youngest, the devastation of Henry's entire plantation by the cruelest of hurricanes—when would the series of tragedies end? Now the widow refused to envision herself carrying on with fewer of her own children. She didn't know how much more sorrow she could bear.

When both horses appeared on the ridge, Callie and two other cooks fell to their knees. Benjamin kept hold of the runaway's reins, so Deefy could more easily support the Trezevant son sharing his saddle. Jamie looked limp and shaken, but alive. His mother sent the kitchen workers to run and move a comfortable settee from the parlor to the back porch where the ventilation was best. Callie stayed alongside her son and brother as they eased the injured youngster down onto wobbly legs. As he let these two support his weight on their shoulders, his feet barely touched the ground, and he was easily transported to the outdoor resting spot.

In some households, a string of recriminations might have quickly tied off joy from the boy's recovery. Margaret Trezevant, though, was true to her own instincts and to the promises she'd made in the days after her husband succumbed in Charleston to bilious fever— *these five precious lives that John passes to my care, these children of ours, will know their mother's love and God's every day…and forgiveness as close to divine as I can provide…if only I am helped by heaven.*

She didn't think her brother was any more likely to scold Jamie for the outing shared with a Trezevant slave boy. After the hurricane devastated his rice plantation, Henry Gignilliat had resorted to bartering with establishments farther north along the Georgia coast to winnow the field hands he'd maintained. The last thirty were mostly men without family ties of their own, but some were aging and had attracted only the lowest bidding even in Charleston where trade was usually competitive. He'd been pained to think what tasks his dispersed crew might be required to take on next, or how long the men past their prime would survive. Margaret believed her brother honest enough to look at every cruel fate as connecting one human to another. She didn't believe he would chastise Jamie for befriending the black youth.

The Dove Shall Fly

One man, nevertheless, in the company of another sometimes felt it important to show a firmer hand than he might among females and children alone. On the chance that Dr. James Pepper, the cousin with whom she and her children stayed in Darien during the school year, should also ride out to the summer house later in the day, the widowed mother felt especially grateful for the hours between Jamie's mishap and his recuperation. By the time her brother and her older son Charles—as well as the Darien doctor and his wife—were spotted coming up the road in two rigs, James Peter Trezevant had enjoyed an array of refreshments from cool mint tea to dumplings. Having squandered the opportunity for a proper bath, he'd managed a basin and wash cloths to make himself presentable. He couldn't completely avert his eyes from a bloodied dishrag wedged between cushions.

"I'm proud you didn't go into detail with Charlotte and George about your accident," his mother said. He nodded and raised himself up on an elbow that wasn't too sore. In fact, he had kept his usual reserve, only telling the youngest ones that he'd fallen and had the breath knocked out of him. "Your brother will certainly share his impressions of the town celebration, but I hope he allows his uncle and my cousin to steer the story-telling."

"You should go and greet them on the front porch, Mother. I'll be able to walk into the parlor on my own. I think my legs are entirely steady." She couldn't help being proud of him. Never mind the unlikely friend, the scuffed boots, or the outlandish riding feat she suspected. She could tell from his expression that a question was on his mind. "Has Deefy come out of the stable? Is he walking all right?"

"Sometime before your bed is turned down this evening," she smiled, "you ought to go find his mother in the kitchen. You should let Callie know you're sorry you got her son worked into such a state of mind."

"I will."

"Then you can go find Deefy and thank him for saving you from wild boars or snakes and bears, and I don't know what else."

"I will."

At dinner, it was the doctor's wife irrepressible in her recollections of the weeklong festivities.

"Ladies in the auxiliary put their servants to hanging crepe for at least three days in advance. Had it rained, Margaret, your children and ours would have had to take up shovels, too, to help clear the main road of a red, white, and blue mess!"

"We did hear thunder off in your direction—"

"But only that, though the parasols folded in and the umbrellas flared out at first warning."

"And the crowds arrived in expected numbers?"

"Well, I don't suppose any count will match the onlookers last year coming through with hopes of seeing Lafayette. Some were so disappointed that our French hero took the road to Macon from Augusta, missing Darien entirely, that they shrugged off the country's fiftieth birthday this time."

"And all manner of speeches were delivered, I'm sure."

"The mayor went on so dryly, I believe someone spurred the parade's start horse early so the din would drown him out."

Margaret appreciated the gentlemen at the table who allowed their rambling talk. Her cousin's wife was a genuinely cheerful lady and gracious enough to accommodate the Trezevant family during the school year. But Henry's reserve and the doctor's gradually struck her as extraordinary self-control. She grew somewhat worried, too, about the uncharacteristic silence of her son Charles.

"Were some classmates of yours in the parade, as you'd hoped?"

"Most all the major events were nearly a week ago, Mother. I've forgotten some facts already." She couldn't account for his subdued response. "Simon and Mr. Lamar's nephews carried the biggest banner. The schoolmaster's son is younger than Jamie, but they let him strap on a drum and march with the rhythm line."

"No doubt, they'll all play some part...in the next round of ceremonial honors..."

What Mrs. Pepper was referring to, Margaret couldn't imagine, but she was quick to read the glance exchanged between her brother and the doctor. Charles looked down at his plate, and the mother at the table studied a side door to the dining room to make sure Charlotte and George had not wandered away from where the youngest children were being fed. Whatever it was making her older son drop his gaze, she felt Jamie and Elizabeth were old enough to hear. Her niece had been gradually sensing momentous news as well.

"What on earth has happened, Papa?"

"We've had a shock. We might none of us have known if I'd left the upper coast a day earlier. Your brother and I were hoping to see a transaction through…a doomed transaction, but that's another matter." He waved away letting the adjective slip, and looked chagrined that he'd taken himself off track so easily. "I intended all along to delay so as to miss the Darien speeches. Everyone in this family steers clear of such crowds these days. It was from Savannah that word passed down to one inlet town and then along to the next…at hurricane speed, you could say…just after the Fourth…"

"What has happened, Henry? If we've made another declaration of war—"

"John Adams and Thomas Jefferson both passed away on Independence Day." Pieces of cutlery at the table and serving dishes in the kitchen went still. "Every bleacher festooned with crepe from here to Boston will be accommodating memorials for the next month."

Mrs. Trezevant and her family and guests all went out to the back porch at twilight. Elizabeth and the two little ones raced back and forth in the grass with miniature flags their uncle had bought them. The doctor allowed them each one sparking wand that Barbara and Charles supervised. When Jamie remained with the adults on the porch, the boy's mishap was explained in the least stirring terms. Margaret had dealt with all the upheaval she cared to weather in a single day.

"He was thrown from the saddle, that's all," she said. "I suppose the most frightful result of the incident is his missed bath."

"I thought you were emitting the potent scent of exertion, young man." The doctor was as likely to tease as his wife was to chat on and on. Uncle Henry's eyebrows rose as he scrutinized his nephew.

"Jamie, how in the world did you come to slide from a saddle?"

"My horse ran me into a thicket."

"Was there a pile of apples or some other treat tempting the animal? I'd wager you to be superior on horseback to every other ten-year-old on the entire Georgia Coast."

"Maybe I was distracted, from expecting company and all."

"Or from wishing you hadn't been left out of the town celebrations?"

"It sounds as if the week had its reversals," Margaret said, turning the topic. "Those who came for the Fourth anticipating nothing but rejoicing were surely sobered by the sad news that washed in days later." Charlotte and George were squealing with delight below, and the children's mother nodded to Liza to let her know it was all right for the youngsters to play more loudly than usual. "We could wonder if those two deaths come as a reminder from above. How fortunate we were to have great minds in charge when America needed them most."

"Or evidence from on high that triumph and tragedy are equals at best in this life," her brother Henry agreed. "Oh, sister, I've almost forgotten to produce a letter that found its way to our postal service, or what's left of it. Contentment is such a remnant these days. To think a carriage used to collect the mail from a docked ship and come all the way up to the grand house. Never mind the abundance we once took for granted on that acreage…"

Everyone enjoying the porch at dusk knew that when Henry Gignilliat uttered the word "Contentment," he would need more than a moment to recover from thoughts of the plantation's destruction. He would need longer to regain his composure from memories of his wife and the five youngest children lost before. The Peppers excused themselves and retired to the parlor.

"We'll visit more after a bit, if you're inclined, Margaret, while the children are being put to bed."

Mrs. Trezevant was glad for the distraction below, where Charles now trotted with George on his back, and Charlotte ran after to make sure she got a turn. She knew that Liza could coax them inside before long and that Barbara would show a mother's tenderness tucking them in. Elizabeth's reluctance to romp amused her. The child was far too big for the oldest brother to carry piggy-back. Suddenly remembering the settee, Margaret was pleased that her second son had curled up on his side and appeared asleep. When she turned again her brother's way, she was struck by how much the boy favored his uncle—a prominent brow and dark hair curling out at the ears. They had the same penetrating, deep-set eyes.

"For a few minutes today, I was afraid I'd lost my darling Jamie." She was giving her brother time to clear his throat, blow his nose and put his handkerchief away. "There are men who wouldn't have been strong enough to persevere after losing as much family as you did, Henry. Most men wouldn't have been anywhere near as strong as you."

"Well…" He shook his head, denying himself the compliment. "What did our doctor finally say about Jamie's head?"

"He couldn't find any sign at all of swelling. I have a sense this sleeping boy of mine is already himself again. But when we all saw his horse wandering back to the barn and him not in the saddle—"

"I am still amazed, sister, that he could be thrown under any circumstances. If he has no other talent than for riding, he'll rise above his peers for that alone."

Margaret Trezevant knew her brother to be shifting the topic from his own sorrows, but she let herself reach for his sleeve and squeeze his wrist.

"I just want you to know that all your nieces and nephews believe you to excel beyond your peers at being an uncle. Your son and Barbara, dear brother, are most fortunate in who they have as a father."

"We certainly can't say that I arrived today with news of improving finances." His chuckle was weak. "I have no idea what investment I can afford to attempt next, no idea whatsoever, but I do apologize for casting a pall at the dinner table."

"The news of Adams and Jefferson does cast a pall, but the country surely reveres them all the more for departing on a day that was already historic." She couldn't let their talk end without one more attempt at comforting him. "Besides, the Peppers are family, too. They might have surmised your business disappointment from your demeanor in town and driven on out here to help cheer you up." Henry was shaking his head again, but he stood up and then bent to place his hands on his sister's shoulders.

"Your husband John shouldn't have died at age twenty-nine, Meg. When he first came down with the fever, I could only see the curse of it and feel pangs of regret about how unlucky he was. But my thinking turned, of course, on the fact that he'd had you for his wife." He straightened himself up before giving her a pat and adding. "He might have been the luckiest man in all South Carolina." On the grounds below, the sparking wands had burnt out, and some of Callie's helpers were bringing lanterns out to the porch stairs. "Let me go see if Elizabeth will let me hoist her up and give her a short ride before they all come in. She's still a child, though she'll be grown like Barbara all too soon." He studied Jamie a moment and touched the boy's hair. "I'll ask someone in the kitchen to bring you a lantern so you can read your letter."

Within a quarter hour the gaiety below ended, and the children had been directed up the stairs and taken to bed. The woman left on the quiet porch could hear men's voices from the parlor and Mrs. Pepper's merry laugh. The frosted shortbread, if Callie had done her usual, dispelled any gloom, and she could imagine Charles and her niece lingering with guests and putting their manners on display. A lantern glowed over by the stables, and another small brilliant arc danced in the dark night. She thought Henry must have distributed the last of the sparking wands and that Deefy might be entertaining Benjamin, who often sat on a stool after his grooming chores.

The widow of John Trezevant read through the letter from her in-laws several times. Her children's grandparents had been in England for the last half year, after learning of an uncle's death in London. The couple's departure from South Carolina had dealt Margaret another shock, but she denied herself wistful yearning. As long as her father-in-law and mother-in-law still lived at the Stoll's Alley home in Charleston, the widow had felt uplifted by their standing invitation to visit. As long as their spacious home remained in the Trezevant family, Margaret had felt tangibly connected to the happy years she and John once shared with the children there. After losing that attachment, though, she wouldn't let nostalgia eclipse fundamental gratitude. How thankful she was that her husband had been so diligent as to secure her a modest annuity in the event of his death. The young lawyer had proven as responsible as he was affectionate. She wanted to put her hand in John's and thank him for his tender care. Nothing at such times would amend the loss of his companionship.

Margaret hadn't even realized she had begun to sob until she felt a different hand on her shoulder, one too small to be her brother's. Jamie was at her side, and his eyes were wide with concern. The boy had never seen his mother cry, and the odd sound she made as her chest shook frightened him.

"Was the letter sad? Did someone else die?" She put her arms around him and smoothed the curl at his forehead.

"Not at all, darling. I was suddenly thinking about your father."

Jamie felt the breath had been knocked out of him again. He didn't want to look where the cushions came together. The bloody rag made his stomach twinge. Now a disturbing image came to him of rags accumulating near his father's deathbed.

"I remember him more than Elizabeth does. He whistled when he wasn't in his study. And sometimes coming back from the courthouse. He always talked to the blacksmith at the end of the alley. He used to lift me up so I could see how the bellows worked," the boy rushed on.

"I didn't know I could still shed tears over losing your daddy."

"I'm sorry I made you worry that I might be…gone, too."

She was glad they had the porch to themselves. In another year or two this son, as well, would think himself too old for her lingering embrace.

"It's a cold-hearted mother who doesn't spend half her day worrying in some way about her children."

"From now on, I promise, I won't try to make any horse run beyond its inclination."

"I should think not."

"Were you crying about President Adams and President Jefferson? Or did Grandfather's letter tell other bad news?" Jamie was realizing that blood had a smell, different from sweat. From recall or premonition, he shuddered to conclude that the bedclothes of the dying smelled much stronger than the damp shirt he'd worn in the morning sun.

"I think I'm overcome with appreciation on both counts, dear."

"I'm sorry Uncle Henry's investment went against his hopes."

"He'll get his footing again, like you've done after your spill. And he'll suffer no more worrying on our account, I'm certain. Grandfather's letter conveys the most wonderful news. Your generous grandparents are sharing an inherited fortune with their children, including us it seems." Immediately, she straightened up and brushed at the corners of her eyes. "You must act as if you were still sleeping when I made such a commotion a minute ago, as if I never discussed this letter with you. Children ought not to be privy to the finances adults agonize over."

"I probably ended up Papa's most quiet child. If my riding skills go in decline, I can still rise above my peers in keeping secrets." The boy's mother nodded in agreement, but it was clear now that Jamie had not been asleep through too much of her talk with Henry.

"We'll all find a house of our own in Darien for next school year, and not impose on the Peppers' generosity any further. I know you'll be as discreet as any adult, Jamie, until that occasion comes about." Her sigh was familiar again. "And now I'll be able to organize Barbara's coming out event, though I'm not sure whether Savannah or Charleston would be her preference. At least my brother won't feel his heart break at not being able to take on that full expense." Her son's attention had already drifted away toward the stables where a few stray sparks were still dancing. "And you James Peter, you and your brother will have no worries about tuition at the college in Columbia."

"I haven't even finished academy yet."

"When the two of you finish in Darien…"

"I can be anything I want?"

"Well, after news from the Fourth, I wouldn't say any young man should aspire to becoming the greatest President of all time."

"When I grow up I'd like to be a man who has just one story about falling off his horse."

The Trezevant boy felt recovered. His dull headache had vanished. Shock over his mother's display of emotion had been erased, but he kept turning over in his mind her fear that he might have been "lost."

The house was quiet except for the soothing sound of adult conversation in the parlor and the muffled clacking of clean dishes being put away in the kitchen. Jamie's mother stayed a moment longer on the porch before folding up the letter and joining her guests. She didn't mind leaving the lantern on the porch so that he could find his way down the steps and across the grounds to the stable. He hesitated at the top plank, shuddering at the inky edges of woodland that rimmed the clearing he aimed to cross. *It's not an idle worry over losing your way, if some dark force can sweep out with no warning and extinguish your light.* Sweat circles spread again at the upper sleeves of his shirt. There was no entirely squelching fear. No boy or man would be surviving any such lethal power.

He wrenched his thinking around to his virtue of keeping confidences. Even that small attribute must have come, in part, from his mother. She'd already joined the people inside. She would keep to herself her assumption that he'd go thank Deefy for saving him from roaming bears and from his own occasional recklessness.

Chapter 5   The Approach of Thunder

For the last hour, the young American kept his horse three lengths behind Juan Seguin's. The captain noted that the Goliad man didn't need to be told to talk steadily to the animal. It was difficult to predict how a horse so newly acquired would behave in battle. It was impossible to foresee whether a great clash might erupt in two days or two minutes, or from what direction.

Seguin strained to listen over his own mount's plodding steps. Any patrol coming over a low rise to the north might be scouts from Sam Houston's army. Hot as the afternoon was growing, he would keep the poncho pulled over his Mexican uniform until he could identify himself. If some of Santa Anna's spies or couriers should appear from the south, he would shed the outerwear and act briefly as if the private riding with him were his prisoner. Trezevant, he felt, had enough to manage without reminders of these contingencies. Suddenly, the officer pointed to drying mud that stretched out between a broad patch of pink blossoms.

"A male panther," he said, lifting his rifle to point in the direction the paw prints went.

"A wildcat?"

"*Si.* Some will call it a mountain lion. No resting under a tree before we inspect the branches."

Instead of heading toward a sturdy live oak to their left, he gestured at a nondescript thicket of scrub trees in the opposite direction. Intending to prod the brushy tufts where the two might sit out the next hour of late afternoon heat, he fixed his bayonet. They'd already edged past one coiled diamondback, and Seguin's horse had danced nervously away from the chilling rattle of another.

The captain nursed no regrets about staying behind on the more perilous mission, though he imagined his comrades' relief upon rejoining the rest of the Tejano company near San Felipe. Flores, Arrocha, Ramirez, Maldonado—and twenty more—they would all be awaiting a decisive battle but making the most of a respite with Houston's army. Captain Mosely Baker surely found a place for Hardaway and the other two Goliad stragglers. This one on the horse behind him wouldn't likely have made it on foot up the Brazos and all the way to Groce's plantation where the independence forces swelled. The trek with mismatched shoes had nearly crippled him. Any Georgia Battalion survivors—half naked and ground up as if they'd been belched from hell's belly—could inspire as much terror as zeal in Texas ranks.

This gaunt youth, Trezevant, had told him about falling off a horse only once as a child. The private didn't need to be informed that a spill on the battlefield meant death. It wouldn't help the young soldier to be forewarned that his horse might be shot from underneath him and a rifle butt slammed against his skull.

"Where are we now?" The soldier sitting atop his horse had let out the reins, and the animal was chewing at a green mound. Seguin was ready to help the young man down if he asked.

"We are close to a fork that Houston, too, will find. To keep the upper trail is to go east and reach Louisiana. The Trinity must be crossed before the Sabine, where they say General Gaines might be waiting with a dozen American units. Not a way that Santa Anna wishes to die, I think."

"When you and your men first found us, you were saying Filisola might go all the way to the eastern border." The Fannin volunteer was breathing better and his sentences came in longer spurts.

"I have heard he is much to the northeast. Perhaps intending to take Nacogdoches first." He regretted letting his thoughts travel there. "My family may be sheltering in that town. If Filisola reaches so far along the Camino Real, my wife and sister-in-law will rush with the niños to St. Augustine and cross the river for Fort Jessup's protection."

While Seguin spoke, the ragged private leaned and let himself slide his right leg from over the horse's tan rump. The boots passed along to him from one of the fleeing women appeared almost too heavy to manage. His dismount was a heartrending accomplishment. Watching him for only a moment, the officer held up a spy glass to examine the stately live oak across the field, to check his emotions, and to let the younger man catch his breath.

"Do you think the Yarico woman and the others have moved on?"

"This was my advice. It is good they crossed the Brazos somewhat upriver of Fort Bend, as we did. Even if Santa Anna is moving his army across at this moment, Yarico and those with her will be beyond his view. I have told her to reach the next river as soon as possible, to keep precisely east."

He took a bite of dried beef after offering the wedge to Trezevant. Seguin could not explain, even to himself, why he had told a little lie to the black woman. It was not a memory he would have shared with a neighbor in San Antonio or even his wife, yet he had told the story—with its small but significant lie—to a total stranger. The boy who fell to his knees weeping, before his returning father could reach him on horseback, this was not in fact how the captain's son had greeted him. The memory was from thirty years earlier. Erasmo, his own father, had let his horse saunter across the plaza to the crying boy, little Juan Seguin himself.

Juanito, can you take the reins for me? What are these tears you have? Did I not tell you I would be back by the next full moon? Dry your cheeks and take the reins for me. Let us look like men when we greet your mother. For her sake, let us keep our eyes dry.

When thunder rumbled off to the north, the officer angled his spy glass away from the limbs of the live oak and aimed at a gray streak underneath expanding white clouds. He wondered whether there might be as many as seven hundred men with Sam Houston, all listening to the same thunder and praying for a light afternoon shower instead of a downpour. Seguin wondered how the rumble might affect the women's flight, whether the threat of rain would spur them on or sap their determination. He pondered reports on the size of Santa Anna's army, dismissing the number as exaggerated. Sesma and Cos, on the other hand, could already have joined him with recovering ranks or hearty recruits. Surely, there were not already as many as a thousand Mexican soldiers crossing the Brazos River at Fort Bend and stepping up their maneuver at the threat of more rain.

It took no longer than twenty minutes for both soldiers to doze, though Seguin had said he would keep first watch. He still sat upright on the folded poncho, with one hand on his rifle and another grasping the spyglass. A spare pistol lay nearby. For another quarter hour, his dulled senses took in no sounds except the creak and scrape of shifting tree limbs and the muted rustle of leaves. A dragonfly zigzagged near his head periodically, and a cardinal guarding its hidden nest sang out. After a while, he heard the thuds of horse dung landing. An acrid and familiar odor reached his nostrils. The officer glanced aside, determining that it had been his own steed, before squinting to shut his eyes tighter. It struck him then, how peculiar the animal's ears had looked, not flopping forward as usual when dung dropped, but twitching backward in response to something far off. There had been no thunder in the last few seconds, and suddenly Captain Juan Seguin was alert and on his knees, crouching, and tapping the American soldier into wakefulness.

The sound of horses, likely no more than two, came from the south. He thought it could be scouts returning toward Houston's position. More likely the riders were Mexican and hunting for any sign of amassing rebels. There was no time for the private to pull himself onto his horse, but it was just as well that approaching soldiers not see Trezevant anywhere close to a weapon. Instead, the independence fighters readied to step out from the clump of stunted trees. When the spy glass made it possible for Seguin to identify uniforms from Santa Anna's army—the gray pants of a lower ranked soldier and the red breast flap of an officer—he walked the American private at rifle point away from the scrawny limbs.

As the Mexican pair came into view, Seguin turned so that the red on his own uniform was visible. Trezevant kept his back to the approaching riders as if he might be relieving himself. He had consumed half the water in a gourd the captain provided, and his rising anxiety made it easy enough to play his role. Seguin waved nonchalantly as the riders drew within earshot. He kept his rifle barrel directed toward the American.

"*Buenas tardes! Un americano aquí!*"

"*Sólo uno?*"

"*Sí, uno!*"

Seeing that the officer on his feet appeared to have the prisoner under control, the two soldiers let their horses approach slowly. Both secured their weapons in leather slings attached to their saddles. The man of lower rank studied the outcrop of scrub oak before shifting his gaze across the field to the heftier tree with wider shade. Relaxed, they directed their mounts close enough to carry on a conversation without shouting at the man in charge, and they both saluted, recognizing superior rank. The prisoner raised his hands before turning to face the men on horseback. His threadbare clothes and cadaverous stature robbed them of casual speech. They leaned, adjusting their saddle slings, to keep from staring.

"*Qué pasó?*" the dismounting lieutenant asked. The other soldier, perhaps not as seasoned a rider, slid stiffly to the ground. He was a slight man with skin of deeper brown and a crude haircut. The senior scout looked inclined to apologize for his awkward companion, but his

The Dove Shall Fly

raised eyebrows betrayed some contempt for the rough appearance of the captain, as well.

"Qué pasó?" Seguin repeated casually. He appeared entirely relaxed. "*Solamente Goliad.*" He didn't need to say more. When he swung his rifle around at the scouting pair, a dark realization canceled the Mexican officer's affable expression like a storm cloud passing over a sunlit meadow. The unsuspecting lieutenant showed his teeth before letting his mouth open wide.

"Cristo." He spat once before the sound of many hooves riveted the attention of all four. Whoops breaking up the afternoon peace might have panicked a less experienced Texan, but Juan Seguin could distinguish the warrior cries of Apache or Comanche from the fearsome salutations that Houston's followers often practiced. Four with Houston's cavalry had boiled out from near the lone oak, but Seguin kept his firearm trained on the two prisoners.

"There's a palomino, two paints, and a roan," Trezevant informed him. The men are in buckskin, except for one with red hair. He has a poncho, like yours. No, one has an American army jacket, but with all that mud—"

"Deaf Smith, it sounds like. Captain Karnes rides a palomino, but don't move your arms. The others may doubt who I am and shoot before asking."

The meeting inspired equal parts caution and fervor in the independence fighters. Greetings confirmed that Karnes and Smith knew the other Texas captain well and from as far back as early action in Gonzales. Seguin asked about Smith's wife—another Tejana who might be sheltering in Nacogdoches—before inquiring about the restiveness of Houston's regiments not thirty miles from where they stood. A rifle barrel aimed at them, the captured patrol of two otherwise went ignored for several minutes. Jamie Trezevant judged the encounter to be well under control, and he moved from the bright sun to the folded poncho in the shade to sit before weakness overcame him.

"So," Seguin began addressing the prisoners, "can one of you *hombres* beg mercy in English?" He doubted his own abilities as translator, especially when precision was critical. "Speak or not, we will soon destroy your army." The Mexican officer made a snorting sound that he attempted to disguise by coughing. It was the other soldier catching their attention, though. His lips would not stop quivering long enough for him to answer. Deaf Smith detached a water gourd from the captive's saddle and allowed the frightened man several sips.

"*Hablo inglés,*" he managed to say, shaking his head. "I mean, I speak a little good English. My father was the librarian of our town. He taught me. This is why I am here with the lieutenant."

"Don't worry about him," Karnes said pointing to the officer under guard. "How he might punish you, that's way down on your list of worries."

"My Spanish, even, it is different. Something else he does not comprehend so easily." He stole a glance at his superior, who scowled seemingly because of his underling's cooperation and not specifics. "I am from what we call Yucatan. Do you know where is this place?"

"Mexico," the corporal with Captain Smith blurted.

"*Si,* yes, but far down the gulf. There they are taking us by force. Conscription ships sail down from Matamoros mostly. We are not soldiers, but they take us and march us to—"

"You want me to reach for my hankie?" The whole group that had ridden across the field with Karnes began to mutter until he waved to quiet them. So far, to avoid alerting any other enemy patrol close by, they'd refrained from using their firearms. A careless and loud argument could prove fatal. "You're serving now under a general that Texans hate worse than a ten-year drought or ten cutthroat Comanches. Where is Santa Anna today and what the hell mission are you two on?"

His Excellency the President of Mexico and leader of the country's army was expecting General Urrea or Cos to be inland, maybe upriver this far. Perhaps Filisola, as well. The officer with him specialized in cartography, and he was carrying maps to show where Mexican regiments would appear next. His Excellency wanted his other generals to immediately head where Santa Anna himself was rushing with the greater part of his army. The import of this capture began sinking in, and the only sound for a few seconds was the buzz of a horsefly and an approaching rumble.

"Well then, where's his goddam excellency rushing to?"

"To Harrisburg, *señor...capitán.* We have news that the rebel named Burnet, the man you call *presidente,* I think, is there with the entire... what General Santa Anna says is *the pirate government of the Texas colony.*"

"He aims to overrun President Burnet and the Texas government that's just moved to Harrisburg..."

"And kill them, yes. He wishes to cut off the head of the snake, señor."

The two men with Smith and Karnes—a corporal and a private—were now going through the satchels secured on the captured lieutenant's horse. None of the Texans paid further attention to the prisoners except to keep them under guard. From where Jamie Trezevant sat to spare his weakened legs, he could see when the conscript began to chew his lip, either from shame that he had so readily divulged important information or from fear that life itself was latching its doors.

The Goliad survivor was trying to read the other prisoner's expression—shame and fear, but also anger and contempt. The proud lieutenant was nowhere near his own weapon, but Trezevant judged the man to be inching away from self-control, too. He thought the prisoner capable of lunging at captors he considered inferior and of forcing gunshots that might warn an outlying company under Santa Anna.

As the others examined a ledger pulled from the guarded officer's belongings, the private traveling with Seguin observed his comrade's rapidly shifting expressions. Some shock, as from an obscenity, disrupted the man's customary demeanor of patience and accommodation. Then a scowl of grief and hatred transformed his face. The seated soldier had grown wary ever since the captain pointed out mountain lion tracks, but he was now bracing himself for the fury of a treed animal. Whatever a beast of prey might look like leaping upon its doomed target, Captain Juan Seguin appeared no less deadly as he charged, growling, at the unarmed lieutenant, forcing him to the ground and tearing into him with a flurry of blows. Trezevant was quick to rise with the Tejano's spare pistol and aim, as a warning, at the soldier from Yucatan. It took the other four men to pry Seguin's fingers from the Mexican lieutenant's throat and to drag him away from the stupefied prisoner.

"Dammit, Juan, he's a map-maker! He's no use to us dead, for crissake!" Seguin shook himself free from Captain Karnes' grasp and straightened himself up as if the recovery of rational behavior were a monumental feat.

"Look at the leather folder, Henry" he managed to say. "Look at the back of the folder!" The corporal still had the cartographer's leather booklet in his hands and he opened it before closing it again and looking at the back flap.

"*WBT*," he said. "His initials, it looks like." A few drops of rain made the horses whinny, and the sharp smell of an advancing storm swept through the gathering.

"William…Barret…Travis," Karnes said, his eyes glistening. He pronounced the name as if he'd swallowed gravel. Juan Seguin breathed through his mouth and cast his gaze now at the threatening sky as if he needed strength from above to maintain self-control.

"More than once, Colonel Travis put this folder into my hands."

An enemy possessing a treasured artifact—any such sacrilege brought on darkest thoughts. The wish to commit murder was unanimous, but so was their unspoken agreement on the potential value of a map expert. The hands of both prisoners were tied, and they were kept on the ground away from one another while the six soldiers pledged to Sam Houston urgently conferred.

"Whatever you order, Henry…" Smith started out. He understood by reading lips, and his voice poured out in monotone. "Which is more dire, getting this message to Houston or to Burnet?"

"Like asking which needed saving, the Alamo or Goliad." Karnes spat in the direction of the bound officer. "We can't fail either. We've got to split up. It won't help much to warn Burnet if Houston isn't on the way. I haven't known any terrain or weather yet, Deaf, to lessen your chances in a fray."

"I can make it to Harrisburg on my own."

"Take your best rider."

"If one of us gets…off track," the older soldier agreed, "the other will get through. We'll see that Burnet and our government boys head on down the coast as close to Galveston as possible. The two of us can get to Harrisburg by this time tomorrow, but it's gonna take twice that to move our whole damn army the same distance."

Giving his anger time to ebb, Captain Seguin let these two settle on practical action. Smith, readying to mount his horse, stroked the animal before running his fingers through his own distinctive red hair. His corporal was checking their provisions, as the other enlisted man brought the captives to their feet.

"Transporting these couriers you've caught will take another two men. My thinking is you need to be one of them, Juan." Under Colonel Sidney Sherman, Henry Karnes had risen to second in command of the cavalry, but he was careful how he articulated his authority. All six Texans might have been wondering whether Seguin could subdue his urge to kill at least one of the enemy in their charge. "I don't think the general will trust the Santa Anna news coming from anyone but you."

"You are right, of course." Seguin grimaced as he rubbed his knuckles. "Your private already knows the way to the farm that is our headquarters now. He can lead. If we don't make General Houston's tents by dusk, Henry, we'll have to wait until morning to reach the outskirts."

"Even in daylight, you'll get your head blowed off without a white badge on your hat," Smith warned in flat intonation. "Back at camp, the rest of your company has itself outfitted with white signal badges. Too many new recruits pouring in can't pick out you Tejanos from Santy Anny's henchmen, otherwise. Where is your dang hat anyway?"

"It fell to the Brazos yesterday morning. Perhaps it floated all the way to the Yucatan by now."

Not having heard his own assignment stated, James Trezevant stepped gingerly to the tan horse, the unfamiliar boots barely keeping him steady. All three captains now gave the Goliad survivor their full attention. None needed to say aloud how wasteful it would be of the young man's diminished energy to have him travel all the way up to Houston's encampment only to take part in a haphazard formation that force-marched back to this starting point.

Captain Karnes looked doubtful. Should the weakened man accompany him to the eastern fork, the partnership might slow him down at a crucial moment. Seguin had said something in their first exchange, though, about the private's skill on horseback. The Yucatan conscript also gave his attention to the Texans. He was standing, and he was nodding as if he could decipher their thoughts as well as their distinct accents. Then, a thunder clap muted the crack of a single pistol shot.

The captured officer fell face down at the feet of Juan Seguin. Hair above his temple was red and matted. He writhed and twitched momentarily before going still.

"He was fixin' to go for your rifle," the corporal with Smith said to Seguin. "I seen him looking at your bayonet." The other enlistee stayed silent and began to fiddle with a stirrup buckle. No one had the stomach to dispute the threat of a prisoner whose hands were well tied.

"He could have been good use!"

"Houston already has a map-maker, captain." Now checking his saddle, the reserved private addressed Karnes but avoided looking at the man who'd fired.

Just moments before the Mexican lieutenant took a bullet, the voices and actions of those gathered had conveyed urgency. Now, a pistol shot was ringing in their ears and blood trickled out from under a body.

Ruthlessness was beginning to rule events the way a sudden downpour transforms a dusty gulch. They awaited Captain Karnes' response.

"You two drag him into the grass and bushes. Weigh some brush down over him with rocks as best you can."

"Better than the boys at the Alamo or Goliad got."

"If his clothes aren't ruined, better see what our Fannin man here can use." Karnes stepped away from the scene and recommended to Deaf Smith that he and the guilty soldier take off to Harrisburg before a full storm broke.

"Looks like you're getting a hat, Juan." Captain Smith gestured without smiling. "Fix a handkerchief or a white scrap on top somehow, or you'll end up like him. Anyways, Houston should be glad to get two more horses, if he can find men that ride half decent. Does Trezevant want to swap?" The Georgia Battalion man was surprised to hear his name.

"No, sir. I'm getting to know this one. He seems to take my commands willingly enough."

James Trezevant wasn't sure how another horse would respond to his odd mounting technique. He wasn't sure he'd have time to achieve some familiarity with another animal, not the mutual trust that bolstered courage when riding into danger. The American volunteer had been wondering in the last few minutes whether he might be the only one in the group who'd witnessed a battle death before. Juan Seguin, having been sent from the Alamo by Travis to seek reinforcements, had narrowly missed the carnage there. Karnes and Smith were among General Houston's regulars and had only heard of the Goliad executions through couriers. Except for scant gunfire exchanged in autumn stand-offs, Trezevant thought the entire Texas army might be as green as he'd been five months ago. Captain Karnes, he realized suddenly, was scrutinizing him. He'd looked up from the dead lieutenant's main map.

"Why the hell is there a star by this town…Refugio? Didn't Fannin and his men only pass through there on the way up the coast to Goliad?"

"Companies with Fannin and those of us with William Ward's battalion, we all stayed there a while before moving on in early January."

"What happened that gave the place stars?" Karnes was keeping his compass steady and looking to the west where all the action had occurred so far.

"Colonel Ward was sent back to Refugio with most of us from Georgia. There were stranded Irish colonists holed up in the church sanctuary where Captain King was supposed to—"

"Refugio? It was you in the mission town Refugio?" The surviving prisoner had spoken up on impulse, but now he seemed to realize he might be killed for divulging that he'd been there, too. "My friends...all *muertos*...in the main street at Refugio. The Americans, they fired from a low wall outside the church, and General Urrea's officers made us go out into the main street again...to get shot and to die."

When Ward's ammunition ran out, Trezevant explained, the battalion had attempted escape to Victoria. A muddy and agonizing retreat followed. But there was no time to piece the past few weeks together.

None in the present gathering doubted that plenty more men would face a lethal barrage while Texas independence was won or discarded as a fool's dream. Before the deceased prisoner was dragged to the thick brush, he was rolled over, his face an unrecognizable wreck. But his clothes were unscathed, and the shirt underneath his blue and red jacket did not stink. He might have changed into it fresh that very morning or the day before. Santa Anna was strict about the appearance of his officers.

The Texans understood James Trezevant's revulsion in accepting the officer's clean shirt. His own tattered clothing reeked, though, of mud and sweat. Since Ward's midnight flight from the church in Refugio, Jamie's shirt and pants had gradually been torn into pieces and shreds, some of which needed to be peeled from his torso. The dead lieutenant's body was stocky, and no one thought the blue trousers would stay up on the emaciated Goliad man. Instead, Trezevant changed into the translator's gray pants.

When the remaining captive pulled on the looser pair, he belted them far below the waistband. His ankles were exposed by three inches, but the salvaged pants would make riding more comfortable than long-johns alone. They could spend no more time taking mercy on the Yucatan soldier who had not chosen to join any fight.

Private Trezevant, Juan Seguin thought, looked a little lost atop the animal he'd been sweet-talking for a day. The young soldier probably wanted to speak some final *adios* to the officer that had found him and three more of Ward's survivors wandering away from Victoria. Seguin reassured himself that Captain Henry Karnes was a good man, and the fork in the road where the Texas army headed was no more than twenty miles east. Karnes and Smith had both packed provisions, so Trezevant could continue food intake gradually. The fellow insisted on keeping the boots given to him by the women and children earlier. He would survive as long as the next day, Seguin reasoned, and perhaps no more could be promised to any of the others, not even President Burnet and General Houston.

The private leading the way back to the Texas general's encampment took charge of the horse with the bound prisoner. Captain Seguin followed with the fourth mount on a tether. He could have benefitted from time with his own thoughts. The enlisted man, though—who'd stayed mostly silent during the scuffle and after the gunfire—grew talkative and spoke frequently over his shoulder. Seguin was generous enough to indulge him, as long as he didn't ask him again to predict Houston's handling of the monogrammed folder.

"There's a new man with the cavalry since you were in camp."

"Is that so?"

"Last name is Lamar, but I'll be flogged if I can pronounce his first name. Something French."

"My father's ancestor was French."

"He signed up at lowest rank, but the way he rides tells me he's due a promotion. He only got to Texas two or three weeks ago. Ships aren't going farther than Galveston since March. He rode some and then took a steamer up to near San Felipe where Houston had his muster rolls. They say Lamar is all the way from Georgia."

"Trezevant might know the name."

"Did you hear we got the two cannons promised from Cincinnati?"

"We won't travel too fast if we're pulling artillery."

"They'll dang sure blow some heads off when we finally get a chance to aim them."

The conversation between the private and Captain Seguin lapsed, each man trying not to think of the head they'd just seen disfigured by pounding and then demolished by gunshot. The captain fixed his thoughts on where the final contact with Santa Anna's military forces might take place. The Mexican general probably had issued special orders about the treatment of traitors to the nation's army. Seguin didn't think his own end would come as easily as his horse collapsing beneath him and his skull getting crushed by a musket ball.

No, he believed there would be special orders to spare the life of any Tejano the Mexicans might find among the independence fighters, especially any officers. Maybe a specific order had been given about the capture of Captain Juan Seguin, whose own father had helped govern the Texas province, whose own father had overseen the early colonization agreements. If he were captured, Seguin thought—*the ungrateful and duplicitous son*—the orders might declare it a patriotic duty to keep the traitor alive so he could be brought before Santa Anna himself. No, the Tejano captain admitted, his death would be slow, and nothing easy about it. If this worst possibility materialized, perhaps he would be able to keep last thoughts on his family. It would be too painful to imagine his wife and his *niños* carrying on without him, but he might be able to withstand some indignity and agony if he could imagine the words of his father and his grandfather and the French relative before.

Juanito, soon you will be able to take the reins and join us. Do not let the enemy shame you to tears and cries for mercy. Did we not tell you this family was destined for a land of freedom? Our ancestral blood is infused with la liberté. Yet it was not in France nor on the mainland of Mexico where we recovered our birthright of independence. Soon you will take the reins and ride away from this earth, but your descendants will live free. Like you, they will honor Texas. Let us look like men, Juanito, let us keep our eyes dry.

Chapter 6 What's in a Name?

"Use my handkerchief, Sophie dear." Red, white, and blue victory stitching had come into vogue again after the War of 1812.

When the two women emerged from Savannah's smaller meeting hall, April sunshine from the west was creeping into the veranda. Activity in the market sprawling before them had peaked hours earlier, but enough shoppers milled in the square to discourage any vendors from packing up. A stroll across the pubic space would provide both women the distraction they needed. The matinée of *Captain Inkle and Yarico* deeply affected them, even with the stage set so pared down. The theater troupe had not expected to perform south of Charleston.

"Just keep it until next time," the more composed lady said about the handkerchief. She was trying to cheer her friend. "I still have that one of yours with the tatted lace." They descended the steps into the tree-lined square before opening their parasols. "If we weren't blessed with ties to staunch theater patrons, we'd have missed the play altogether. Most of Savannah did. Now, you and I can count the South Carolina measles outbreak as good fortune."

Her statement appeared to shock more than uplift the woman with her. Overcome by the production they'd just attended, Sophie Pagnol dabbed at her eyes.

"That performance took everything out of me. How can they call it a comedy?"

"The version that Roland and I saw in Covent Garden had the heroine dying at the end, too, as well as her child. Too terribly sad. You and Guy must consider a trip to England, before all this embargo nonsense gets out of hand." She looked again at the pamphlet about the play. "Two weeks ago, Philadelphia audiences at Walnut Street were applauding it, and if measles hadn't gripped Charleston—"

"I know, Miriam, but if someone hears you call any outbreak fortunate…"

"Anyway, the three of you would adore London. What is Delphine now, six? You should all go before we end up in a third war over who rules this country."

Mrs. Pagnol did believe the friend hugging her elbow too often made comments intended to startle. But Miriam Tuttle had a remarkably open mind, and there were some topics she could broach with her and no other female acquaintance in the town of five thousand. Both ladies were trying to conceal how the controversial play had affected them, and Sophie didn't mind her companion's provocative banter.

"If I had as much influence over my husband as you have on yours, I'd make him produce funds for building a proper theater. Savannah's population will demand one soon enough."

A vendor with a German accent tipped his straw hat and waved his hand over a display of golden chains. He next withdrew his own pocket watch to demonstrate the item. An array of cuff links glinted on black velvet, and Sophie felt a surge of pride that her husband had minimal interest in such accessories.

"Guy hasn't decided what to with the Hugues Pagnol inheritance yet. I think he's still in shock over the amount. He never communicated with that brother very often."

"All that was, what, a year ago? Give your advocate notice that you want the next spacious home coming available on Ellis square. A small domicile went up last week. I almost forgot to mention it, a house not quite large enough for staging a theater production in the parlor. I don't blame the troupe for not hauling in the set, but weren't the costumes splendid?"

"Mr. Ledbetter came in from Tybee just a few days ago," Sophie confided. She stopped short of mentioning that the lawyer had made three trips to their home in as many months, much less that the attorney's cook was caring for Delphine that very afternoon. "More papers to sign about the indigo trade left to us, but Guy is perfectly content living two blocks off River Street. His walk from our house to the cotton exchange takes no time, and I can stroll in any direction I like with our daughter."

Her friend, who felt the Pagnols needed a second rig for in-town social calls, did not respond right away. Both ladies paused to gaze at the tops of the live oaks planted according to the city's original layout. The tree limbs had begun to widen and sprawl in recent years and they'd observed on other excursions that the square would one day be in the shade of their arc from morning to dusk. They wondered if the astonishing display of finery and edibles would appear so colorful and tempting in full shadow.

"You and your dear Guy have no suspense or drama in your life. The three of you are far too happy," Miriam said at last.

Sophie Pagnol appreciated her friend's company. She did not wish her to push the boundaries of their confidence, however, by asking how the couple was coping with their inability to have more children. Their only daughter would soon turn six and more than one physician had told Mrs. Pagnol that she was lucky to have carried one baby to term. Childless themselves, the Tuttles had considered adopting from the town's Bethesda home, which sheltered male orphans. But Miriam admitted an abiding preference for baby girls. The two women moved quickly past a familiar Irish couple offering embroidered infant bibs, as well as aprons and pillow case edging.

"Lace for your Sunday collar? Ribbon for your daughter's braids?" If Delphine had been with Sophie, the vendor's wife would have offered them a small bow as a sample.

The Pagnol woman shook her head pleasantly before her thoughts returned to the unscheduled theater production. She could not convey to her afternoon companion how much the first act had jolted her. When the Indian maiden Yarico knelt giving care on the beach to a shipwrecked captain, Sophie felt an overpowering kinship with both characters. The castaway officer's plight reminded her of Guy Pagnol's susceptibility to falling sickness. This secret, though, was kept strictly between husband and wife. She reminded herself to keep watch for anyone in the market offering herbal remedies and to make the most of an opportunity to purchase more mugwort without Miriam's notice. A tea made from the herbal leaves would usually soothe Guy after an attack. Fortunately, the infrequent seizures came with enough warning that the respected accountant could walk home quickly before succumbing. Sophie had knelt to tend to him more than a dozen times.

"If I ever complain about my circumstances in life, I hope you will remind me of the tragedy we just watched. I fail to see its comedic elements."

"It's cheerful enough when they first discover love," Sophie's friend said, "but I remember my own husband's comment after the Covent Garden opening—*A female native should have known her affection for an English captain would end badly.*" Usually ready to laugh, she let the corners of her mouth tighten before going on. "Saved the captain after he washed ashore, basked in mutual love until he sold her off as a slave, and then had to face life with a child out of wedlock."

Sophie agreed by nodding and then shaking her head. She folded the patriotic handkerchief inside out as they continued their walk along the square. No adult citizen of Savannah was ignorant of the port's beginnings, which included an agreement with the native Yamacraw settlement below the city's bluff. However, any reference to the Indian wife of Savannah's original trader, Mrs. Pagnol feared, would likely fade from school lessons well before the live oaks overhead completed their embrace. In a burst of confidentiality a few years ago, Miriam Tuttle had even confessed lineage with John's Rolfe's spouse Pocahontas, though Sophie felt it was not her place to bring that fact into their current conversation.

"Lemons! Straight from the Floridas! Plantains from the Antilles!"

Mrs. Pagnol saw her friend gesture at a lively stand across the pavilion where fresh harvest was offered, but she encouraged her afternoon companion to go make a purchase without her. The aromatic tables of bright fruit, below dangling fish and plucked chickens, made her queasy. She had felt shaken and ill ever since Captain Inkle took money from the Hispaniola slave trader in exchange for Yarico.

Nearby haggling, opposite the produce section, pulled Sophie away from somber reflection. One shopper walked off from an arrangement of parlor doilies, and a trader's wife let her arms cross at her bosom. Behind the next display table, draped in astonishing magenta and rose, sat a woman easily recognized as among the free black residents of Savannah. The vendor offered an array of fans—from feathered to linen to varnished paper pleats—as well as oyster shell hair combs and pearl brooches. Miriam would have loosened grasp on her elbow if she'd been with her, and Mrs. Pagnol enjoyed being able to walk directly toward the gaily dressed merchant and bid her good day.

"And *bonjour* to you, too, madame."

"My daughter is not with me today. I recall she likes to practice her French with you."

"*Moi aussi*, I remember, madame. So *charmante*, your petite girl."

There was something else, Sophie felt, that the familiar individual was about to say, but the moment passed and the woman opened her palms to accentuate the wide selection. Although the spring afternoon would not turn hot enough to necessitate cooling oneself, such days and long stretches were coming soon.

Sophie Pagnol already possessed fans for sundry occasions, and she didn't delight in unnecessary purchases, as many ladies did. A fan with elegant stenciled panels lay tucked inside her handbag, and she'd thought of retrieving it when the tense drama had made her cheeks flush. She grew compelled, however, to buy one item from Delphine's favorite vendor. The woman's tranquil features glistened, and her eyes shone beneath a mauve headdress. She had a self-possession subdued in people of color who served Savannah's homes. It was a quality rarely observed in shackled slaves at auction near her husband's accounting office.

The fan merchant, who spoke two languages, could have plucked any castaway from swirling water, Mrs. Pagnol believed. She wanted to make a purchase whether she needed a new fan or not. She opened one with pleats that snapped when it closed, but she thought the ivory handle excessive.

"Have you seen these, madame? From the south of France. They are *aide-à-memoire*, not so *ravissant* at first glance, not for everyone. But open this one, tell me what you find and if its…*raison d'être*…is to your liking."

When Sophie realized there was fancy script in patches across the open pleats, she folded her parasol and let sunlight better reveal the lettering. She could then see the faint outline of geographical borders. Countries were listed alongside their capitals, with European destinations prominent, though Lima, Peru, appeared on one wedge. Before she could comment on the United States listing, the smiling vendor apologized.

"Some are still thinking our capital is Philadelphia."

"So I see," Sophie agreed.

"You can say to some people what you know to be true, what you have seen as witness," she shrugged, "and still they will believe what they prefer."

"I suppose that's always been the case." The woman's philosophical observation took her by surprise, and she could think of no other response except to comment on the fan's dual purpose, which was new to her. "What a remarkable idea, to include within the pleats some learning as well as decoration. Most ladies will admit to have felt their entire education evaporate on a hot summer afternoon, along with topics for discussion. Fanning alone does not always revive intelligent conversation."

"And so madame, this memory-helper, this *aide-à-memoire*, will stimulate the dialogue, *non*? Even if you wish to point out the flaw in this one, you shall laugh to comment that Philadelphia has not been our capital for quite some time."

Flustered, Sophie was trying to locate her coin purse, because she intended to buy that very fan. She tried to assess her enjoyment of their exchange, which had lifted her melancholy more than chatting with Miriam. The amiable merchant had likely noticed the two ladies strolling before with their parasols, and Sophie glanced across the pavilion as the other shopper was starting back with a parcel of lemons.

"Thank you, yes," she said, handing over several coins. Turning, she caught Miriam's eye and waved. "My daughter will love this. I expect we'll study the globe this evening." She wished the girl, at ease with every stranger, were there to smooth the transaction's end.

"Then, madame, if you permit…" The merchant withdrew another fan from a satchel behind the vivid table, and at first Mrs. Pagnol was struck by how rapidly she could re-stock her display. When the black woman slipped a second *aide-à-memoire* into Sophie's open handbag, however, the accountant's wife couldn't react. "May I ask you to give this of the same kind to Désirée Martin?" The item was already purchased apparently, and to be passed along to a third party. When she saw her friend Miriam Tuttle approaching, she managed to stammer.

"Is it Flora that you know? Madame Martin is taking her place today. Do you and Flora attend the same church? Or do you know Madame Martin?" The sparkle in the vendor's eyes was extinguished, and the conversation closed off. The mysterious woman opened her hands and used her bright palms again to accentuate her offerings. Miriam, only a few paces behind her, looked eager to move on along the pavilion.

The ladies walked in the direction of the river without alluding to any acquisition just made. With the soothing noise of the marketplace, neither felt pressed to talk, but Miriam eventually took up their most recent topic.

"Did your Mr. Ledbetter bring his cook with him this time? I wonder, as slender as that man stays, if she can be very good at her task."

"He says it's an attorney's constant worry that dampens his appetite. I'm certain he wants Guy to accept the entire estate, so his poor brother's case can be tied off." The lawyer's cook was on Sophie's mind, too. Flora, the domestic in charge of the Pagnols' small kitchen, had needed to visit a physician that morning about female troubles. The doctor welcoming "coloreds" lived many blocks from Savannah's market sector, and Flora had seemed relieved that her secondary duty—occasional supervision of Delphine—would be handled by the Martin woman, who doted on her own lively toddler. "Madame Martin's little child appears plump and healthy." Sophie reminded herself not to say much more.

"Named for an empress, but dark like tea from India. Her mother is as pale as gold," Miriam remembered. "Surely there's some drama in that child's parentage waiting to be acted on stage. In the first scene, the name *Josephine* would be changed to one more fitting a house slave than Napoleon's wife. The Martin woman must worry whether the girl's looks, pretty but so brown, will make her suitable for household service."

"An observation Guy's older brother has often made, as if it were his domain. He's out of sorts that nothing in the will last year was bequeathed to his own name, so he has nothing but harsh judgment of every other affair Mr. Ledbetter manages. He becomes easily irate about how tenderly Madame Martin and her baby appear treated." Sophie Pagnol still felt queasy and she knew she should drop the topic, but her revulsion against cruelty had been piqued at the theater. She let herself go on. "One day, he told Guy that spoiled house help and coddled field hands were worthless and might as well be strung up." Both women shook their heads in disgust.

Mrs. Pagnol and her friend were in complete agreement about one issue debated in Savannah. Both felt strongly that trusted house servants should freely join Sunday service with the town's black congregation. They should find their own spiritual peace, as anyone in God's creation had a right to do. When the two women reached the corner for parting ways, Mrs. Tuttle handed over the program while opening her handbag to retrieve something else.

"It won't do to have this pamphlet lying around. Your husband is much more appreciative than mine of the dramatic arts. He'd remind me that seeing *Captain Inkle and Yarico* in London was by default in the first place. *Hamlet* was entirely sold out last spring. Next, he'd tutor me that England's stance against slavery is due to its fervent hope for our country's economic failure." She had Sophie's attention, but she still paused to underscore a parting caution. "Then, he would ask me if I remember what happened to Savannah's last blithe proponent of abolition."

"As if women could change history as easily as men do," Sophie said. Still, she was thinking about how Pocahontas had intervened and saved the legendary Captain Smith from certain death. But she knew her friend was right. Her own Huguenot family had lauded abolition in France during the 1789 revolution, but marriage to a Southerner had complicated her perspective. Her husband would often raise his arms and drag his hands through his hair before asking *how the oppression of any people could be blessed as righteous behavior.* Then came the next rhetorical question—*how could the homeland's agrarian economy thrive without enslaved labor upon which it was built?*

Sophie Pagnol and her husband kept independence as best they could from the harshest positions of Savannah citizenry. From any viewpoint, the world was wide and political forces were always shifting. They knew from Mr. Ledbetter and from the few times he spoke of the deceased Pagnol cousin—an eccentric who died fleeing Haiti with no possessions except the family cook—that waves of change could wash back any which way. Sophie, too, thought it likely that the full story of Madame Martin would be a drama poignant enough for the stage. One larger truth was known: injustice and violence could tear at anyone's shore. At least the Pagnol men, except for the older brother, had shown themselves to be calm moderates.

"I will be very circumspect about the play," she reassured Miriam.

"Then, take this newspaper edition, too. Roland thinks I have no use for such pages except to hand Mattie something for sopping porch puddles after a storm." Sophie watched her friend fold the paper and slip it into her tapestry bag. Her parting comment was familiar. "I wish he were more like Guy. You're so fortunate, my dear."

When Sophie Pagnol turned the glass doorknob of the house set back elegantly from the walkway, she stood in the foyer trying to suppress an abdominal pang. Stealing a glance into the adjoining dining room, she saw that Delphine and the visiting toddler were marching around the table. One chair had been turned to the outside and Madame Martin, singing away in French, provided a game of musical chairs. The children cared little that spring was not the season for *Auld Lang Syne,* and Delphine looked delighted to join the chorus—

Oui nous nous reverrons mes chères

Ce n'est qu'un au revoir.

"We'll see each other again, my dears…It's only 'til the next time!" The plump woman from Haiti clapped her hands as she translated in English, perhaps not sure of Delphine's comprehension. Too tiny to climb, little Josephine could only clamp her arms down upon the vacant seat and laugh when she found herself the winner of that round. The older girl stepped over to give the two-year-old a congratulatory hug.

None of them had heard the lady of the house enter, and despite her uneasy stomach, Sophie withdrew entirely from view to retrieve from her handbag what she feared was contraband. She tucked the newspaper and pamphlet under her arm and withdrew the item slipped to her by the fan vendor. What might be folded inside the other *aide-à-memoire* gift sent pain into her head as well as her abdomen—cash perhaps or forged identification or a packet of lethal powder?

The Martin woman started up singing again, but after Delphine turned the open fan over and over she felt flushed with relief. This conversation piece contained only listings of familiar Georgia Islands, including Tybee and Skid-away, and alongside were inscribed the names of equally familiar trade vessels. A flaw came with this fan, as well, though it appeared the correction had already been made in a slightly different lettering. Whatever had prompted the familiar merchant to pass it along in Madame Martin's direction, the women's motives were proving innocuous. It was likely nothing more than a gesture of thanks from Flora to the lawyer's pleasant helper for looking after Delphine.

"Maman!" Delphine called upon suddenly glimpsing her.

As Sophie looked in from the doorway, the Martin woman stood erect and Josephine rushed to her side. Mrs. Pagnol set her belongings down on the dining table before embracing her own daughter.

"I think you three have enjoyed your entertainment today more than I did my own outing."

"We did not hear you, madame. We had been listening for Miss Flora, but she has not come back yet. My singing is too loud. I have been told this before—"

"No, no, it's a pity to have to wait a year to revive that song," Sophie said, "and your changing *mes frères* to *mes chers* has the girls smiling."

"Ah, I think it was my own *maman* who sang it so." The Martin woman paused as if hearing a distant voice. "But perhaps it was the whole island that knew the words this way." Then her expression changed from wistfulness to alarm. "Are you not well, madame?"

"It would do me some good to shed this corset as soon as possible."

"The afternoon sun, it grew warmer today than usual." As a borrowed servant, she was unsure of her place in the house, but she went on in concern. "Shall I assist you in making a change of dress, madame?"

"No, thank you. I can manage on my own." Her daughter was showing the charming toddler how to hold fingers to make a church steeple. "If you could look after Delphine for a few minutes longer. I might just lie down for a while with a loosened sash. If you'd look after the girls."

"Of course, of course, madame. And we shall amuse ourselves more quietly. And listen for Flora at the side door, *bien sûr*."

It wasn't until Sophie Pagnol lay in an airy robe and felt the pangs of the afternoon floating away that she realized she had not mentioned the second *aide-à-memoire* fan to the Martin woman, but had only set down her own new purchase and Miriam's pages. The dining room grew quiet, except for an occasional faint giggle, and she was embarrassed as she finally dressed that she'd let nearly an hour slip by.

This time she tiptoed from the master suite to the room where Madame Martin and the children occupied themselves. In one dining chair, Delphine sat examining script on the newly bought fan. She'd been able to read print since she was four, and her mother was certain she had at least identified the theme of the information written longhand. Folding and unfolding a fan made from the wrapping paper, little Josephine amused herself next to her. Mr. Ledbetter's plump cook occupied a chair at the end of the table. Laid out directly in front of her were the pamphlet from the theater performance and the morning edition of *The Savannah Republican*. The servant held her head in her hands, and it was clear she had been quietly crying.

"Are you all right?" To answer, the Martin woman could only nod. Sophie's daughter might just have asked her the same question.

"She's just sad, but she's all right," the six-year-old said.

"Was it something…" Her mother couldn't think of the right way to put it in front of the children.

"It was something she *read*," Delphine explained gravely. "She knows the words in French and in English, Maman. But Josephine and I won't talk about it outside, will we?" The toddler turned her head from side to side.

"It's all right," Sophie reassured the overcome woman. "I taught our Flora to read a word or two—she has to manage a grocery list, doesn't she? And then, we worked on entire passages from the *Bible*. It's no wonder, keeping the kitchen for an attorney, that you often come across lettering in his household."

"Maman, she doesn't even move her lips." At that compliment, the stricken woman looked up with a shudder and smiled.

"I don't know why I confessed such a thing to the child," she said. "I'll keep learning to myself from now on."

New laws forbidding literacy among slaves were considered by many Savannah residents to be an overreaction to plantation rebellions. In this case, the lady of the house had no misgivings that their Flora or Mr. Ledbetter's enlightened cook would use such knowledge to foment any uprising. The connection was hardly what worried the white adult in the room. Seeing the opened pamphlet in front of the Martin woman, Sophie was pained to think that a synopsis of the drama had struck someone else as deeply as the production had affected her.

"Let's go talk in the foyer," she said, putting her hand on Désirée's shoulder before helping to pull out the woman's chair. "I have something of yours in my handbag, anyway. I meant to give it to you earlier."

Madame Martin scooped up the printed items in front of her and the two stepped gingerly away from the children and into the home's wide entryway. The lawyer's cook spoke first, as Sophie reached for the second fan.

"Heaven forbid you would ever have to choose between your husband and your child, madame, but what would you do? I weep to think of such sad choices, and I have to ask God if there is to be no comfort on earth for love torn asunder so."

Sophie looked at her in puzzlement and wondered if the pamphlet, which she'd not yet perused, had mischaracterized the Captain Inkle narrative. Or perhaps the cook's literacy was only rudimentary.

"No, the maiden Yarico never faced that particular dilemma," she wanted to make clear. "Sadly, though, the captain forsook her without warning."

"Yarico?" The two women sensed a broader misunderstanding. "Oh, yes, the theater program. I saw the title but did not recognize the story." Sophie handed her Miriam Tuttle's handkerchief and hoped she'd go on. "No, madame. I tried to interest myself in the play after I'd read the newspaper. But I was too overwrought. Monsieur Ledbetter is right, I think, to keep the daily journals out of the office rooms where I stay with la petite Josephine."

"Was there tragic news today? I'm afraid the drama put me in another world entirely," Sophie said. "Did something happen on the Savannah coast? Elsewhere in the country?"

"There must be such notices every day, but I am kept in cheerful ignorance by the kind lawyer's consideration." She opened the newspaper and turned to the third page. "Runaway French Negro," she read, "named *Grand Louis Telatte*. The name *Telatte* was not uncommon on our island," she said, intimating the reason for her initial shock. "Then, to read on, that he is wearing shoes with no shoelaces, that a reward of twenty dollars is offered for his capture. Such a pitiful image came to my mind." She pressed the handkerchief again to her eyes. "I once had a brother who might have been lost like this."

"I cannot well comprehend the suffering of so many," Sophie admitted, "or explain how God ordains such starkly different stations in life."

"How can a woman happily choose between a child and a sweetheart?" Madame Martin asked again. "On the same page is a notice about Rose—*a yellow woman who has likely eloped in the last two days.*" Both women, shocked, put their hands to their mouths. "She is suspected of boarding a ship that's friendly, for a price. For her capture, the reward is two hundred dollars."

"Do you know a woman named Rose? Is she leaving her own people behind?" Mr. Ledbetter's cook appeared to shake herself out of a fog. The dialogue had grown ill-advised, and her eyes conveyed a fear of having confided too much.

"The considerate lawyer spares me all distressing news, certainly no report of abandoned children." At that moment both of them looked down to see that Josephine had toddled up and was pulling at her mother's skirt to be lifted. "May I, madame?"

"Of course, of course."

Sophie had delivered the second *aide-à-memoire* fan, but now felt renewed concern that she'd become an unwilling participant in some furtive scheme. Her own observant daughter, however, was standing in the doorway, and the child's solemn stare worried her more. A sudden noise at the side entry alerted everyone that Flora was finally returning from her medical appointment.

"Forgive me, madame. The precious petite is all but weaned. My emotions overflow these days, even as my milk subsides."

Only minutes later, conversation on the front steps gave the women scant time to compose themselves further. Guy Pagnol went immediately to give his wife a kiss on the cheek and put his arm around Delphine. Mrs. Pagnol studied the lawyer from Tybee with greater sympathy this time, wondering why she had never attributed to him the quality of kindness as his cook so readily did. Except for the surviving brother-in-law, Pagnol men had proven their distaste for oppression. Their choice of attorney surely aligned with their own inclinations and temperament.

Sophie was struck with wonder, nevertheless, at the solicitous gaze Mr. Ledbetter directed at his domestic and the tiny girl. He'd taken off his hat upon entering the house, but stood awkwardly and immobile in the crowded hallway. An older man most careful with his posture, he appeared somewhat stooped today, and his hair seemed a shade grayer. The two-year-old in Madame Martin's arms wriggled and waved in his direction, and Sophie looked down to hide her surprise at the bachelor's sudden smile.

The estate of Hugues Pagnol was indeed coming to a conclusion. Only mentioned as an aside, the estranged cousin drowned en route to Tybee appeared to have no impact on the indigo trader's will. A handwritten codicil in the mix of Pagnol papers confirmed transfer of the plump cook to Mr. Ledbetter's assets to count against the drowned relative's debt. Sophie and her husband knew better than to pry. Whatever else the will stated about transferring personal property to her husband's name, there were likely details that the lawyer was committed never to divulge.

The Savannah couple and their daughter would certainly never suffer financial dilemma. That was all they needed to know, her husband reassured her that evening. Her customary calm was restored by the next week, when Mr. Ledbetter came by to walk with Guy in town. His cook, collected this time and even reserved, left the little toddler to play with Delphine a while—"if madame permits." Flora was happy to take on the responsibility of watching both girls. No mention was made of the theater drama or newspaper notices that stirred their last encounter.

On the following Tuesday the same exchange took place, and the Pagnols expected the next Tuesday to go by in the same way. Delphine's parents delighted in the children's easy rapport. They wondered if their daughter thought teaching was always as easily accomplished as it was with the precocious two-year-old.

"She knows A, B, and C. Watch her point to the letters, Maman. Look, Flora." The tiny black girl would study the carpet first at such praise, but whenever she looked up into Delphine's admiring countenance, she broke into a smile that could have won over a shipload of stodgy lawyers and accountants.

Sophie Pagnol had already let turn in her mind how she would initiate a dialogue with Mr. Ledbetter, and with the lawyer's cook at the right time, about making the child's stay permanent. Eventually, they could provide her a place in their home as a domestic with light duties, not so far from Tybee and her fond mother. Clearly, Delphine had taken after the child as a sister.

Late one morning, there was surprise in Flora's voice as she answered the service door. It was Thursday, and Madame Martin had not been anticipated. Guy Pagnol had already walked to his office near the river, and Delphine was reading with no expectation that the lively toddler would be her companion for the day. Sophie met the mother and child in the foyer.

"I didn't know Mr. Ledbetter had meetings in town today." The greeting appeared to fluster the lawyer's cook for a moment.

"If it is not too much trouble to leave her with you," she said. Her daughter wriggled down and headed for the sunny dining room in search of the older girl.

"Not at all, but my husband wasn't expecting a conference, I don't think." Then the woman held out an unmarked envelope.

"When he comes here…shortly…Mr. Ledbetter, he will need this." Her expression brightened when Delphine came to a doorway off the hall, hand-in-hand with the tiny girl. "While I go to an appointment, madame, perhaps these two will entertain each other."

"Of course," Sophie said before daring to go on. "There is something, in fact, I would like to discuss when you return. You daughter has become so dear to ours. They dote on one another, as you see, and—"

"*Nous, nous reverrons*, mes chères petites!" the cook said, blowing a kiss to the children. The line from the sentimental song, or perhaps some ailment, brought the cheerful woman to stoic tears.

"Are you not well? Should Flora accompany you…to the doctor?"

"Oh no, madame, I shall manage on my own."

"Well, then *à bientôt*." Mr. Ledbetter's helper seemed not well enough to respond in kind. Sophie wondered if the woman's appointment might prove to take more time than the lawyer's generosity allowed. She would vouch for the black woman's somber demeanor and testify that her trip to the physician looked necessary.

The next two hours passed in tranquility, as Sophie penned letters to friends in Charleston and Darien. The envelope left for Mr. Ledbetter reminded her that she was behind in correspondence. Flora was baking cinnamon tartines for afternoon tea, and the two girls had the dining room for their own entertainment. She heard Delphine explaining to the younger child how to fold a fan from paper, how to curtsey, and how to tie a bow. Madame Martin's daughter spoke a word or two, but mostly laughed in response to the older girl's chatter and instruction. Quiet fell in the dining room for a while, and then she heard the toddler cry out "Delphine!" Both Sophie and Flora came running from opposite ends of the house and at first were alarmed to see the Pagnol daughter lying on the carpet near one of the wooden chairs. Then, she easily sat up.

"It's only a game, Maman! We're on a theater stage. The chair legs are parts of a ship."

"Darling, when we heard your name called out, we—"

"I'm still *Delphine*, but she's *Yarico*," the older girl went on. "She runs to rescue me when she finds me washed up on the shore."

As the afternoon wore, one worry after another swept over Sophie Pagnol. More than odd was the tiny black girl's disinterest in answering to "Josephine." She responded only to *Yarico* long after the children ended their enactment and moved on to tossing a bean bag. Clearly, Madame Martin had looked over the pamphlet from the play weeks and weeks ago and had shared some of the story with the girls. Clearly, the woman had counted on a warm reception of the two-year-old into the home off River Street. Just as apparent, was the cook's unwillingness to make her own movements predictable. The envelope on the table gave Sophie a twinge of culpability that she'd experienced before. Somewhere among her daughter's possessions, she'd recently noticed the second *aide-à-memoire* fan mixed in. She'd thought nothing of it. There was some message inside, she now feared. Madame Martin had tucked some information securely in her memory, making the fan itself superfluous.

The unmarked envelope whispered to Sophie each time she passed by the entry stand where it lay. When, as Madame Martin predicted, the Tybee attorney knocked at the Pagnol door, he looked both agitated and forlorn. A faint smile countered his expression as the toddler embraced his knee. Flora rushed the girls to the kitchen for their cinnamon treat, and Sophie led the visitor to the dining room where he could peruse in private the letter left for him. She looked in on him periodically and was grateful that Guy had not arrived home for the day. Mr. Ledbetter's shoulders shook for a while. It took close to half an hour for the graying gentleman to compose himself. Though his previous interaction had been almost exclusively with Sophie's husband, he seemed grateful to have her company when she returned at length to the dining room. Trying to regain his erect posture, he still sat clutching two handwritten pages. Mrs. Pagnol only nodded while he rambled as she had never heard him do before.

"I would have gone, too, but she wouldn't have me—wouldn't have me risk so much. She thought you or your husband might have guessed that in Haiti, she is a Pagnol, too, you see, married there to your family's cousin." The lawyer smiled at Sophie as he had smiled at the toddler earlier. "But no such alliance could be countenanced here, never in these parts." He sighed in resignation. "I confess to you now, though, that I offered to accompany Désirée to her island…to marry her there, but she was adamant in her refusal. She said she would never forgive herself if I were murdered after her first husband escaped that fate. Or, God forbid…" He needed a full minute before he could finish articulating the unthinkable. "In Haiti, there are too many, she says, that would murder any offspring portending a Louverture dynasty. This is the thanks the dead hero receives for winning his people their independence."

"She was married to cousin Nicholas," Sophie repeated as if to help herself believe. "But is Madame Martin—Madame Pagnol—also related to the general?" She looked off toward the kitchen where the girls were safely occupied.

"Désirée? No, though you are right to think of dear petite Josephine… our *Yarico*, as she thought it best to call the darling girl now. The child is a grand-niece to the martyred hero."

"But your cook, Mr. Ledbetter…your employee, Madame…Pagnol…" Sophie could not fully comprehend the black woman's reason for fleeing to Haiti. Free blacks, in small numbers, could live discreetly in Savannah. Where was the wisdom in leaving such hospitable work conditions, if the woman's homeland were still in turmoil? How could she jettison the affection of the child in her care since infancy?

"She was a trusted confidante of the child's deceased mother," Mr. Ledbetter said at last. "My Désirée was afraid she'd be forgotten by her own daughter, Claire, sent back to the island and raised by friends of color who have known only freedom."

Sophie allowed herself some time to sit, as the lawyer had done, with her head in her hands. She did not know which revelation shocked her more—that her husband and she were related by marriage to the Haïtienne, that the friendly woman had never hinted about Josephine not being her own child, or that she had a daughter of her own elsewhere.

Hearing the family lawyer use the possessive as a term of endearment was equally disconcerting. *My Désirée,* he'd said. Sophie felt no less disoriented and overcome than when she'd left a theater performance weeks earlier. Adrift, she held the edges of the table to sit up.

"Little Josephine is a descendant of Toussaint Louverture."

"The gospel according to Madame Martin." Mr. Ledbetter smiled wanly.

"Our darling empress."

"Better for her in the long run to answer now as *Yarico,*" he said. "Désirée read her every book I bought them, English and French," he went on with pride. "There was implicit trust in your husband's compassion. The child was yours all along, transferred—in this imperfect world—to next of kin in the Pagnol will. Her loving caretaker, though, that lovely kind-hearted woman, was never to be mine."

When the girls came into the room moments later, Delphine was shy in the gentleman's presence, sidling up to her mother to offer a subdued hug. The two-year-old went directly to Mr. Ledbetter and put her hands on his knee.

"Where madame?" Sophie could see that the child's eyelashes curled almost into a circle and that her lips pursed with seriousness. With such tender worry in her voice, the child might have said *maman.* Delphine, as well, noted the little girl's concern.

"She said she'd see us, Yarico, remember?" The Pagnol daughter sang a few notes of the musical-chair song. "She'll see us again."

"But…where madame?" The tiny girl grew alarmed by the lawyer's inability to speak.

"Yarico is staying with us now," Sophie said, "Isn't that so Mr. Ledbetter? And you'll come by to visit often." Just then, Flora stepped into the room and brushed a last trace of cinnamon from her apron. "Would you show the children to Delphine's room upstairs? Little Yarico will be staying with us—"

"She's used to a pallet," the attorney managed to say.

"We'll arrange one, won't we, Flora?" Sophie thought she heard her husband on the front steps, but she harbored no doubts that the lawyer and Madame Martin had read Guy's kind nature correctly. "Let's arrange a pile of blankets and pillows on Delphine's floor up there. They can both sleep as if they've been washed up on a peaceful shore."

Adeline Harper was keeping watch as Yarico slept fitfully on damp ground near the Trinity River. The only traveler in the group to have denied herself a respite on horseback, the exhausted woman turned and groaned while unconscious. Beset by bad dreams, like everyone else escaping toward the American border, she spoke scraps of sentences in her sleep.

"Where...Josephine?" she mumbled.

"Shhh, it's all right, Yarico." Adeline thought she might be having nightmares about a baby who'd crawled off the night before from a group of Brazoria siblings. Bears didn't roam the coastal plains of Texas, the fleeing settlers felt sure, but tan panthers would wait in the fringes of tall prairie grass for an opportunity. Someone from Kentucky called the predators *mountain lions*, even though the terrain was relentlessly flat. Hope of finding the Brazoria baby had rapidly evaporated. When Yarico turned again in her sleep, she still appeared locked in a distressing dream.

"Madame...where Josephine?"

"Wake up, Yarico." It seemed best to nudge her back into this world. "Mrs. Wainwright is getting the children roused. Aunt Maggie went and curled up with Little Abel a while ago. The storm has passed. People are wanting to get on to the other side of this river. Time to move again soon. It'll be all right, *belle-mère*," she whispered.

The woman bolted upright and looked around her as if she'd been deposited on the colorless moon. Then she remembered the green swirling clouds that threatened earlier. Those fleeing had surged toward the shelter of small trees along the riverbank. But when the menacing clouds spared the Harpers and Wainwrights, along with hundreds more converging on the Trinity, they'd all dropped to the ground and rested as if dead.

"You kept watch," Yarico finally said to Adeline. "It's good you kept watch." Neither of them wanted to speak about cries and shouts heard during the previous night's frantic search.

"You were talking to *madame* in your sleep. At first, I thought you were remembering Madame Genet in New Orleans. I kept listening for more French."

"I was back in Savannah."

The conversation subsided for a while. Simple talk was an energy drain to half-starved people on the run for more than a fortnight. But there was some comfort in recalling a bygone era, when pursuit by a cutthroat army would have been unimaginable. At least Yarico's tense dream had not featured Santa Anna. For a moment, the two Harper women envisioned a future as secure and uneventful as life in Savannah or Macon.

"You were with Madame Martin and Mama?" Adeline asked at last. "Was Mama in the dream?"

"Yes. Mixed up with what your grandmother told us later and from the letters Madame Martin sometimes wrote."

"I'm glad I remember Mama."

"You were so little when your papa passed away," Yarico recollected. "About the same age I was when I came to your grandmother's home in Savannah." A din slowly rose around them. Clumps of muddy stragglers for a mile along the western side of the Trinity were forcing themselves out of their afternoon stupor. It was time to attempt the crossing. "I'm sorry you don't remember Mr. Harper much. He was as good to me as you and your mama were."

Adeline stood first and helped Yarico to her knees and then to her feet. Their remaining horses looked up from the trampled grass and snorted. The seven traveling together would get their logistics straight about who would ride which horse.

Maybe another life, Yarico silently hoped, would start up upon their arrival at the opposite shore. As worrisome as the crossing would be, maybe some serenity would take root east of the river where they all believed the Mexican army had no desire to go. Maybe they would not have to flee in desperation all the way to the Sabine. Surely some renewal lay ahead, some embrace of life as they had known it before.

Lord knows there would be gratitude for some freedom and tranquility before it comes time to cross the proverbial River Jordan.

The Wainwright girls were awake and talking to each other, and the two trying to get steady on their feet could hear Aunt Maggie answer Little Abel about riding a horse with her. It made Adeline think to ask Yarico one more question about her fitful sleep.

"Yarico, when you were dreaming," she began, "who was in your dream with my mother and grandmother, besides Madame Martin, I mean?" A breeze brought in the scent of the flowing river. "Who is *Josephine*, Yarico?"

Chapter 7   Along Comes Chaos

"You worried about Captain Smith?"

Karnes answered with a shrug. He had his back to the Georgia Battalion survivor. The officer stood another minute scanning the horizon to the southeast. Harrisburg couldn't be much more than thirty miles away, the two soldiers had figured. They wanted to believe that Santa Anna's army would be slower making the distance than the Texan scouts who'd sped that way at noon the day before. Someone needed to warn the designated president, Mr. Burnet, and the rest of the rebel government to retreat to wherever they could.

"It doesn't feel right, the captain and me going in opposite directions. Could be bad luck."

"Did you and Smith find your way into all this at the same time?" Jamie Trezevant was glad for the slow-paced talk. This was only the second day of his feeling well enough to start off a sentence on his own. Captain Henry Wax Karnes took even more time with this question, as if he found it nearly impossible to fix his attention on the past instead of what might happen in the next few hours. The younger man went on thinking aloud. "You and he could almost be brothers, with that red hair. It looked like his has some gray."

At first the officer just smiled. Jamie had seen that kind of smile before on people whose thoughts aligned more with dread than a light heart.

"I give him a hard time about it," Karnes said. "Deaf's been in Texas a long while, way before the colonies started up. Visited as a youngster and then came back on his own. Never left. His wife is Mexican, so he was none too eager to see himself on the side of independence."

"They say Jim Bowie had a Mexican wife, too." The private could tell that he'd touched a nerve with the comment. Swearing under his breath, the soldier in charge took out his spyglass and stared at the bland prairie he'd just scoured.

"Deaf Smith is no drunk or swindler or murderer, so I don't hold with those judging him for his family."

"It was just an idle recollection," Trezevant admitted. "It's only just now coming back to me how to keep any conversation going." He could feel his face growing hot, and he thought maybe that, too, was a sign of recovery. He was coming back to life enough to feel embarrassment.

"I gotta report to the latrine again," the captain said stalking off. He moved toward a clump of mesquite without taking his eyes from the swath of grassland. "You should, too. There's no hell like taking a desperate gallop and feeling a leak in your trousers." Almost at the designated brush, he turned briefly. "Put your ear to the ground again." He was giving an order. "If Houston has anything like seven hundred men, you'll be able to catch their rumble from a mile off."

The officer had recognized his apology, Private Trezevant felt, but he couldn't bring himself to propose a different method of detecting the Texas army's approach. He didn't want to paint himself as too weak in any way to join the clash ahead. He knew, though, that the position most secure for him was sitting, if he could lean against something solid like the empty supply chest where he'd done his share of the watch. Possessions jettisoned by fleeing settlers littered the plains. Sitting astride a horse also suited the Goliad survivor. He had a dread, however, of lying directly on the ground. Dreams invariably came back to him of the childhood spill he'd taken at the family's summer home. But, in his nightmare, it wasn't Deefy who discovered him in a tangle of vines. It was a pair of Mexican infantrymen with lances readied to violate flesh.

When he leaned over onto the moist ground, he took no care to secure an oilcloth square under his head. He allowed the broad top of his skull to touch to dirt first, then his ear. His temple finally pressed down close to the earth, and he wondered what he would be able to hear other than pounding blood. To ward off stupor, he concentrated on the familiar smells of spring.

During these weeks of battle and flight, the private's deeper needs overruled his other senses. The internal warnings while on the run from the Guadalupe swamps near Victoria—*Don't stop, Don't relax, Don't sleep*—subsided after encountering Juan Seguin's men. *Let go*, his body was telling him now, *You are among comrades now. Rest. Rest. Recovery may take the rest of your life.*

The pounding at Jamie's temple gave him something to count. He heard no other rumble or sound. The damp Texas earth smelled different from the spring fields in Georgia and South Carolina. More clay and shell made up the soil in these parts, he thought, nothing like the acidic mix that included pine needles until closer to the Sabine border of Texas. The Goliad survivor struggled to mentally catalog wildflowers from the regions of his childhood as opposed to where he now lay. Back at the summer home outside Darien, Charlotte used to hold a hand-picked bouquet under his nose.

"Close your eyes, Jamie. Smell this and tell me if it's yellow or pink."

"It smells purple."

"You're not trying."

"I don't know my flowers like you do."

"They're not the same as the ones in Charleston," his sister went on. "I'll tell you what they are. Open your eyes."

"They won't open."

"Wake up. I didn't tell you to fall asleep."

"I can't wake up."

"How do you spell *Trezevant*—"

"You know—"

"Tell me or I'll leave you for Urrea to roast over this fire."

The dazed private sat upright, blinking at the mid-morning sun and the officer.

"T-r-e..."

"I've got that much," Karnes said. He gripped a pocket-sized notebook with frayed pages already curling loose. He scowled but then shook his head in sympathy. "Look, you don't want to let yourself doze off early in the day. I've seen it before. Some were like that up near San Felipe, the ones who nearly killed their horse goin' at a pace to escape one Mexican army or another, even just to get as far as the Colorado."

"I'm awake. I didn't hear anything."

"Take it in spurts. When you get your ear all the way down, count to a hundred." He was studying the man who'd evaded Urrea's patrols from Victoria to the Brazos. "Better just count to fifty and then sit up awhile."

Trezevant was embarrassed again, but relieved that he could obey the order. His pulse was making the same roar, he realized, but maybe a little louder. Captain Karnes was right about soldiers on the retreat, how they reacted to reaching relative safety at last. There were difficult stages to recovery, the private admitted. He wondered if he would ever forget.

His fingers and his toes throbbed and burned at the same time, like that winter term at the college in Columbia. He'd been dared to follow his class-mates barefoot out into the snowy courtyard. The rare scene enticed them all. Back in his dormitory, he'd not been warned against plunging his feet into a hot bath. Two years later on a Texas prairie, Jamie's breathing held its slower and deeper rhythm. When he allowed himself to inhale completely, though, a pain jabbed up under his ribcage like the pierce of pitchfork tines. The twenty-year-old also acknowledged the dulling of an agony in his abdomen. He'd taken solid nourishment, a little each day, for more than a week now, and his body was commanding him to avoid any more paths to slow starvation. Something else solidified in James Peter Trezevant's mind.

He'd begun to identify himself as among the living.

How could the Columbia college boy have guessed—even as an admirer of Ulysses and modern military maneuvers—that a prolonged effort to avoid death might be different from the recovered will to live.

The irony of this day, April 20, 1836, made his skin prickle. When he clenched his teeth, he bit the inside of his cheek. Though he'd maneuvered a scouting horse to outrun death in the creek banks near Refugio; though musket balls had zinged past his head at the church wall there; though he'd tramped through dark swamps to avoid capture; though he'd raced like a madman with other survivors—Hardaway, Andrews, Moses—Private Trezevant had not reclaimed his own desire to live until that very morning.

He wanted to know where Charlotte was now, whether she was naming flowers as she picked them. He didn't want to imagine bouquets in remembrance of the Georgia Battalion. He was sure no Mexican foot-soldiers told before nightfall to burn his body, along with a pile of other slaughtered rebels, would take time to carve a date into a burial cross.

"I can't say I hear anything exactly," he said, "but the ground is vibrating."

"Mount up!" Karnes stashed his notebook into his vest and rushed to sling himself onto his horse. "A thousand range beeves could kill us just as fast as two Mexican companies, but I'll wager it's General Houston!" He shook his head at the Goliad man's slow maneuver. "Mount up or I'll leave you here as a decoy."

The two directed their horses to scrap trees and brush that marked the latrine. If these vibrations came from enemy troops, there would be no outrunning them after smoke from the abandoned campsite drew attention. Cattle or lesser livestock would give the fire a narrow berth, leaving the Texans some safety within that space. If Sam Houston were to direct his men eastward and out of the campfire's view, Karnes and Trezevant could take time to douse the flames. There was enough risk to face that day without adding the vagaries of a grass fire.

Recalling a burning ship at the New Orleans wharf, the private turned his head away from the shallow urinal. A docked steamship from up the Mississippi— not one of the schooners the volunteers were set to take to Texas—had become engulfed. He fended off thoughts of a galley cook whose remains were discovered the next day in the ruined vessel. Ladies with perfumed handkerchiefs waved at the departing battalion later that week, but few who'd seen the charred steamer could forget the stench of burning flesh. Jamie tried to ward off images of bodies he'd heard were put to flames outside Goliad's walls. He couldn't keep a vile smell from affecting his stomach now, however, and he wondered if Captain Karnes, too, were suffering from poorly digested dandelion greens.

A stink in the breeze overpowered the two hidden men before they detected a sound. Just off to the north of their campsite, scrawny trees appeared to wiggle on the horizon. The brushstroke of activity soon widened and the officer handed over his lookout piece. If ever asked to name his first suffering as a soldier, James Trezevant would simply answer...*marching in winter.* Close to three hundred had staggered one icy January day from Refugio to Goliad where another four companies were already dug in with Fannin.

The swarm of fighters presently under General Houston amounted to maybe twice that. While most of Fannin's volunteers had left civilized towns and regular bathing habits only weeks before their slaughter, the army Jamie was scanning looked to have gone unwashed for years. Houston's men were mostly settlers long wary of disarming and stripping as bathwater heated on a fire. Their collective hue was the gray of river-bottom sludge.

The private was both elated and repelled by the approaching mass of revolutionaries. He didn't think any Mexican army could emerge unscathed from battling them. He didn't think the wild mob coming their way had entertained the full will to live since the fall of the Alamo.

"There's the general!"

Karnes pointed out a mounted soldier distinct from scores of other mud-covered fighters. Jamie still held the spyglass. He saw that it was not the color of Houston's clothing that distinguished him. The tall leader of the Texas army loomed even over other men fortunate enough to be on horseback. He wore a fur hat with a warped brim, and a string of animal pelts draped his broad shoulders. His jacket was as fringed as it was grimy, and when one foot swung out regularly from the horse's flank it was clear he wore ankle-high moccasins. He rocked oddly in the saddle. The general appeared as he was regularly described, though Trezevant observed no flask in his hand.

"You think he's drunk?" he asked before wincing at his own impertinence.

"Most likely." Two cannons drawn by oxen jostled into view, and the captain looked to be wrestling down a decision. "I'm gonna make sure he got word about Harrisburg and the fix Burnet is in. It could be he hasn't decided whether to keep fallin' back or call out the sons of bitches under Santa Anna."

"If you think I should—"

"Wait here." Both men had noticed a band of black-haired soldiers with white badges on their hats. Uniforms still distinguished that company off to the side where Brazos crossings were possible. The two couldn't pick out Juan Seguin among the Tejanos, but they knew he'd be in charge. Karnes took in the breadth of the Texas army and then looked off toward the Sabine route. Louisiana meant safety.

"If there's a direct eastward retreat," the captain began, before shaking his head. "Even if he calls for that, I'm still riding out for Harrisburg. I still aim to join up with Deaf."

"I'll go along—"

"Come along in the same direction, if you want, but I'll be goin' at a gallop."

"I can…"

"Follow my angle at a slower pace." Trezevant could keep up with the officer's line of thinking, at least. "If me and Captain Smith crisscross without seeing each other, he'll likely run into you."

Nodding as Karnes rode off toward General Houston, the young soldier knew he was steadier on an ambling mount. He'd worried about how fast the Harper women's horse could be prodded to go, but he wasn't at all sure his legs were strong enough to grip the flanks of a racing animal.

What Jamie observed next helped him brush off his self-doubt. He could see when Captain Karnes approached and caught the attention of the rough commander at the army's front edge. Hundreds of regulars continued their slow progress more southward than east. Jamie saw General Houston take off his hat for a moment and wipe his brow. It must be sinking in, he thought, about what odds the Texas army would face by opposing Santa Anna.

At the general's doffing his hat, one soldier near the front line shouted, "Remember the Alamo!" After a resounding echo of that cry, another voice called out, "Remember Goliad!"

Apparently, the general had decided to ignore the odds and face up to the Mexico's elite troops. But even if Houston settled on retreat, there was no redirecting his angry fighters. As an afterthought, the general lifted his rifle authoritatively and pointed in the direction of Harrisburg.

Jamie Trezevant felt the stench and clamor closing in on him, but he fixed his eyes on Karnes. At first he thought the captain had forgotten him. The officer edging away from the tall general looked set to run his horse alongside the front ranks. No individual shout would have risen above the tumult, but the cavalryman rushing ahead turned toward the private for a moment. He raised an arm and twice gestured forward.

Follow my direction, Karnes was ordering again.

A dung fly made Trezevant slap his ear. He was more surprised by how fast the tan horse jerked forward at his urging. Animals sensed the danger in mobs, he supposed, as easily as they recognized the peril of wildfire. He kept his mount at a canter and gave the animal's thick mane an appreciative tug. Putting some distance between himself and Houston's wild army, he grimaced at his preference for the sharp odor of horse sweat over human grime and excrement.

With Houston's wild army not too far behind, the lone rider shuddered to consider how his Mexican pants and shirt might be misconstrued in the heat of battle. He counted in his favor the donated saddle, easily recognizable as American. His skin was fair even for most English speakers, and his hair went into curly tufts. His relatively clean shirt was not tucked in, as the lowliest foot-soldier with Santa Anna would have done. It billowed as he leaned over the horse's neck. No, Jamie reassured himself, he would not likely be mistaken for a sharpshooter with Urrea, Cos, or the detested dictator.

Still, the mounted soldier felt some dread of being exposed in bright open spaces. At least, the sun made southeast easy to gauge, and he didn't fault Karnes for riding off with the lookout piece. Jamie had done perilous moonlight scouting when Ward's battalion was pinned down at the Refugio church and its perimeter wall. Though on solitary duty, he'd suffered no alienation from comrades meeting the street assault. Measles had kept their captain from going inland with the company, but the officer's absence only made their cohesion greater. Most with battalion leader William Ward would have chosen the sanctuary or the church's rock barrier over the rough ravines that Trezevant was ordered to assess. Retreat routes were desperately needed. Ward needed his spies to locate enemy patrols. Jamie had felt indispensable. The entire Georgia Battalion depended on him, along with a scattering of other practiced riders, to sound the alert if Urrea's men approached from behind. The same difficult terrain did serve that final midnight as the battalion's only means of escape.

The current flat and treeless landscape, Trezevant instinctively judged, would ease any night retreat. In daylight, it gave the private stomach cramps. For another two miles, he shrugged off the warning Karnes gave about relieving low pangs before battle. After slowing his horse to a walk, he spotted a cluster of willow saplings somewhat obscured by thick grass. Scant shelter was better than none. He was easing down from the saddle when a growl and furious scramble within the thicket made him land awkwardly with one foot barely out of the stirrup. Jamie's startled horse bolted back from a branch where he had hoped to tie him. He put a hand up to prevent the animal's rump from backing into him and knocking him off balance, but not before a rear hoof set down upon one of his borrowed boots. When he shouted from the pain, a snarling prairie wolf darted out from its hiding place and raced off in a blur.

Jamie hopped on the other foot for a minute, but he managed to calm his horse enough to retrieve his rifle and aim it at the parted grass where the predator had hidden. If there were pups, the dangerous adult might return. Not wanting to alert any Mexican scouts within earshot, Jamie fixed his bayonet and poked. His right foot wouldn't take his weight and he hobbled forward as he prodded the grass. What he soon saw in the grassy hollow pained him in worse ways. At first he identified only a bloody infant nightgown. It had an edging of dainty pink roses. Nearby lay a shredded pink ribbon. When he realized he was looking at a small crooked bone that had been a thigh and a knee and an ankle, he bent over and vomited on his good shoe.

The horse sensed the man's panic and wouldn't let him mount. For minutes, the animal turned and turned from the private's approach. At last Jamie pulled himself up, and the horse sped off at a gallop without instruction. In a half hour, they were both exhausted and no more in control of their progress than the crazed Texas Army.

The Dove Shall Fly

The soldier wanted to get his bearings, and he still needed to relieve his bladder. His horse had to be retaught who was in command. Not far ahead, a lofty oak drew his eye, but any of Urrea's patrols in the vicinity would also have their spyglasses trained on it. Heading to a shallow gully no more than a quarter mile from the tree, Trezevant wondered if the ditch could mark half way to Harrisburg. Karnes might already have reached the makeshift capital to see what action was taken after Deaf Smith's alert. If he lay down to stretch, Jamie promised himself, he'd sit up or stand upon counting to fifty.

The private banished the image of the doomed baby's gown but couldn't help imagining what dangers the woman Yarico and the Georgia girl still faced. The pang in his stomach persisted. If he recalled his own sister Charlotte when she'd been a crawling baby, he might be throwing up on his shoes forever.

Whatever training had taught Private Trezevant about keeping watch, when he allowed his head to rest on the ground—to listen for Houston's approaching army!—his body's needs took over. *Sleep, sleep,* he heard as his shoulder and neck relaxed. *Recovery might take all the rest of your days!*

"Where in tarnation did you git them boots?" It was the same question that Deefy's uncle had asked long ago, as the three made their way back to the summer house after the riding accident. Jamie's childhood friend had interpreted the question well enough and responded with a flurry of gestures.

The soldier addressed sat up to make sure he wasn't dreaming. His vision was fuzzy at first, but his hearing was good. The speaker was no more than a boy, towheaded and too young to possess a deepened voice.

"Don't you lie! I know whose boots you got on! I seen this horse before, too. Where'd you git 'em?"

"A settler woman offered me these," he said. The toe of one boot was mashed beyond repair. "She and her children were retreating with friends. The horse is one the other ladies gave over." Jamie's eyesight sharpened again, and the boy's trigger finger made him slow down and take great care with his words. "There were two families. Just women and children. They were smart to cross upriver from Fort Bend. The crowds there were dangerous."

"What did the mother look like? You'd best not lie." Instead of lowering his musket, he raised it and appeared to take aim at the ridge between Jamie's eyebrows.

"She wasn't much taller than you, if any. Her hair was somewhat dark. She had her little ones with her. Two neighbors and their servant traveled with them. They came from the same camp up near San Felipe."

"If so many was together, how come anyone freed up a horse?"

"I wouldn't have dared ask. It was Captain Seguin who made the request." The boy squinted and made a sucking sound.

"He's one that's friendly."

"He and his men found four of us on the run out from Victoria. Otherwise, we could have been caught again and carted back…to Goliad." Mere mention of the execution site gave the youth pause.

"What company you in?"

"I'm mostly with Captain Karnes, but I haven't mustered with the regulars yet." The soldier sitting on the ground straightened his back so that he could breathe. The youngster's musket gradually came to rest across his arms. His manner of speech, a southern accent different from the captain's, was reassuring.

"Name's Ned Wainwright. My mama let me have Nickel," he said at last. "She'll do most anything for the cause." Mollified, he was nodding. "You got on my daddy's boots."

"She switched footwear out of generosity. No one would have asked her to contribute more than the saddle she'd offered up."

"Daddy's other pair is holding together," the younger soldier said. "We're not on our feet so much as most regulars. We signed on official with Mosely Baker on account of he takes some with horses. They both wanted me to ride the edge where fightin' won't be worst. The captain said I'd do some good on scout anyhow." For a moment, he studied Jamie the way Seguin's men had, with the respect due any man who'd traipsed through hell. "So how long ago did you come across my mother and the Harper women? You think all them families can get out of Santy Anny's way fast enough? Were the young'uns gettin' by? Did you notice if my sisters and Little Abel thought to help Mama with the new baby?"

"What's your name again?" Jamie rushed to ask. "I'm Private Trezevant from South Carolina." He couldn't feel chagrin at his overly formal introduction, because he was too horrified by the boy's mention of a baby. "Do you hear anything off to the south? Or from over that way where Houston's men should be coming at our heels?" He'd asked only as a distraction, so he was surprised when the boy began to nod more vigorously.

The Dove Shall Fly

"Both of what you said. There's only just one rider comin' now from where Harrisburg is at. But, if you squint the other way, past that big oak, it looks like every fighter with Houston is scrambling out into view up yonder."

They eased back into the open to meet a courier from the southeast, who told them breathlessly that Santa Anna had already burnt everything in the makeshift capital. The good news was that Deaf had been able to warn President Burnet's men beforehand.

"They had me stay behind on the fringes. It could be some of that town is still afire," the rider went on. "It must have been a whole day that I skirted the scrub forest near what was left of the mill and the village. Finally, two of our scouts came back through with news. Burnet managed to high-tail it to New Washington on the coast. It's not but twenty miles away. Then the whole government caught skiffs across the bay and made it to Galveston."

"Did it look like the Mexicans went on after them?"

"Naw..." The courier took time to size up the private and his unusual clothing, as well as the boy straddling a farm horse. "Enemy officers show some strategy. I'll give 'em that. I reckon they didn't want their armies cut down and sunk to the bottom of the gulf." He turned his horse toward Houston's approaching ranks again. "Oh, word is they found a black woman hidden away in one of the New Washington homes. A female that caught Santa Anna's eye. She can show her official free papers, so it might be she'll be paraded to dampen the spirits of any American slave-holders slow to skedaddle."

"Señorita West, I imagine." Seguin had speculated about the woman's value to both sides. He'd thought she might mingle without suspicion and assess Mexican plans. "You want us to go on and pass your news to General Houston?"

"I'm almost out of air from telling it to you two," he admitted. "That's for sure. But I promised Captain Karnes I'd say it direct to Houston."

"So Karnes made it to Harrisburg—"

"He was there with me when Deaf Smith rode back from New Washington to report what's what." The soldier with one stripe on his armband angled his horse toward the ungainly general coming into clear view. "You and the boy should ride on ahead and keep lookout for any repeat threat near the burnt town or at the bayou our army aims to cross."

Less than a minute after news reached the general, his elite riders charged out distinct from the mass of regulars. No horses could have stayed ahead of the Texas Army's foremost cavalry unit. At least thirty horsemen overtook Jamie and Ned, including one in clothing dapper enough to identify him as a newcomer.

"Keep up!" the man called out. "There's a bridge near Harrisburg in need of securing! We might do better tearing it apart to build ourselves a ferry. Captain Sherman is giving orders, but we're obliged to hold fire until we all cross one way or another!" His horse rose up on its hind legs briefly, and the private with recurring dreams of Georgia felt sure he'd seen the gentleman before, maybe at a parade in Darien.

"Hold fire?" the Wainwright boy asked. "But all them Mexicans went on to New Washington, sir!" The tenor of his voice made the other two blink. He might have been no more than twelve.

"True, son, but they'll likely turn back our way!"

The distinguished rider was done with informing them, and he sped after the main contingent. Trezevant and the youngster urged their horses to follow. Ned made just one more comment audible over pounding hooves.

"Hope Santy Anna halts to hold a hat dance! Our bunch won't take less than a day to git past a mud puddle!"

Two hours later, they were putting their shirtsleeves over their mouths to block out the acrid smell of burnt timber. Harrisburg still smoldered a quarter mile away from a narrow bridge better crafted to hold a single donkey cart than an army. Its timbers might have been logged from not too far away. A sawmill wrecked by the fire suggested the proximity of trees large enough to harvest. The Goliad survivor had grown aware of the changing terrain as the two rode farther southeast. Still, he thought the boulders that shored up the trestle on either end might have been hauled from Anahuac, a town the Georgia Battalion had spotted from schooners passing out of Louisiana waters into the Mexican coast.

"Sherman's already located a giant oak one mile easterly where the general can make camp," a sentry told them as they crossed. "As for gettin' all of us to the other side of this bayou, the general is having the floorboards tore out of a farmhouse you likely passed. Makeshift ferries will get us on over quicker than this foot trestle. We'll be looking for a better bridge soon after at a place called Vince's." Again, Jamie's attire drew notice.

The Dove Shall Fly

"He was at Goliad," Mrs. Wainwright's son explained before getting distracted. "Is that someone burnt up over there?"

"It's an old man that Karnes and another scout hauled out of the fire. Either of you two speak German? We can't figure if he overheard any plans while the town was getting torched. It's nothing but German he's talking now, as far as we can tell." Another mounted officer approached.

"Have the boy stay with Mr. Erlich." The injured man was thought to have run the town's livery and had possessed the only building large enough to house a fledgling government. "We think he might have stayed on in his barn after Burnet and the others took off. He could have been hiding there when Santa Anna's men swept in, maybe hearing something of plans. A Harrisburg couple taking cover in the woods over this way says Erlich speaks passable English and Spanish, too."

"I don't speak anything 'cept American."

"You stay with him anyway," the officer said before turning to the older private. "Are you with Captain Lamar?" Jamie shook his head, but the name was coming back to him.

"A Mirabeau Lamar has brothers, I think, and cousins from my part of Georgia."

"That's him. He hasn't been on Texas soil much longer than two weeks." Then the officer gave the man on the tan horse a closer look. "I heard the boy say *Goliad*. You come here with William Ward's battalion?" All those at the narrow bridge cast their eyes toward the burn victim, and Jamie nodded.

"About two hundred of us came over with Colonel Ward. I did some scouting for him." He swallowed before going on. "Now I'm supposed to ride with Karnes."

"Well, if he doesn't find camp in the next few hours, sign on with my men. We're infantry—" The rumble of the approaching Texas Army made further talk difficult. "Captain Hockley and my company are looking after the cannons!" In minutes the wooden structure spanning the bayou would be overwhelmed. "There's no unit that can't use scouts! Sign up under Moreland if you don't find Captain Karnes!"

Before moving on to advise how floor boards might be lashed together, he pulled his horse back close enough to Jamie's to point and give a final order. "We've got some of our spies hidden over on that southeastern rise. Off where Houston aims to camp is a river ferry we intercepted earlier. There's a bayou to cross every time you blink in these parts, but a good meal is coming our way because of that supply heist." A band of trees

111

edged grasslands gently inclining to that point. "If you've served watch on horseback, you'll likely do most good there. Getting over these water barriers will take through tonight. Let any captains over that way know we need to get clean past this crossing. Another Santa Anna general might be bearing down this same way!" Noise of the approaching rebels was drowning out his voice, and he turned to go but paused once more. "Houston says to hold fire until we cross and form up! But Sherman has the last say on maintaining that guard line!"

Taking the borrowed horse at a run, Jamie believed Captain Moreland had spoken orders mostly to review his own intentions. The officer reminded him a bit of his grandfather, and the private felt some encouragement that seasoned men were overseeing vital maneuvers. He didn't let himself look back at the boy tending the elderly Harrisburg man. Again, he fought off anxiety about being the lone rider in an open field. When the image of a prairie wolf and an infant gown flickered, he spurred the Harpers' horse on.

At first, James Peter Trezevant thought he was entering a lonely lookout post again, but he soon realized how many mounted spies hid among the sycamores and hackberries. Their gray sleeves and trouser legs blended in with branches and bent trunks. Fortunately, showy spring leaves caught attention first, and the rise in the land helped hide them. The ridge would keep anyone just south from spotting the Texas Army. Twenty cavalrymen waiting at the thicket line maintained an eerie quiet. The two riders closest to him waved at him silently, warning him to make no sound.

They were all watching Mexican scouts make their way toward another line of trees less than a mile east. One dressed like Jamie loitered behind the patrol and dismounted, assessing the terrain. The others continued in the direction of the San Jacinto, a short river eventually joining the curved bayou Houston's men would cross upstream. There was no telling whether they already knew supplies had been stolen and the ferry there disabled.

Jamie also wondered if Santa Anna and two thousand men under him might have learned from their own spies about the proximity of the Texas companies. A determined Mexican army could have followed the coastline east of New Washington and come back up into the southern plains to assemble on one bank of the San Jacinto or the other. The small patrol heading to the river might still be taken on before they alerted Santa Anna to Houston's approach.

As if Jamie's worries and those hidden with him were one, a cavalryman suddenly bolted from cover. Two more in the unit followed him. The lone opponent who'd been inspecting the grounds jumped onto his horse and fired a pistol shot. His comrades off to the east stopped instantly.

"Damn it, Sherman!" Mirabeau Lamar slapped his thigh as he swore.

"Look over that-a-way not far! There's another party towing their cannon, sir. He must have spotted our men!"

"You three come with me. Everyone else stay put!" Private Trezevant was one of the riders ordered forward. "If we all rush out, they'll go get more help. Every firearm in Mexico will point our way!"

The young man on the tan horse had no more time to reflect than any other Texans rushing out into the field. The enemy patrol had reversed course and appeared ready to face adversaries in equal numbers. Riders on both sides managed their reins, as well as a rifle or musket, but only the solider who'd inspected the ground took aim. His horse held steady, even when his weapon discharged.

Captain Sherman's fall came about like a nightmare. An instant after the officer's rifle was blasted from his grip, his mount bucked and threw him. Jamie fired in the assailant's direction, but his effort was out of range. The explosion gave the Mexican time to retreat a short distance to reload. Meanwhile his comrades fired their cannon to no effect, and then pulled it back from the fracas.

Sherman, seemingly unhurt, frantically searched for his firearm. In the next chilling moment, it looked certain he would be cut down by the patrol racing closer. Mirabeau Lamar boiled in their direction and forced them to waiver as other Texans moved in. He then edged closer to Sherman, making a move that Jamie had only imagined in militia classes. Lamar reached down far enough to let the stranded cavalry chief reach up for an arm and hoist himself securely behind.

"Get his horse!" he ordered Jamie. "Back away, men! Fall back to the ridge while they tamp their powder!"

A few more shots went off, but no one engaged out in the open faced any further danger. Other mounted Texans within the tree-line remained out of sight.

Whispers of the skirmish flamed up among the Texans just crossing the bayou. Jamie kept looking back at the ridge as he secured Sherman's horse near the partly staked officer shelter. While searching the crowd for any Karnes men or Ned Wainwright, he regularly scanned the vacated lookout spot for first signs of an attack. Whatever hostile maneuver might be coming, General Houston's army kept crossing as quietly as possible through late afternoon. By nightfall they had traipsed a mile eastward and assembled near the San Jacinto River. No enemy front line erupted from across the field. The private tending at last to the tan horse wondered whose command he should now follow. His ears still rang. Everyone near the army's makeshift livery spoke in hushed tones. News of an officer shift shocked them all.

"It's Mirabeau Lamar he's put in charge of us—"

"Is Captain Sherman in irons?"

"No, but the general was mad as hell for a while about him drawin' fire…"

"Did you see Lamar swoop out ahead for the rescue?"

"That Sherman…"

"He was right to act on seeing a cannon set to fire our way."

"He could've brought a million Mexicans down on us to—"

"Wish you'd seen the general thrash his hat against a tree. He was in a fury…" The men calming their horses fell silent for a while. They would not have wanted to weather Sam Houston's rage much more than Santa Anna's.

"I heard Deaf Smith might take some men back over toward those westerly bayou bridges we just crossed," one soldier finally whispered.

"What can they do in the dark?"

"They'll likely wait 'til near daybreak—"

"To do what?" The repeated question was barely audible.

"Back over yonder where we took that wider bridge to get here—it was Vince's or Sim's. No matter its name, he'll find it again."

"Captain Moreland fears another Mexican army could come down in from that way soon." Jamie was surprised by his own low voice. "Sherman might have thought it best to face smaller numbers."

"Well, come mornin' Deaf will have orders to burn that bridge down to tar, too."

"No fresh Mexican ranks will be able to get at us then," said a man swigging water from a gourd. "Or none of them villains escape if we pin them down from this side."

A subdued murmur of approval rose up, but one soldier waved away their enthusiasm. "Ain't *none of us* escaping by any burnt bridge neither." Carrying away his saddle, he disappeared into the dark.

Private Trezevant wasn't sure who'd ordered him to stay near the cluster of horses. Six others also had guard duty. He couldn't have hauled his saddle far, and he judged the Harpers' horse to be resting well enough without his weight. He felt sure that Captain Karnes or Lamar—Major Lamar now?—would make the rounds at night or have orders passed along. The last he heard before taking a turn at rest was the news that Captain Hockley's cannons had successfully been stationed not far from the first ridge of trees. His men and Moreland's company allowed themselves only one torch to light their way.

"I'll thump you when it's your watch again," an older man was telling him. "Who'd you say you're with?"

"I'm not asleep. I'm just resting my eyes."

"Let the fella be. He was with Fannin," Jamie heard a different guard say. "Did you see him lean head first near the captain's horse to get the danglin' reins?" The others might have nodded, but the only sound was a piqued army stifling its fury for the night, the low rumble of rage. "There's at least two other Goliad men who escaped this far," the guard whispered again. "Even the muster sergeant was broke down to tears. I don't know how this one grabbed hold of the saddle horn to reach for Sherman's reins. He looks no stronger than a skeleton."

If their talk went on, James Peter Trezevant didn't hear. There was a blur in his imaginings of the sickening voyage from New Orleans to Velasco. The freezing trek inland to the gray stone fort played next, and then the day that he and another scout first learned of the Alamo's fate. He'd managed that afternoon not to vomit on his shoe. He couldn't let his thoughts revisit desperation in the swamps outside Victoria. The men escaping in those brutal wetlands at night would stop when they could and nudge one another.

"Are you asleep? Or are you just resting your eyes?"

The Georgia Battalion man drifted off disbelieving that midterm exams had been his greatest worry only six months earlier.

Chapter 8 Farewell, Light Heart

The upperclassman at the window watched his militia unit disband on the campus lawn below. Through poplar branches just shed of their leaves, James Trezevant counted about half the usual number of gray military coats near the main building at South Carolina College. Those finished with midterms had been directed to spend their morning productively. Jamie didn't mind that his remaining French exam kept him from marching formation, but he envied any classmates who could now resume cavalry maneuvers.

On his desk, an iron held his textbook open to a verb chart. Expressions needing the subjunctive kept slipping his mind. He was relieved, at least, to have completed his Latin requirement the previous year. That barrier frequently denied his peers promotion, and Jamie felt a mix of sympathy and disdain about his roommate's refusal to review noun declensions. The poor fool, whose second attempt to pass Latin was hours away, had already failed his other courses.

"How are you going to practice law if you don't know your Latin?"

"You sound like my mother," his chum Pleasant would answer.

Having grown weary of either pronouncing or spelling *Trezevant*, Jamie was one of the few young Columbia men who'd never needled the weaker student for his name. He didn't envy Pleasant Goodnight for anything, but he still grumbled to himself as he sat down again at his cramped desk. There were strict college rules about staying near books during exam week. With the spectacle in the courtyard ended, the nineteen-year-old sharing Trezevant's dormitory space would probably breeze in soon with a dozen distractions.

"Your first French question," his roommate asked him after barging in moments later. "Subjunctive or not—*Honte y soit qui mal y pense.*"

"You can quote French without studying it, but you keep failing Latin…"

"*Shame to those who think ill of it,*" Pleasant translated. "No, I haven't gone down in battle with Caesar yet. That calamity isn't until four this afternoon, the same time you'll be sparring in *the language of love.*"

There were worse roommates, Jamie admitted to himself. But he looked from the lanky, light-haired fellow before him to the open window to his French grammar chart and felt a rising sense of futility. He'd calculated he could show adequate proficiency without mastering the subjunctive, but he didn't want to earn a borderline grade. He'd already started one letter to his mother and one to a sweetheart in Augusta. Students at the exclusive college really had no news to report other than credit progress, so Jamie didn't think it boastful to list honor scores so far.

The unfinished letters tempted him, and he placed the hand-iron again on his textbook. He would tell them both simply that a high enough mark on the French exam should free up another spring slot for a military course or added militia hours. The worst outcome simply meant he'd have one more term in his ancestors' language.

"You're not going to win over Yvette if you tell her you hate French."

"I don't hate it," Jamie said. "And I don't tell her everything. I'm keeping my letters brief this time." He had barely dipped his pen in the inkwell when Pleasant interrupted him again.

"How do you say *good night* in French?"

"We both know it's *bon soir* or *bonne nuit*—but I don't think that will be my hardest question."

Steadying his pen, he realized that the courtyard had already claimed his roommate's attention. During midterms, there was often a prankster or two darting across the open space in flagrant opposition to conduct codes. It was no use advising his roommate to review notes, since Jamie was also otherwise occupied.

He didn't like how he'd started the letter to his mother. It sounded too much like the forlorn, childish messages he'd sent her after his father died, when he and Charles remained in South Carolina with relatives as Mrs. Trezevant resettled the family in Georgia. The ink was beginning to dry on the pen tip, but he couldn't make himself write a sentence about finishing college in another year. He avoided any reference to his older brother and what positions the recent graduate was already pursuing in Charleston.

Lately Jamie was overcome by a desire to live out ambitions uniquely his own. He doubted he would find the right words for explaining to his mother. She'd be disappointed in him if he came across as petulant and selfish. Jamie slipped that stationery sheet underneath a letter he'd started to Yvette. When his emotions shifted to anything like fervor, he thought of her. They'd exchanged correspondence three times since meeting at a cotillion in Augusta the previous spring. It was his turn to reply to her latest cheerful note. He sensed the danger in professing love, so he wracked his brain for a phrase to suggest she wait for him until he possessed a degree.

In one short year and a half, I shall be in a position to describe my future with enough certainty that you might judge it worthy of...

Jamie's inability to finish the sentence made him stab his pen into the aromatic inkwell. A dark, liquid bead splashed out onto the desktop and he was quick to press the blotter down over it. Was he writing of *respect* or *loyalty* or *sacred devotion*? Was he admitting on his own part an enduring affection worthy of matrimony?

"Here come the Rutherford brothers," Pleasant said suddenly. "Angus and Mathias are in your militia unit, aren't they? They're always with three others. You know, those naves caught setting a graphite fire in the bath house."

"Didn't our pyromaniacs get expelled?" Jamie gave up on both letters and began looking over a copy of the *Augusta Sentinel* that he'd spent too much allowance on.

"One of them has a relation in the state legislature. This time, they only suffered a lecture and probation. But Professor Crowder is on the hunt to oust them." Jamie was tempted to step to the window and see what the Rutherford brothers and their mates were up to, but the article on Texas developments called to him. He was only half listening as Pleasant went on about their antics below. "They shouldn't waste their graphite on a courtyard fire, not if they mean to subdue the Negro Church once exams end."

"What are you talking about?"

"Not necessarily...only if there's proof of rebellion plots...they were all just talking, I imagine..." Jamie's roommate knew better than to advocate violence against Columbia blacks gathering for worship.

"There's nothing like a Nat Turner uprising anywhere in South Carolina."

"I know. I know." The young man at the window made a calming gesture. "You've told me all about your peaceful dealings with the children of Africa."

The Dove Shall Fly

"Do you mean that church three blocks from the college?"

"Just purge it from your mind," Pleasant said. "They're probably going to let all their powder go up in flames shortly anyway. What are you reading? I thought you were studying." Jamie knew his roommate was side-stepping a divisive topic, but the subject of Texas was inherently more compelling than college pranks.

"Those candlelight speeches in Macon some weeks ago. It looks like several dozen signed on for the Texas campaign that night. A battalion under Captain William Ward is already on its way to Montgomery. Then they'll go down the Alabama to Mobile, it says here." As Jamie picked up reading silently where he'd left off, there was stifled laughter at the window. The daredevils down in the courtyard didn't appear too worried about expulsion.

"What do they aim to do in Texas? Tar and feather Santa Anna?"

"Secure the safety of American colonists, at least." Jamie had just read about Hugh McLeod's rousing call to action. That last name, Lamar, and others mentioned in the article were familiar to him as families established in either direction from Macon. "Self-governance was promised to all those colonies more than a decade ago."

"It doesn't sound like the Mexican general knows how the dramatic story of King George ended in these parts—Oh Lord!" Pleasant made a loud choking sound and waved frantically to someone below before planting himself out of sight along the inside edge of the window casement.

"What's going on?"

"I think I just saw Professor Crowder come out of the faculty hall across the way."

"Did that put an end to..." Jamie felt suddenly sick of all this juvenile behavior. "Is it over now? Whatever they were up to?"

Without having finished the Texas news, he gave up on trying to concentrate. He needed to stretch his legs, and the open window made him mildly curious about what might still be observed in the commons. When he stepped to the sill, he didn't see anyone at first. The broad grassy space appeared calm between his observation point and the older red brick halls in the horseshoe. Bare trees allowed visibility across the wide lawn, and the more serious roommate appreciated the stately arrangement of three-story buildings. Ground had already been broken on one end for a final structure, to be used exclusively for the college library. He was proud his credentials would include a degree from such an esteemed institution. It wasn't until he cast his eyes on evergreens at the edge of a nearby walkway, that he realized the Rutherford brothers were still preparing for mischief.

"Mathias!" he hissed to his literature classmate. Both hidden men responded to his warning and bolted toward a corner, but Jamie punctuated his alert with a louder call in their direction. "Crowder will erase you from the rolls if you show yourselves again in daylight!"

"It is you I see, Mr. Trezevant!" Pleasant shrank back farther from the window frame, but Jamie found himself frozen in disbelief. The professor had stepped out of nowhere, it seemed, and directly below windows of the upperclassmen dormitories. "You wish to know who is about to be expunged from Columbia rolls? Do you, Mr. James P. Trezevant?"

"Loitering in the commons is expressly against rules…I knew that…I was only letting them—"

"Aiding and abetting!" Professor Crowder shouted. "Count yourself as the miscreant expelled from this college today, sir. The very idea!"

The next three hours went by in a sickening swirl. At first, both young men hoped the professor might let the sharp reprimand suffice. Then, a crisp rap at their door shook them from that optimism. An envelope slipped underneath the barrier. Inside was a document about removal protocol, and in a blank near the top Jamie's full name was written. After the posting of exam scores each term, class rosters were updated and published. The winnowing process was most often explained by failing performance in coursework, but this special form was available to instructors for documenting "any deed or deeds counter to gentlemanly deportment."

James Peter Trezevant was mortified to see himself named for such an accusation. Pleasant's chatter in his defense gave him no comfort.

"It wasn't even you! It was the Rutherford boys. And he just wants to show he can eject someone, even if it isn't fair. I should have told you not to go to the window, but I thought the old man had gone back into the faculty quarters! You ought to take a rig out to that uncle of yours. He and your aunt have as much sway as any state legislator, don't they? Every influential family in Columbia seems to know them. And, anyway, you could let Crowder know you still have advocates in Charleston who were in the law with your father, connections I mean. Attorneys never forget their colleagues. And besides, you have nothing but honor scores, except in French, I'm supposing." Pleasant took a breath and tried to read Jamie's unchanging expression. "Are you missing your French exam right now? Has it started, or—"

"It no longer matters." Jamie had been numb, but his hands moved out in front of him. The motion made him sit up straighter in his chair. He folded both unfinished letters and put them inside their envelopes and into an inner coat pocket. He set the iron back on its stand and closed his textbook, so that the cover aligned with the edge of his desk. He took care to get the original creases back in the *Augusta Sentinel*. From a smaller inside pocket he took out his mother's banknote for the upcoming spring term. He was trying to think, but Pleasant couldn't contain himself.

"I know I missed my Latin hour, but what good does anyone think I can do on a second attempt? I might as well go home to Augusta and find a clerkship. They could let me whitewash fences in town, if they want. Well, oversee their maintenance anyway. I'm not cut out for higher study and fine achievements like you Trezevants are, so—"

The young man he addressed looked as if a different voice held his attention. Jamie gradually sat even more erect, likely readying himself to make his own pronouncement on the disaster, but a full minute of silence stretched out.

"I had a strange feeling about today," he confided. He glanced at the Latin dunce, whose pale, disheveled hair seemed fitting. He surveyed their cramped quarters and their identical study tables, too tiny for full use. He opened and closed again his mother's tuition check, even though he knew the amount. That envelope slipped into the inner pocket. "The only thing that's made sense all day is this article on the battalion going to Texas." Jamie's roommate stopped breathing. Awaiting a final statement, the prattler held his tongue and hunched over to listen. "I'm taking the late coach to Hamburg."

"In the morning, you can cross the bridge to Augusta. Yvette will be—"

"Your cousin's cousin may or may not be at home when I stop by with her letter."

"In another day or so, the two of us can walk back over to this side and take the train to Charleston—the longest continuous rail line in the world! You can brag to any family and friends you still have there."

"I'm not going to Charleston," Jamie said. His tone motivated Pleasant to try diverting the conversation differently.

"You could help that city halt any church burnings planned. The Rutherford boys aren't the only ones aiming to dampen the next Negro revolt and get credit for—"

"I'm going to Texas," Jamie said calmly. "If I start the journey today, I can meet Ward's battalion in New Orleans."

There was not enough privacy for candid talk on the coach line from Columbia to the state line at the village Hamburg. Sitting across from each other in a packed coach, the roommates communicated with glances. Pleasant winced when a stout older lady squeezed next to him. An elixir salesman boarded at a crossroads, and a medicinal odor made the blond student turn his head and slide open a window panel, even though the air had turned chilly. At the last stop before the South Carolina border, a howling baby prompted both college friends to cross and uncross their arms and legs. Otherwise, Jamie's response was to shrug. His mind was on weightier matters.

The stage route that ended in Hamburg was next to a recently finished train depot. Benches on the covered walkway appeared newly hewn. Before going to locate the outhouse, Pleasant reminded his companion once more how entertaining it would be to travel over a hundred miles by rail to Charleston. But Jamie took no notice. He'd already seated himself and retrieved his two unfinished letters. He blew on his fingers to make them more limber.

In one short year and a half, I shall be in a position to describe my future with enough certainty that you might judge it worthy of... "...the Trezevant name," he concluded.

Between Columbia and this border town, he'd spent the hours contemplating heritage and reputation. Even without the respect due his surname, Jamie understood how a truly noble cause might outweigh life itself. He couldn't explain how deeply he'd absorbed his earliest history lessons—Huguenots abandoning France during the purge, refugees fleeing across the English Channel, their descendants embarking for free worship in the Carolinas, patriots risking all during the Revolution.

"May my service in Texas help turn the tide there," he wrote.

Jamie was suddenly struck by the inspiration to conclude both letters with the same simple statements. Every rousing speech calling for American volunteers was printed in newspapers from Charleston to New Orleans, as well as a dozen Georgia towns. No words of his own would better convey the logic and honor in rescuing stranded Texas colonists from a despot. Both Yvette and his mother, should they make public his decision to serve, would be embraced and hailed with congratulations. Even Professor Crowder might feel compelled to withdraw his pedestrian complaint amid the cheers, "Hear! Hear!"

It didn't really matter to Jamie, though, what the college instructor might do. He had been riveted for weeks by any column he could find labeled *News from Texas!* He'd not tried to win over anyone else to his line of thinking, but he had posed one question to himself again and again. *If, sixty years earlier, the farmer near Lexington had excused himself during harvest, or the Boston merchant had asked for a waiver in order to tend merchandise and cash box, who would have fought for the country's independence?* Jamie could not well argue the reverse case about a young man's duty to tackle the subjunctive. It was clear to him that ideals and lives were at stake. He could not make himself care whether others understood.

Standing two hours later in the grand foyer owned by the Lachapelles of Augusta, the honorable Mr. Trezevant was less self-assured. As he caught his image in a gilded mirror, he felt more like a dubious youth who had just turned twenty. Yvette and her mother, he had been told by a servant, were on the back veranda with a guest.

"Miss Lachapelle will be made aware of your presence."

The new caller was inclined to pace, but the reflection in the mirror unnerved him. Both Columbia College students had done their best to freshen up from the coach journey. They'd splashed water on their faces and taken damp handkerchiefs to their necks. They'd shaken their coats to air them out and brushed road grit from their lapels. Before heading for his own home, Pleasant had given himself a quick spritz of cologne to please his surprised mother and soften her up for the inevitable talk later with the Goodnight patriarch. Jamie had declined any scent from Paris, but now he kept catching an image of his hair and wishing his hat hadn't flattened the broad curl next to his part.

He sat down in an upholstered armchair and checked both letters to make sure which one he'd be reaching for. He intended to engage Yvette in only the briefest conversation, before leaving her the letter to read at her leisure. He shuddered to consider her reaction should he give her the wrong envelope. There would be no recovery from mistakenly handing her the page headed, *My dearest Mother*.

A more recent issue of the *Sentinel* lay on a marble top table next to his chair. On the third page was updated news from Texas, and one sentence helped revive Jamie's confidence. "...for it is true that most of the volunteers are youthful men and boys. Surely those young in years will well withstand such fatigue as those mustered with Captain Ward have in store."

The observation made him rise and give in to pacing. In a few steps, he was at the rear windows looking out onto the back veranda. What he saw made him absentmindedly roll the newspaper into a funnel. An officer, maybe ten years Jamie's senior was resettling Yvette's shawl around her shoulders. Then the striking gentleman walked to Mrs. Lachapelle and took her hand. His lips touched her fingers, but they didn't linger there as long as when he bid Yvette adieu in the same manner. Her expression as she gazed up at him needed no interpretation. They were exchanging final courtesies when Jamie whirled around to face the parlor servant, the same man who'd welcomed him into the foyer.

"With regret, Mr. Trezevant, I have not yet been able to let mademoiselle know of your presence." His voice conveyed compassion, appropriately reserved. The graying, dark-skinned man allowed the shaken visitor to recover on his own.

"I am leaving immediately," Jamie said. "Do me a service, please, and never mention to Miss Yvette that I was here."

"As you wish, sir." He said it as if it would have been his advice.

"I have an envelope I might post instead." The servant made a slight bow before speaking again.

"If you are in haste to leave, allow me to set the news pages straight."

When Jamie arrived at the livery a short time later, his demeanor convinced Pleasant not to question him about the encounter with Yvette. For a while, the two travelers inched toward the ticket counter in silence.

"My mother has already inquired with three Augusta law offices," the blond man said at last. "She has sway with more notables here than my father does, as do many wives, I suppose." The allusion to marriage roles elicited no comment about promises made in the Lachapelle household. "If I take a local position, I'll have plenty of opportunities to test the train to Charleston. I think I should accompany you at least to Milledgeville, probably on to Macon. We'll use that time to settle on my wisest course of action."

"Single ticket to Macon," Jamie said to the cashier. He turned to his friend with genuine affability. "You should look to your own future, of course."

Over the next week, neither young man found time to record thoughts in a journal. Again and again, they stood in line for a coach ticket. Macon made itself an indelible memory. It seemed as if the volunteers under William Ward and Hugh McLeod had marched away from its main street only hours earlier, and as if the candlelight speeches had attracted throngs only the day before. A paper boy peddling the *Macon Messenger* called out from the walkway, "Read all about Macon's own boys on the way to Texas!"

While waiting in the next town for the Columbus connection, they overheard Colonel Troutman tell a visiting dignitary how his daughter Joanna had crafted a flag with a single star, how she had handed it to Captain McLeod as the soldiers passed through. Knoxville men were inspired to volunteer. Townspeople of Columbus talked of nothing but McLeod's regret as he bid farewell to the battalion. He'd formally requested leave from his West Point commission in order to take a command in Texas. In the meantime, Captain Ward led the swelling ranks on to New Orleans. "As soon as our McLeod gets official permission at Fort Jessup, he'll be chargin' across that border to challenge Santa Anna!"

It wasn't until Montgomery, where both travelers were taken aback by the city's rough edges, that Jamie wondered aloud how far his friend meant to accompany him.

"Mobile will be my last chance to turn back," Pleasant figured. He'd counted his folding currency twice. "I do want to go down the Alabama with you, if you'll agree to wait for a berth on a proper steamer. I'm not forgetting the dock worker who told us more than half the battalion boarded flatboats. I know, but the volunteers will face enough hardship in Mexican territory, don't you think? It doesn't seem wise to squander a final opportunity for rest and civilized meals."

"It could be Ward favors toughening his men before they experience true privation."

"Remember that ship captain saying his brother has sailed to Velasco a half dozen times? His other claim was bound to be exaggeration, about its being a good four days on horseback from any town in Texas to the next. It was likely an outright fiction that butcher shops can't be found inland there at all, that dried beef as tough as shoe leather is all some families eat for half the year."

"La Salle's diaries describe such food scarcity...we read his reports in Military History."

"La Salle? I thought he went ashore near New Orleans." The blond student's knowledge in this field was as weak as his Latin.

"He made land about where Ward's battalion is headed," Jamie said. "His fleet was woefully off course. Natives on that coast were used to eating only oysters and wild fruit for four months." A graphic chapter had convinced him that an army's quartermasters were indispensable. *"The starving time* is what the savages called the other part of the year."

"Well, starvation is a process no one claims to be better started early. Pass me some cash, and I'll go purchase our steamship billets."

In Mobile, Pleasant Goodnight drew the attention of tourists still hoping to spot Texas volunteers on parade. A Louisiana family, who'd traveled to attend a wedding, insisted on treating the sociable fellow and his friend to an elaborate evening supper at their hotel. The pair and their two adult children drank in the lanky man's commentary about Texas. Speaking as if he'd volunteered at first opportunity, he tested Jamie's patience and reserve.

"We soldiers don't always stand out for gallant dressing," Pleasant admitted, "but Mr. Trezevant and I apologize for our truly worn appearance. Some reports say the uniforms waiting for us at the Texas coast are a muted ochre, but others claim the jackets will be cornflower blue. The territory is known for blossoms that shade in spring."

"Either choice will set off your flaxen hair, Mr. Goodnight." Madame Robinet's son and daughter, barely in their twenties as well, appeared helpless to stem their mother's flattery. "Those Spanish villains will be dazzled before they flee, I dare say." She nodded in Jamie's direction. "I hope whatever attire Colonel Fannin has in store for our American army will be some color that energizes your companion. I imagine he ceases his aloof carriage on the battlefield."

"His energy is currently in reserve," Pleasant said, giving his roommate a nudge under the inn's wide table. "He's a different man when called to action."

"I hope I shall be," Jamie murmured. He appreciated Mr. Robinet's silent nod of approval. The family offered to host the pair in New Orleans until ships sailed for Texas, an invitation that likely erased Pleasant's financial concerns. Whether or not his friend meant to sign on with Captain Ward's recruits, Jamie could locate the Georgia Battalion muster sergeant on his own. No matter how Pleasant's intent seesawed, he felt no need to explain his own commitment. He knew before putting his signature on a list when to hold his tongue and maintain a serious air. A chatterbox would not be able to follow an order he'd never heard.

"Theo will introduce you to some of our youthful acquaintances," Mrs. Robinet went on. Her son murmured agreement, but he winked at Pleasant and Jamie when his mother turned to the watch a *tarte au noix* sliced.

"They may have trouble finding Lafayette Square on their own," he said. The sister suppressed a giggle and glanced at him.

"A dozen uniform colors are applauded there every Sunday afternoon." She'd spoken for the first time, and all eyes turned to her. "Theo and I paused to view the activity a fortnight ago, Mother. You remember when we called on the Solange family. It was just after their grandfather's funeral—"

"Certainly I remember sending you two to convey our condolences, but I do not recall permitting your travel through center of town afterward and on to Lafayette—"

"My wife and I were both raised in New Orleans, gentlemen," Mr. Robinet broke in. "Coming of age, we learned to avoid certain avenues where refined youth might encounter a shocking difference in cultural mores." He put his napkin to the corners of his mouth. "And it's not only thievery I'm insinuating." No one at the table expected him to elaborate.

"The guidance we give our own children is no different from how we were raised." Mrs. Robinet accepted the way her husband had tied off the subject, but she couldn't resist one further warning. "I trust my son to speed you safely through any pick-pocket districts en route to the barracks of the Georgia Battalion."

"Entire families come to watch companies parade in Lafayette Square, Mother." Theo swirled the burgundy in his glass, taking a sip before going on. "As distinct as each is in military dress, I'm sure they are all like-minded in their patriotism. Alike as well in their resistance to corrupting influences along the way."

In New Orleans one week later, Mrs. Robinet had Pleasant Goodnight escorted to a guest suite in their villa. She turned her back to Jamie, who'd declined the family's lodging offer as graciously as possible. Childhood memories flooded back to him of Charleston homes likewise enclosing a courtyard, though he preferred his grandparents' less showy house in Stoll's Alley as a secluded space for an affectionate family. He was in a hurry to dissolve into this astonishing city, find his own sleeping arrangements, and learn as soon as possible how near Captain Ward's volunteers were to final preparations. He was desperate to escape yet another awkward departure from an elegant foyer.

"Please thank your parents," Jamie said upon finding Theo. "I'll send word of my whereabouts as soon as I'm able. My friend Mr. Goodnight will want to keep apprised."

"Baptiste is always at the outer door. He can be trusted with your message should we not be at home." The young gentleman shook his hand. "There will be no shame in returning to us if you're unable to find a civilized room. Ever since the Texas crisis, New Orleans inns have little space to let—gun sellers and gawkers, what not."

"If there's a cot left at the barracks…"

"I suppose it's more my own shame for not mustering, too, and making my father proud." Theo was not winking, and it took Jamie a moment to conclude he wasn't being wry.

"An only son is born to a greater slate of duties."

"And drawn to distractions more easily, in my case."

"Well, let Pleasant know, won't you, that I cast no judgment on anyone—"

"On anyone who has a change of heart?"

"He's accompanied me this far out of friendship, I think. He may not find battalion maneuvers as…stirring as I do." His discreet explanation impressed the Robinets' son, who avoided further candor by smiling broadly.

"And, even if your laudable purpose fails to entice others, we shirkers may yet draw you into distractions for which New Orleans is acclaimed… the roulette wheel and pastel petticoats!"

By midnight, James Peter Trezevant regretted his haste in declining a good meal and a fair bed. The only room available at a dingy lodge three blocks from Esplanade had originally been a domestic's quarters. The first four rows of entry tile in Augusta's Lachapelle home covered more square feet than the entire *petite chambre* there. In contrast, the cramped dormitory he'd shared at Columbia seemed a master suite. There was no table, much less a chiffarobe, on which he could set his travel satchel. It lay at his feet when he stretched out on a rough coverlet and dozed off.

The next morning, he realized he'd slept in his clothes. One narrow window let a shaft of light squeeze in. Spare trousers and a fresh shirt were folded in the lightly packed satchel, and he took time to change before bundling the soiled clothing he'd worn for a fortnight to hand to the clerk downstairs. He attended to two more tasks before leaving his room. He folded a card on which he'd written his lodging address, next printing out Pleasant's name in care of the Robinets. Then he made his bed with precision. No chamber maid would judge the mattress in need of tidying. Even a thief determined to shake out the bedding would miss the slim folds of cash tucked at one leg of the frame, a trick he and his college roommate had devised. At the counter on the first floor, a sullen man assured Jamie that a laundress came daily. If *monsieur* was in a hurry, her helpers were known for working magic with bellows in their drying room. The inn could have his clothing articles back by the end of the day.

Slipping the lightened wallet inside his coat, Jamie took satisfaction in calculating his financial reserves. After paying the laundry fee, the first night's lodging bill, and the delivery charge for the note to Pleasant, he verified that his wallet still held enough to cover a round-trip from the inn to Lafayette Square. The remaining money hidden at his bed frame would cover the rest of his stay and allow a worthy sum to offer Captain Ward toward costs of the mission. The Ward family's part in financing the effort had been noted in every Georgia newspaper. While his Trezevant donation would not inspire any article, Jamie felt some pride about his conservative use of funds for travel to New Orleans. Whatever amount he had left on mustering day, he would contribute in the family name to the Georgia Battalion.

Coach services took over an hour to arrange, but Jamie was glad for the warmth of the mid-morning sun. Every other day since Mobile had turned more balmy than blustery, and he'd almost forgotten that the calendar was already counting off December. Window shoppers along the boardwalks and vendors in the alleys suggested the gaiety of the season. Inside the swift carriage rolling away from the Vieux Carré and on to Lafayette Square, Jamie gradually recognized the thrum of drumbeats. Even though he anticipated appreciative sightseers at parade maneuvers, his pride soared as he made his way through the throng.

He found a space at the roped off walkway, just as a Louisiana battalion in smart gray attire stepped before him in tight formation. Militia practice at Columbia College could not have won such admiration from bystanders. Cheers rang out until they passed by. He'd read plenty about contrasting tactics during the American Revolution, though, and he considered the spectacle with greater objectivity. He doubted that form perfection would serve volunteers against Mexico any more than grand style had given the Torries a winning advantage.

A man on his left was reminding his wife that Georgia's battalion did its practice on Saturdays and Mondays, if that was whom she'd hoped to see. Sunday use of the square had already been allotted to a dozen units permanently headquartered in the American District. Since docking in New Orleans, Jamie kept an alert ear for any talk of the companies overseen by William Ward of Georgia. Every time he turned his head this morning, he caught a new snippet of conversation above the thrilling line drums. Two men on his right, he gradually concluded, were volunteers with the battalion. Their tone was sober, and their discussion seemed to come from a page in Jamie's military handbook.

"I've been accounting for all the necessities." A slender, tan-haired fellow spoke to a companion with a drooping mustache. "Then I feel just as hard pressed to imagine what provisions we might use in the heat of it—what unlikely things, taken for granted here, could make a difference in some scrape we can't imagine." Their exchange went on, and Jamie found himself nodding in approval as the plainclothes soldier with the ledger printed the word "twine."

Applause again drowned out all talk, but Jamie was remembering the time Deefy's uncle had tied a sapling splint to the broken leg of a hound pup. When the man with the mustache spoke again, it seemed at first that their topic had changed.

"Remember the day Malacai came to us?" There was a short interlude of quiet in the square, and the man lowered his voice. "Cousins know confidences about each other that would make them shy to testify."

"I climbed up higher in that sycamore than I ever had before."

"We were both as ginned up as eight-year-olds could be."

"Told to stay in sight of your house until our new cousin's arrival. But we let the horses amble a mile off anyway." Their conversation stopped for a moment, and Jamie fiddled with his inside pocket before taking off his coat.

"Sometimes I tell Malacai his expected arrival from Ireland got me so excited that I went right out and tried to break my neck."

"How many branches do you reckon you crashed through? You were a good nine feet above ground when you came to rest."

"I wasn't quite resting. I was only half conscious by the time I hit that lowest limb." Both men groaned.

"I thought you might be half dead. I was full sure your neck would snap if you crashed on down to the dirt."

"Not much consolation to our mothers if told a new son was gained mere hours after another was lost."

"What made me remember just now is…the twine."

"You kept your wits. You're the one who assembled something of a ladder."

"You're the one who thought to keep a rope coil in your saddle bag." Both men gave in to subdued laughter. The soldier with the ledger underscored the word he'd just printed and closed the cover of the tablet.

"Let's hope some in our companies are superior equestrians," he said. "Those plow horses we used to ride were mere pets."

"I'm just saying they've put you to good use asking your advice on supplies." A group in black and gold began forming up on the opposite side of the square.

"Well, make me another rope ladder, will you, if I'm up a tree somewhere with a supply list when our lives depend on every man's rifle aim." The cousins went on amiably, and Jamie was struck with an odd loneliness. He'd been traveling with Pleasant, but their connection as roommates lacked any such depth.

"You might put down an extra container of lard," he found himself saying to the first soldier. In another short sentence, he spoke his name and his intention to join the battalion. "After you count what's needed for biscuits, lard will serve as salve for cracked fingers and palms." They shook hands, and Jamie said he hoped to end up in their company.

"One of our Macon boys can't shake off his fever," the man named Francis said. "A doctor should tell him in a day or two whether he's out of the mission. There's no space in the barracks just now. We already have two sleeping on a stair landing, but come march with us tomorrow. During the week, the crowds aren't so unnerving."

"You'll meet some of our boys in a while if you have time," his cousin Joseph said. "Most of the fellows we know walked on down to the docks to see where the fire was last night." Jamie had attributed a lingering stench to smoldering trash heaps only blocks from his inn.

"I think I would have slept through cannon thunder yesterday evening."

"Our first fear was for the barracks, but word is a steamship burned where it was tied—"

"Francis! Joseph!" Coming their way was a lively man whose curls shook as he called out. He cradled bakery goods in one hand. His other arm rested across the shoulder of a solemn, dark-haired youth. "I found us a Weeks! Here's another Weeks, lads!"

Jamie stepped back to allow space at the ropes for Malacai and others, and he sensed vaguely that the couple to his left had moved on. The Georgia men exchanged greetings and reports from the dock. He admired their rapport and wondered if any who'd signed on in Macon might have come from as far away as Darien. He shifted his coat from arm to arm in response to their energy or from the rising temperature. An approaching formation caused the crowd to erupt in applause, and everyone at the roped off perimeter pressed in, jostling one another until the ranks finished striding by.

A half hour later, he set out to speak to the sergeant in charge of mustering volunteers. The three Macon cousins had pointed out the brick building where officers kept daily count of supplies and enlistees. Jamie was rehearsing a clear concise statement of intent, when he thought he might look more mature with his coat back on and partly buttoned. There were bound to be school boys turned away from official rosters for looking wary of a mother's disapproval. It wasn't until Jamie pulled at his coat sleeves and smoothed his lapels that he judged his inner pocket to be far too light.

His wallet had disappeared.

His first instinct was to retrace his steps, all the way back to the edge of spectators where he'd met the Macon men. He thought he might spot the husband and wife who'd watched alongside him, ask them if they'd noticed any hooligans mingling and dashing away.

When he reached the spot where he'd stood, he saw no one he recognized, much less any valuable lying on the cobblestones. This was New Orleans, he reminded himself, not Augusta or Columbia or Darien. In a city this size people looked out for themselves, not one another. Jamie was too rattled to discuss enlistment at battalion headquarters as he'd planned. Instead, he took on as deserved punishment the endless stretch of blocks between Lafayette Square and his lodging district. Had he taken greater care with his coat, he'd be sightseeing from a carriage.

Walking briskly, he felt sure he could retrace the path his morning coach had taken, but near the center of town, narrow avenues began to abut at odd angles. When he inquired at one *auberge* for directions, a friendly matron knew nothing of the inn he could describe but not name. A disgruntled doorman shrugged in satisfaction.

It was late afternoon by the time he recognized the dingy structure where he'd at least secured a bed and privacy for the evening. *La Bougie*, he recited in disgust. He growled at himself for not recalling basic facts. No wonder the subjunctive had kept slipping his mind. But how could he have forgotten the pick-pocket warnings? He had no energy to react with surprise when he was told at the counter that his friend had already claimed the key, as well as his laundry.

"It was the same gentleman you ordered a note carried to, just this morning, monsieur." Jamie only nodded, in no mood to debate hotel procedure. He was uplifted to think the only friend he had in New Orleans might be standing at the narrow window with stories to tell. His feet ached as he climbed three flights of winding stairs. When he reached the familiar door, he was not alarmed to find it locked. Just above the last full floor, there were only two other small rooms alongside his. The night before, he too had certainly closed the bolt inside.

"Pleasant? It's me, Jamie." He was about to knock again when he heard an odd sound coming from a housekeeping closet down the short hall.

"In here!" a muffled call came again.

"Pleasant?" Jamie asked, though he could clearly see who it was standing mostly unclothed among the brooms and dust mops.

"I took a coach right after your message came." One of his bruised eyes opened slightly. Pleasant's only additional statement made clear that he no longer possessed the room key. After wheedling in the lobby to borrow a duplicate, Jamie came back upstairs, his head pounding from the size and swiftness of doom.

He could have let his fingers drift down right away to the secret place at the edge of the mattress frame, but he sat stiffly next to Pleasant and permitted him to spin his tale of misfortune. The failed student had gone the previous night with Theo Robinet to see the roulette wheels firsthand and had lost the rest of his cash. Pleasant was sure Theo would have covered a final round of bad luck, but the Robinet heir had also drunk too much and wasted a fortune. They'd been escorted from the gambling hall after turning over their coats and watches for partial payment. Both young men had staggered from the center of town out to the family's villa, where Baptiste was true to his reputation and brought them each a spare jacket as well as his assurances of discretion.

"Your message was a godsend," Pleasant said recovering himself. He ran his fingers through his limp hair. Jamie thought his friend's worst eye could swell more over the next hours. "I knew Theo's mother would corner him for an explanation this afternoon, so I used some coins loose in the coat pocket and hopped a coachman's ledge out here."

"Where's the spare jacket, Pleasant?" His hand twitched but he still didn't permit it to stretch down toward the hiding place. "Where are your trousers?"

"I'm trying to tell you, Jamie. Look, these roulette salons have more than just doormen. These places have other hulking men, hired special. I don't know what the ruffians are called. They follow you out of the betting halls, if you haven't yet made good on your debt."

"And they follow you home?"

"Yes," Pleasant stammered. "They'll wait overnight, if they have to, and—"

"Assault you and take your clothes. They'll threaten you about the rest of the amount you owe…" Jamie's fingertips explored along the leg of the frame and found nothing.

"It's gone, Jamie. After the beating up here in the hallway…the black eyes…he made me tell. He might have killed me if you hadn't tucked your extra in…"

"In the secret place." Pleasant Goodnight had risen while making his excuses and was standing before him, but his pale image began to blend in with the blank walls, the pitiful space that Jamie couldn't now afford for even one more night. Fortunately, he'd thought to pay his first charges, but now he wondered if the sullen cashier in the lobby had a muscled associate hired to accost freeloaders.

"Jamie? Mrs. Robinet enjoys scolding, but I'm sure she'll be happy to—"

"The Robinets will certainly take you back in for a while. They seem generous people. They'll trust you to repay your fare back to Augusta."

"I should go with you to Texas. I was meaning to." There were worse roommates than Pleasant, James Peter Trezevant reminded himself, but he didn't think he could feign enthusiasm for enlisting his friend in the Texas mission.

The Dove Shall Fly

"Hand me the laundry bundle, will you? I'm going to swap trousers and shirt. Mine were fresh this morning, but the walk across the city put a deep sweat back in." The next moments brought him a premonition of battle travails. "By the end of January, I'll likely laugh at myself for qualms over a dank shirt." He was changing into the laundered clothes anyway, not wanting to spark his friend's further regret.

"Don't worry. Baptiste can pass mine to the Robinet's laundry woman. Let me handle your letters, though," Pleasant stammered. "It's the least I can do."

"If you'll put the envelope to my mother in the post." For once, his roommate held his tongue about Yvette. Jamie stood as straight as the militia men he'd seen marching in the square. He pumped Pleasant's hand and gave him a friendly pat on the back. "We'd best vacate the room."

"We'll both have stories to tell at the spring cotillion." The hapless fellow's voice quavered. Here was a twenty-year-old far more boy than man, Jamie thought

"Safe travels…and best wishes." The parting seemed final. "Best wishes for every spring to come."

The separation released in him an unexpected and strange energy. He trudged back in the direction of the American District, but either his feet hurt less or sundry pain had lost its impact. On another occasion, Spanish grillwork and lacquered carriages might have won his attention. Feeling released from worldly attachments, Jamie directed his concentration to the path directly ahead. When kitchen aromas wafted out from a well-lit lodge, he remembered he'd not eaten since accepting a beignet from the Irish private. He stepped up his pace. Light was fading in the west by the time he recognized the square crowded earlier with soldiers and spectators. When he entered the barracks stairway for the first time, he felt at home.

"You'll want to get a blanket from the orderly, Trezevant." The man named Francis spoke, and his cousin Malacai was climbing the stairs right after.

"If you haven't had a bite since bakery fare this morning, ask cook for a ladle of beans. There's a wee bit of pork still left in the pot."

"Can you march with a musket?" the other cousin asked him. "Ward aims to wear us out tomorrow."

"That's what I came back for," Jamie nodded. "I'm ready," he said as a blanket was passed down to the landing. An hour later, he had consumed a cup of bean stew and rinsed a tin plate.

Quiet soon pervaded the sleeping quarters. Roulette wheels in the center of town had not yet begun to spin, but the battalion's station was as still as a church chapel. Captain William Ward must have dutifully read his training book. A soldier was by necessity separated from his mother, his sweetheart, and likely his childhood friends. It was up to a commander to keep all night temptations from reach. An able commander led his men toward cohesion at least six days a week. When possible, Sunday might be saved for prayer.

"It's early, I know," said another Georgia private stretched out on the wooden steps. "If you can't fall asleep tonight, you'll drop off in an instant tomorrow after marching all day."

"I'm ready," Jamie whispered back. "This is what I came for."

Chapter 9   No Way But Forward

A mile east from the web of bayous near Harrisburg, a private on final night-watch stepped under the livery awning to see who else was awake inside the tent. The morning was turning gray, and the smell of scorched coffee grew stronger in the camp. One soldier sat cross-legged on his pallet, but his eyes were still closed.

"We got a Mexican out here looking for someone in particular," the guard announced softly. The sitting man's eyes opened wide as he reached for his firearm. Another watchman, who'd been dozing, raised himself up on an elbow. "No, not one of Santa Anna's. One of our own Mexicans. One of them fellas with Seguin."

"Who's he want?"

"I already told him there's no way to find Karnes or Deaf Smith. We got a man with us named *Tressant?*"

"I think you're talkin' about JT over there."

"Moreland came by and said to let him sleep through watch."

"He done good yesterday, but Captain says the poor soul hadn't slept a full night since Goliad."

"He outrun the firing squads?"

"Naw, he was stuck before that with Ward and all those Georgia men that lost their way… Most were rounded up over near the coast at Victoria, but a few escaped through the swamps."

"Well, wake him up. Does he speak English?"

"Hell yes, but don't ask me to pronounce his last name." The soldier sitting with his weapon went on gesturing at Jamie. "You go on and wake him up, but do it easy. Like I said, he earned some rest."

"JT? You awake? There's a Seguin man out here with a message for you." He bent over and wiggled the private's shoulder. "You awake?"

"I'm ready," Jamie blurted out, bolting upright. "It's what I came for."

"Good. I hope you understand Mexican better than I do. There's a soldier outside with a note from Seguin. It can't go into any hands but yours or two officers that are Lord knows where." He looked with some exasperation at the other guards who'd been little help. "I gotta go finish my watch. Don't drink all the coffee, boys. Everyone's gonna need it today."

Captain Seguin's courier waited near the horses for Jamie, who came out holding two tin cups by their top edges. His foot pained him, and he was eager to ride again. The stocky messenger nodded instead of saying *gracias*, as if he'd been alerted to the danger of expressing himself in the native language of Mexico. Sentences on the page were short, Jamie saw right away, and he was glad Seguin knew to get to the point. His unit had successfully spied on enemy movements. Scrub trees along the riverbanks gave his men cover.

Santa Anna's last companies had struggled across the Brazos the day before, the note said. By this morning they'd have joined the main contingent a few acres south of the prairie between Harrisburg and Lynch's Ferry. Cumbersome wagons had not joined in on the rout of Burnet, the chase to New Washington, or the race back up the banks of the San Jacinto. The approximate location of Santa Anna was common knowledge by now, but Seguin's next statement was news that made Jamie's pulse race. His spies were on lookout for fresh ranks under General Cos! There was something else, though. Something about Santa Anna's stragglers needed confidential discussion. A lone Seguin scout had observed the odd maneuver. Their river crossing included a strange action which needed interpretation. Señor James Trezevant, if he could be spared in the morning—and if Captains Karnes and Smith were already on scout—should ride out with the courier and judge for himself.

Jamie wondered if he might be astride the wrong horse as he followed Seguin's courier at a canter. No, it was the same tan mount who'd let him charge out in response to Mirabeau Lamar's order the previous afternoon. Maybe the battlefield performance had given the animal confidence. The possibility prompted Jamie to reach out and pat its coarse mane.

"Good boy, Harper." The creature deserved a name. Jamie was realizing that he too felt different this morning. Recuperation did come in stages. He was on his way to meet the Tejano who'd offered protection and mobility only a week ago to the battalion band escaping from Victoria's swamps. Then, the two days with Karnes had allowed Jamie's digestive system some recovery. This morning, he acknowledged a new surge of energy. He could not remember how long he'd survived on mere scraps of sleep, maybe since the second week at Velasco when their captain had come down with measles. He might have succumbed to a death-like numbness on occasions since then. Did exhaustion after marching in sleet to Goliad equal rest? After the army's miserable failure to reach and rescue San Antonio, the paralysis taking over Fannin's men surely did not count.

In the hours before April 21st, with Santa Anna himself likely bedded down not six miles away, James Peter Trezevant had slept more soundly than he had since accepting a blanket in a barracks stairwell off Lafayette Square. The colors infusing dawn sparked in him the small steady flame of inevitability. If he did not believe himself invincible, as a youth does taking his horse on a dangerous leap, he at least acknowledged a growing fever to engage in the clash ahead.

Before leading the way across a natural shallow where two lesser bayous joined, Seguin's man paused inexplicably. The day before, Houston's restive army had made its way over on Vince's Bridge, a sturdy structure just up the bend. Whatever the messenger stopped to inspect, he kept a mystery. He let his mount trot in circles while he scrutinized the gray terrain. In the faint light, Jamie could not decipher the courier's purpose. Then the man made a clicking noise, bolted into the water and splashed across. Jamie followed, soon letting Harper break into a full gallop, and the two riding away from sunrise drew close at last to a cluster of oaks concealing Seguin's men.

Houston's recent meeting with Karnes suddenly resurfaced in Jamie's thoughts. The chant he'd heard from mud-slicked rebels made his head pound—"Remember the Alamo! Remember Goliad!"

No Texian fighter had walked away from the Alamo. Only a handful or two from Fannin's volunteer companies had escaped the firing squads at Goliad. Who now could make better use of rage than those who'd staggered from the executions or from the earlier manhunt in the Guadalupe wetlands? It was pride, as well as anger, helping Jamie hold his shoulders back straight as the two riders approached Seguin's hidden camp. The Tejano officer and Captain Karnes and Deaf Smith were among the very few Texas Regulars who'd witnessed shots so far in the fight for independence. Their direct engagement went back as far as Gonzales and Concepcion.

"Remember Refugio!" The call roared in Jamie's mind as he dismounted, favoring his injured toes. Yes, it was pitiful to see General

Urrea's fallen soldiers sprawled across one another near the low wall at the church. Before retreat was a necessity, Jamie's company at the sanctuary's rock perimeter had taken down dozens. Their heart-rending pleas spilled out in Spanish, but a French line also surfaced in Jamie's recollection. *Honte y soit qui mal y pense!* Thinking of Pleasant's blithe translation, he couldn't swallow. *Shame on any who think ill of it.* The last shrieks among Urrea's infantry were unforgettable, but American soldiers had been wounded and left for dead at Refugio, too. Their final utterances were no less compelling. Rage had begun to fuel Jamie's energy, but he recognized a strangely calming measure of gratitude. It would not be his dear, foolish roommate Pleasant mortally wounded and stretched out before him by the day's end. The next deadly struggle would unfold among strangers.

Captain Seguin stepped out from a secluded arrangement of sitting mats. He must have been expecting the private, but he made the sign of the cross as if he were witnessing a ghost.

"You came back, Trezevant. You are nearly yourself," he said. "The saints will count me a blasphemer if I say you rose from the dead on the third day." Jamie saluted.

"I've been able to eat. And sleep, finally."

"Come walk a few steps with me, if you can manage," he said noting the partly crushed boot. Just beyond the thicket, the captain lowered his voice. "One of my spies came to me with a report. He is trusted." Others in his patrol had ridden off from the Brazos lookout the day before near sundown. They went to see if Cos might be approaching from the south, but this man stayed with his spyglass and the grackles. Seguin was digging into his pocket. "He brought me the evidence in a bandana. Look here. It is little proof, all he could carry. But he is someone I trust." The transport units, they both knew, had no part in chasing President Burnet to Galveston. "After Santa Anna's last wagons made it to this side of the river, my scout went back over. He went to where he'd seen load after load of this go into the water."

"Grape shot." Jamie identified what the Tejano held in his hands. He waited for a full explanation.

"My *hombre* watched. Sixteen boxes lowered to sink into the river."

"That would have lightened their wagons and made it easier to cross."

"And then, two more cartloads to the bottom of the Brazos."

"More grape shot?"

"And rounds full size, big like your fist." Jamie was trying to visualize the scene. He imagined what daring it had taken for Seguin's spy to ride closer in fading light, to dive at dark for grape shot in the silt.

"Santa Anna has held the same army together since before Matamoros, isn't that right? We've both heard some with him came up all the way from the Yucatan. His men can't be recovered completely from the Alamo siege. That's impossible."

"Only two cavalry companies stayed with the chase of Burnet. This is our understanding by a witness from New Washington. *El jefe's* men are past tired, I am sure. And these coming last, with six ox for every wagon. Too worn to drag the heaviest across even one more river." Jamie wanted a pounding in his head to subside so he could take in the implications. "And there's another thought I have," the captain said tentatively.

"They must be…" Jamie began. He imagined the orders being passed down to an officer in charge of artillery and on to those soldiers driving the laden carts. He visualized the dumping of grape and cannon balls. He reasoned out the chain of command for such a maneuver. "Mexican officers must think…Santa Anna himself must believe…that he's already won the war."

A mockingbird nearby sang out a series of notes and then telegraphed an elaborate pattern. The morning took on clarity like a stirring hymn, and Captain Seguin was nodding. Jamie stepped closer to hear the Tejano, who spoke on in a near whisper.

"The general is perhaps still abed only a few miles from here. His companies will take their time arranging breastworks. We saw twelve beeves cross the river yesterday at this hour. Santa Anna's *cocina* men will prepare a fine meal when the sun is high, a feast, at least for his favored officers."

"He must have his own spies watching us," Jamie said.

"Yes, but he is not impressed. I comprehend this proud general, how he keeps his love for handsome uniforms." Captain Seguin pressed a sideburn with one hand, and Jamie felt some chagrin over his own appearance. "Witnesses swear that he keeps his admiration for beautiful women, too. The lady Emily West was sighted near the officer tents." Both men kept silent about what dangers females might face among conquering soldiers. "Our Napoleon fears nothing from what he hears of Sam Houston's army. He is asking himself. *What can the muddy rebels do to professionals that shine?* His answer is to send cannon shot to the bottom of the river."

"Santa Anna thinks he's already won."

Jamie was on horseback again as he waited for Seguin's courier to finish a confidential talk with his superior. The captain listened intently before swearing and making a gesture of exasperation. Feverishly, he wrote out more short sentences, refolded the message, and handed it over. Then he waved the stout aide on his way and called out to others in the hideout that it was time to abandon the post.

The route back to Houston's encampment was due east. Jamie knew he could find the two smaller bayous without a guide, but he was still glad for the company of Seguin's courier. On the hour-long ride, no conversation distracted from the riveting meaning behind discarded ammunition. He understood the importance of the message, and he also shared Seguin's wariness about dispersal of facts.

Rumor could throw the regulars with Houston into panic and disarray. Half might abandon the revolution, and the others storm on in suicidal reflex against greater numbers. Worse, the dumping of shot could be misinterpreted as surrender. Any advantage given Texians by Mexican overconfidence could be easily reversed if independence fighters were to put down arms and give in to celebration.

And there was something else. On the way back, Trezevant wondered what other developments Seguin's stocky messenger might have reported. What he'd not yet passed on to the private surely had to do with his pause at daybreak to read marks where two lesser bayous merged. Some new information gained south of Vince's Bridge had altered the courier's expression. His mouth was now thin as if he'd just put a hot cup to his lips. Jamie did not envy the man's knowledge or General Houston's obligation to decide the next move.

Earlier, on the westerly ride out to Seguin's post, the Georgia Battalion man had felt a surge in energy. An epiphany struck next.

Depending on how the conflict ended, perhaps this very day, English speakers from Georgia and Mississippi and New York and Tennessee might take their horses and wagons as far west as they liked. America might well expand its borders all the way to the legendary Pacific. Or, the Sabine River might forever stand as Mexico's barrier to pioneering by non-natives. Loss at the hands of Santa Anna could stanch any further American claims west of the Louisiana Purchase.

Jamie could tell that Seguin's man was leading them upstream from where they'd made a bayou crossing an hour before. As the courier kept angling, the battalion survivor wondered if they would now miss Vince's

Bridge altogether. It made sense to straighten the route of their return and cut their riding time. It was also prudent, perhaps, to avoid any structure so out in the open and vulnerable to attack as a broad bridge. If they rode back up as far as the makeshift rafts at Buffalo Bayou, though, they'd negate any time saved.

"Shhh," the messenger said, indicating his own misgivings. "I do not hear any marching. I do not see newer signs of Mexico's army." His facility with English came as a surprise, and Jamie studied the ground again. He had assumed Houston's companies to have left the ruts and hoof marks and flattened prairie grass.

"Are we going up as far as Harrisburg? What's left of it?"

"*El capitán* wishes to make sure. When we are there, we speak for a *momento*."

The two steered clear of the town's ruined grist mill and blackened huts. They cut over on the trestle to where rafts had been fashioned from a domicile's ripped floorboard. Private Trezevant didn't see the body of Mr. Erlich until his horse set a front hoof down on the victim's bloated backside, rolling him over. Water had darkened the dead man's graying beard. He'd floated long enough at the bayou's edge that his limbs swelled too, and burnt flesh had burst.

"How did he make it to the river?" Jamie wondered aloud.

"They put him here. If he was fortunate, he was already *muerto*."

"They? Who?"

"If he was not fortunate, they enjoyed to hear him beg."

"Our men have not lost their souls along the way." Jamie was ready to defend the ragtag fighters following the Texas general. "Houston's men wouldn't—"

"The army under General Cos. They made it through here late last night."

"But, weren't all you with Seguin watching for him to come from the west or south or—"

"Yet the ground says he came this way. He marched his companies to the bridge called *Vince*. Some crossed there. Some moved on a little to the low place where we went over, too, only this morning."

"How many do you think—"

"It looks five hundred. By now, they will be with Santa Anna, but first they came through here at night. Quietly, except for the cries of this poor man. First, they made their fun with him." Reflexively, both men bent to see if Mr. Erlich's remains could be pulled from the water. At least, they could keep his corpse from polluting the waterway. There was no time for burial, but he might be dragged to tall grass, if nothing else. Each soldier had gripped a swollen arm, and it seemed initially as if they'd recoiled in unison from the horror of their task, until Jamie realized the stockier man had jerked back first. Only in response had he, too, staggered away.

The cottonmouth obscured inside Mr. Erlich's sodden shirt now had its fangs in the Tejano's wrist. Then the writhing creature struck again at the man's upper arm and shoulder and neck. Seguin's courier was dead only moments after he landed in the water. There were scant seconds to comprehend what had happened before a wailing sound rose up from the trestle bridge and the boulder holding it in place across the bayou.

"Aheeeeeha! Get 'im! Did ya get 'im, Tressant?"

"Wha—Ned?"

"Cut that bastard like they did the old man! And my horse, too, Tressant—they cut down Nickel without no reason! Git that one for me!"

"Hush!" Jamie called out as he backed off from the fatal encounter. "Lower your voice, Ned. This one was our friend. But there could be others—hush now," he repeated. "And get yourself out of this water. A snake got Seguin's man. It could be the kind that swarm together. Get up onto the grass!"

The facts seemed to serve as a slap would have, and the spot over by the foundation boulder went quiet. Jamie saw the Wainwright boy rise up and steady himself before exiting the far bank on all fours. Then the youth stood limp and transfixed as he watched the older soldier tether the Mexican's horse and navigate the trestle again. Raft pieces lying about had been trampled by Cos to prevent their further use.

"We don't have time to do right by them. I know it's a shame, but there could be worse coming." Ned began pointing in another direction, and Jamie thought he might have spotted more snakes.

"Last night, when I heard them a-comin', I up and left the old man where I was tending him."

"They would have killed you too."

"What they did to him was devil's work, and the same as what they gave Nickel for no reason." The boy still pointed, but Jamie intended to edge away in any direction that would spare them both the sight of a bloating horse.

"Here," he said, getting down from the familiar saddle. This one knows you from up the Brazos where your family and the Harpers were camped. I think he wants a rider he already counts as a friend." Jamie handed over the reins of the tan horse.

"The way they was all laughing…before they put a knife into his neck…I reckon they thought a plow horse wasn't worth any more than a cow paddy."

"Look, Ned. He recognizes your smell. We've got to get going."

"I left the old man, and then I plain forgot about where Nickel had wandered to."

"You didn't have time. There's no blame on you."

The Wainwright boy hoisted himself up, and Jamie thought he had calmed himself enough to stay quiet, but the youth suddenly began to sob.

"Is this what it's gonna be like, Private Tressant?" He choked and gasped for breath. "Stickin' knives into old men and horses and boys that's with their daddies and laughing even when someone's already on his way to dyin' or has his hands up?" A swatch of pale hair fell across his eyes. His chest was heaving and the Harpers' horse began to back up. "Is this what it's gonna be like?"

James Trezevant, barely past his teens, felt as if he'd lived twenty years and a hundred more.

"That's what I expect," he said putting a hand on the boy's arm. "Before the day's over, we could see things we hope never to remember. Your daddy wouldn't want you warned otherwise, or your mama."

Ned Wainwright looked down at the borrowed boots and shook his head, as if their being worn by a virtual stranger were proof itself of worst circumstances.

As Jamie spoke to the boy, he took another look at the folded alert from Seguin. He knew that information had to get to General Houston. Santa Anna's brother-in-law Cos had brought five hundred men down between bayous right after the Texas army in the dead of night. Even without them, the Mexican dictator was so dismissive of the rebelling colonists that he'd ordered loads of cannon shot discarded at the Brazos.

"It's best not to leave an important message in the hands of just one man," he said, tucking the folded page into the youth's thin coat. "You can't tell what will turn up out here. Everything wild is on the move this time in spring. Snakes and desert panthers and coyotes. Everything."

"Mexican devils."

"And Tejanos more than friendly, like Seguin." Again, the boy sucked air through his teeth, and it looked as if his tears were over.

"I can take his message straight to Houston if need be. I seen the general up close before. He was near eight foot and covered in bearskins. Like as not he was too drunk to remember me."

"I'm leading the way. That's how this horse is accustomed." When Jamie looked back, Ned was patting Harper on the neck. "If anything makes me fall out of the saddle, you just keep heading straight east for Houston's camp. You won't miss it. It's not more than thirty minutes from here."

In less than a quarter hour, strong smoke drifting from the direction of the smaller bayous caught their attention. Either Houston's patrols or the Mexicans had set fire to Vince's Bridge, Jamie surmised. It was too dangerous to verify which by taking on the job of a spy. He and the Wainwright boy made steady progress across the prairie closed now on most every side by bayou, river, or swamp. They passed by more and more clumps of grimy Texas men. Wherever two were tearing at flatbread or oiling their rifles, four others kept their eyes trained on the far band of trees. Cavalry regulars had reins in hand or their horses tethered within reach, but the livery tent Jamie had slept in the night before had disappeared, been designated moot and dismantled. The twin cannons Moreland had spoken of were positioned in clear view halfway up the incline. As General Houston's sheltering spot came into view, a guard, his rifle resting across his forearm, rode up alongside.

"Stray horsemen are all fixin' to set out toward the Sim's and Vince's, those that weren't on hand already to see the bridge burnt down." He sized up Jamie's attire. "You ought to get down and roll in some of this dirt, son. I don't like how your borrowed shirt shows up bright."

"He can dirty it up," Ned offered tersely.

"Most of you fellas on mount, you're all under Lamar now. He's already forming up over that way. It was Deaf Smith, though, and others riding scout that put torch to the bridge yonder."

"We were hoping the smoke meant our upper-hand."

"Mexicans who came that way last night won't find their exit so easy. If they don't grasp yet what riles Houston, they'll learn soon eough." The guard expelled a glob of spittle. "'Course that works both ways, as far as getting out goes." The oddly dressed private and the boy let their mouths open a bit.

"He knows about fresh companies joining Santa Anna?"

"Followed the same route we came through. In the dead of night, as far as we can tell. But no one can get an estimate on how many."

"Five hundred, according to a soldier who read the ground," Jamie said. The guard squinted at the Wainwright boy, who was already scowling back.

"That there your trail expert?"

"No, he's dead," Ned informed him. "And so is an old Harrisburg man. And so is my own horse, without no godly reason." The guard was as unsettled by the child's voice as by his report.

"I can pass your number estimate on to Houston."

"I have to get a new piece of information to the general," Jamie said. "Captain Seguin made us promise to hand a message over to no one ranked less than his first officer."

"Well…" Something in Jamie's tone made the guard avoid further delay. He brought his horse up close enough that his own voice was just audible. "Have the youngster stick close." Then it struck Jamie that the entire army, though out in the open, was hushed in its communication and moving about furtively as if a thousand Mexican spyglasses might train on them at any moment. The band of trees across the field and up the rise remained still, but it was no use trying to suppress memory of the skirmish the day before. The Twin Cannons brought to the Texas cause all the way from Cincinnati looked ready to advance on short order. "You two stay together. And get yourself some soil on that white shirt."

James Trezevant and Ned Wainwright let their horses amble on across the glistening prairie grass toward a giant live oak where a coterie of top officers was gathering. The private knew they'd be stopped and questioned again before getting much closer to the roughest rebel among them. Nearly a foot taller than many men, even without his misshapen hat, Sam Houston paced from one soldier to another. An orderly tended to the general's massive dark stallion.

The private and the boy remained astride at the perimeter. Jamie looked for the current cavalry commander, Mirabeau Lamar, but decided the guard must have been right about his having maneuvered out along the western edge. Sidney Sherman, though, he recognized from the previous day's clash. The officer now in charge of infantry shook hands with Houston. Then the general clapped him on the shoulder appreciatively while pointing east, toward the San Jacinto River. Lynch's ferry had been dismantled there the afternoon before, and whatever order Houston had sent out about holding fire, the Texas commander appeared to hold no grudge. He gestured again in that direction and put both hands on Sherman's shoulders. Every ranking man in the inner circle stole glances to read the exchange.

"Did you find Karnes?" Jamie hadn't noticed the individual approaching on foot and taking his horse's bridle. It was the soldier who'd stayed calm as the Texas army swarmed near the Harrisburg trestle. It was the officer who'd directed him minutes later to do what good he could at the tree-line beyond. "You get signed up with anyone?"

"No, sir. Not yet." Captain Moreland looked to see if Houston had gathered his officers up close. Then he turned again to hear the older private explain. "Seguin sent for me at sun-up. He wanted to make sure the general gets this message." Jamie let Ned hand over the folded page. While the man read, his eyes and brow went crooked, and the corners of his mouth tightened.

"You apprised yourself of this yet?"

"Seguin spoke to me about the sighting," Jamie said nodding. "We agreed on what it meant." Moreland was moving his head in assent, either to him or to a captain not far off who might have been Burleson or Mosely. General Houston wanted to confer with all of them together.

"I'll show him Seguin's message. It may well add fire to his decision, but don't speak a word of it. "

"No, sir."

"Go on and find Colonel Lamar's line. You two had better fork up some meat into flatbread on the way. Houston's already ordered us done by high noon with anything that'll work our bellies."

Grandfather Trezevant had used that expression occasionally. He'd advised Jamie one Saturday to stop running with his older brother for a while. *Stop while that blackberry cobbler is still working in your belly.* In Charleston, the phrase had struck the boy as oddly rural. Again, Jamie found it encouraging that some soldiers adhering to the battlefield were seasoned, and that not too many appeared mere pups. He couldn't decide whether it would be good fortune or ill to happen across Ned Wainwright's daddy as the two obeyed Captain Moreland's command.

With so many fighting men amassed in the San Jacinto prairie, there should have been a tumult, but the agitated assembly remained eerily quiet. When he and the boy were finally handed a bite of beef in a tortilla,

Jamie was surprised to note the sun as directly overhead. How fast the next few hours swept by proved an indelible shock.

The men under Lamar dismounted to tighten their stirrups and climbed up again and patted the animals for keeping their hooves still. Jamie caught glimpses of red hair and thought either Captain Karnes or Smith had finished his last scouting mission. Maybe the other was risking a foray across the next meadow south, the final space abutting where Santa Anna reportedly bivouacked. Another premature skirmish could prove disastrous. The cavalry stayed to the rear of infantry units that had begun a slow advance. Texans on horseback took position as the final impediment to any Mexicans trying retreat.

Some small commotion drew attention in the trees up the incline. Across the breadth of the Texas army, rifles went up to eye level and some with pistols also unsheathed their sabers. It was a small patrol of Houston's men, though, hacking their way through the last vines and undergrowth at the tree-line. They were clearing the way, so that oxen could tow the Twin Sisters on through to the next field south. As infantry under Sherman moved forward, they also stretched out east in the direction of the San Jacinto. General Houston, keeping abreast of companies minding the artillery, signaled to hold the all-quiet.

On the western side, cavalry under Colonel Mirabeau Lamar couldn't help admiring the new leader. If not for Seguin and his unit, he might have been the only fighter that day whose clothing matched his carriage and attitude. Jamie was proud to have followed the Georgia man out into the fray just the day before. As difficult as it was to wait astride an excitable horse, the private knew from his military studies that an initial assault is best dealt by infantry. Mounted soldiers can sweep through afterward and take down any stunned enemy, as well as those scrambling for an exit.

The angle of the sun shifted, and James Peter Trezevant, who'd dreamt at last rest of semesters and coach miles, judged it to be at least two in the afternoon. Had he been in charge of Texas Independence fighters, he would have insisted on knowing the posture of Mexican troops less than a mile away. He would have wanted to ascertain what kind of watch Santa Anna put at the breastworks and whether their artillery was situated for damaging effect, even without ammunition for third and fourth rounds.

Sam Houston surely understood his own limitations. The general was holding up his sword at an angle commanding silence, but soldiers on foot and on horseback kept inching closer to that first row of trees regardless. The chief of the Texas army held his men back as best he could. Once across the next open field, however, Texians would be close enough to view Santa Anna's encampment. No order would have stopped their initial advancement toward Harrisburg. There would be no stopping this final rush.

The quiet was a miracle, and Jamie wondered if every other soldier on the field might be imagining, "Remember the Alamo! Remember Goliad!"

A wide line of scouts in pairs emerged from the ridge of trees to report to their superiors. The nine hundred under General Houston soon stretched out according to new orders and advanced to take cover in the spring thicket ahead. In an hour, the band of rebels progressed to form a deadly perimeter to yet one last field. Some bold spies on horseback needed to locate Mexican guard posts, guess where officers would be thickest, and get the lay of the battleground, which appeared to drift down again.

A breeze brought an aroma from the Mexican cook wagons across their encampment meadow. Even the horses at the rear of the Texas army shifted from side to side upon smelling civilization so near.

Jamie and Ned drifted somewhat apart. With a borrowed spyglass, the youth was straining to see where Captain Mosely and his father might be on the field. The older private supposed Sam Hardaway and other battalion survivors—Moses and Andrews—might also be on the far eastern side of the assault formation. But similar expressions, he was finding, made individuals in the army no more distinguishable than their clothing. The majority wore skins and stained jackets the color of raw earth. Never mind the delicate hues of bluebonnets and pink primrose. Every countenance communicated savage intent.

When two scouts emerged from the final perimeter to parlay with General Houston, he sent them out in opposite directions to spread latest information at a whisper.

There were no guards at the breastworks! No patrols showed at the bivouac's borders. Their artillery was positioned in such a way that it wouldn't have any effect once the Texians approached close enough. The soft scrape of tin pots against wash kettles came from several *cocina* wagons, where a hearty meal must have been offered earlier. Otherwise, a pleasant silence reigned. The entire Mexican Army—Santa Anna, Cos, Almonte, all of them—appeared to be taking a *siesta*. Two thousand enemy soldiers rested in the assumption that any clash would take place another day!

Chapter 10 The Shortest Dreams of Mercy

Abel Wainwright saw Captain Mosely hold up both hands to signal just ten minutes before the order to attack. The private's rifle was primed to fire, and he patted his vest pocket to feel for his pouch of powder. If the men to either side observed Abel peeking at a gold watch wrapped in oilcloth, the action might have been mistaken for vanity. But he only wanted a reading of the approximate time he might die. Mr. Wainwright was rather sure the date was April 21.

Responsible for five children now, he felt relieved that he'd not seen Ned in days. It was comforting to think of his oldest boy as off in a westerly direction, maybe as far away as the Brazos and somewhat protected by experienced cavalry. The father and son had enjoyed only a brief look at the new baby, Wendel, before leaving the family camp near San Felipe and mustering with General Houston in March.

He wondered if anyone finding his body before the day's end might discover the watch protected in his pocket and see that it got back to Ned. It was a comforting little dream.

Abel shook off an image of his wife and younger children trudging across sodden river banks toward Louisiana. He said a little prayer on their behalf but tried not to think of their faces. He didn't want to wipe away a tear with the same hand that managed the powder pouch. He thought to test the hold of leather strands securing a hatchet at his waist. The hour was four in the afternoon.

He could easily see down the gradual slope. Movement in the enemy camp continued at a leisurely pace. Near one end of a shallow barrier made from cut brush, a soldier scraped a blade across his whiskers. Another low-ranking man in gray leggings sat on a stone and polished his boots. A soldier still wearing an apron stood, blowing to cool something in a serving spoon. Two men assigned to tend a small cannon were writing letters. Silent activity continued, and not one active Mexican scrutinized the meadow tilting up with its border of trees.

Texans hidden among the hackberries and cedar elms responded to the first strains of "Come to the Bower" as they might have reacted to harp music from golden clouds. The words to the tune, though, would have made an angel blush. Houston's men were smiling in spite of their disbelief. Soldiers who'd waited in the trees lurched forward, as line drums began to accompany the fife music.

The private to Abel's left stalled at the last tree to drop his trousers and relieve his bowels. Whatever might stain the field ahead, Ned's father ordered himself not to submit until he'd lost the last of his own blood.

Ahead, a Mexican soldier let one shiny boot slip from his grasp where he'd been sitting. He lunged clumsily for his musket. The man surprised while shaving could only stand, dumbfounded. Paper fluttered to the ground where two had been penning letters. Jerking into action at the cannon, they seemed not to recall the correct sequence for priming and firing. The cook let his spoon fly into the air as the first hundred Texans poured out from hiding.

"Fight for the Alamo!" From the center of Houston's attack line came the shout, and Abel Wainwright growled involuntarily when he saw the general's magnificent dark stallion felled before the second whoop rang out. "Fight for Goliad!"

In an instant, an aide on horseback galloped to the commander's side and leapt to the ground to give over his mount. Bloodied at the leg, Houston limped to the replacement steed and bellowed his own call to charge. "Gates of hell!"

Staccato notes from a Mexican bugle broke out and officers in long-johns stumbled from their tents. The soldier who'd set a match to the cannon fuse looked perplexed as shot flew far over the heads of the attacking rebels, landing harmlessly behind their stretched line. His hands were shaking in the attempt to light a second round when Abel Wainwright sank a hunting knife into his neck. Ned's father sensed only a flicker of relief that he'd put off firing his rifle, because he needed that weapon immediately to take down a soldier dashing to a tethered horse. Falling back, the cavalryman clutched at a wet spot spreading across his undershirt.

Shock tore through the Mexican camp. Neither officer nor foot-soldier could maintain composure or gain an upper-hand.

"Remember Goliad!"

The half-dressed men who'd been settling only minutes before into the deeper bliss of rest could not now muster cogent response. One commander gestured as if ordering a retreat. Another man wearing the red breast-plate of rank waved his arms as an order to form up and stand ground. Neither could make himself heard above the shrieks of terror and agony.

Onward through Santa Anna's encampment stormed the hundreds under General Sam Houston. Nowhere, among the scores that Wainwright and his company overtook, did the Mexican dictator stand out in the fray. Only one appearance caused the father and his comrades to blink and pause momentarily. A dark-skinned woman, a beauty in a blue skirt and matching shawl, stood immobile not far from an open tent flap. She made no movement or noise, and her presence had the effect of a deity's approval on mortals winning in combat.

Ever closer to watery edges General Houston's army drove the fleeing Mexicans. Where Sherman's men were venting their rage successfully, Santa Anna's eastern flank was being forced down the banks of the San Jacinto River. Juan Seguin and the mounted men under Colonel Lamar would cut down anyone peeling off to the smaller bayous on the north and west. Those with Mosely Baker, including Ned Wainwright's father, deduced as they pressed forward that Mexicans fleeing due south had reached a barrier there. More and more thickly the conquered soldiers bunched up at a swamp's edge and begged for mercy.

"Me no Alamo! Me no Goliad!"

A strange methodical calm overtook the Texans as they amassed upon the last of solid ground. The steps to tamping down powder and loading shot took on the self-assurance of sacrament. Abel waited until his weapon was ready before deciding which trapped opponent to dispatch. Others in his company called out their intentions as they prepared their rifles and muskets.

"I got that fella prayin' like a preacher!"

"Let me take the one waving his hands!"

"That one yonder cryin' for his mama!"

"The heathen splashing away!" An axe flew and buried itself in the man's back.

"Remember how Goliad went! Weren't no mercy at that bloodbath neither!"

Mr. Wainwright didn't intend to scrutinize any Mexican's face as the slaughter went on. Near the end of the killing, though, he had no choice. A knot of gray hair dangled across the brow of the last one he shot, and the man squinted up at Abel as if curious about who'd given him a mortal wound. It was the same look any soldier might give his timepiece before the start of a battle.

So this is about what time it was when I died. So this is who's been waiting for me at the crossroads. This is the person—strange and familiar—who's brought my life to an end.

The banks of the San Jacinto fell into a hush. Then the solid ground at the southern swamp grew quiet, and even the northern bayou edge up near Vince's calmed briefly. It was the kind of startling silence that makes a person notice his own pulse. A dragonfly buzzed past Abel's shoulder and sped erratically across the bloody water. The father stood up straight and rested the butt of his rifle on the ground. He patted his pocket to feel for the watch he'd tucked there. Others in his company also recognized the freedom to pause. Somewhere over near Sherman's flank, a friendly bugle sounded its short victory strain.

The elder Private Wainwright unwrapped his watch for the second time that afternoon. The minute hand was only eighteen marks past when he'd last looked. Texas independence had been won in little more than a quarter hour.

Chapter 11 Riding the Aftermath

Victory yelps echoed out from the big river and the swamp where Sherman and Houston directed Texas fighters. Along the more open western perimeters, though, harrowing encounters increased. For the first minutes of battle, James Peter Trezevant stayed aware of young Wainwright's position. After the mature private steadied his aim and sent one Mexican scout flying from a colorful saddle blanket, it seemed a blessing to spot the boy's horse skirting lethal encounters at a trot.

As more with Santa Anna scattered in the cavalry's direction, however, there was time to consider only one's own survival. Jamie didn't know how the other mounted men with Captain Karnes managed to voice their rage between killings. As they rode down the next wave of fleeing Mexicans, he was stunned by the chorus of battle shouts. "Here's for the Alamo! Remember the massacre at Goliad!"

Jamie was proving skilled in mortal attack, the grim reflex honed by any who'd survived battle at Refugio. But he was well aware his voice was of no use. When he did find himself within a span of calm, he spied the Ned engaged in life-or-death struggle. The eleven-year-old was being dragged from the Harpers' horse but somehow managed to reverse his adversary's bayonet with deadly force. Immediately, another wounded *soldado* rose and staggered in the youth's direction. From Jamie's throat came a deep, gravelly sound too muted for impact. On instinct, the boy performed an about-face and made second use of the blade. Another exhortation came to Private Trezevant, as two from the Mexican infantry dashed in desperation toward a mesquite thicket. Jamie made the guttural sound again and pursued, his battle cry unintelligible.

Honte y soit qui mal y pense!

Word reached those under Lamar that the entire unit with Santa Anna's general Almonte had surrendered and somehow avoided annihilation just to their south. Texans on horseback spent the last hours of daylight responding to sporadic fire nearer the bayous of Harrisburg.

Mexican soldiers still scattering from the carnage at the San Jacinto continued their effort to reach the remnants of Vince's bridge. Sometimes the scramble from a clump of sage alerted Lamar's men to an escape attempt. Sometimes a musket ball zinged past the ear of a Texan on horseback, before he and his comrades fired back at the source.

Jamie shuddered at the fading light, but he could still make out the company answering to Captain Juan Seguin, their white badges catching the setting sun. They were turning west again toward the banks of the Brazos, prepared to thwart enemy retreat at Fort Bend's ferry.

Nearer his own position, Karnes and one lieutenant suddenly rode off in the direction of a single rifle blast. Other officers in that company held their position, though, and the cavalry's demeanor mostly signaled a time for respite. Any soldier riding with a torch at night made an easy target. Besides, every member of the Texas army deserved a short space for breathing and resting and for taking in the magnitude of an utterly decisive win.

Jamie's purpose shifted quickly to locating Ned Wainwright. He wouldn't drift into even the briefest sleep if the boy might be lying injured somewhere out in the dark. Favoring one foot, he walked his mount among random clusters of men and horses. One band answering directly to Lamar sprawled near a prairie willow. As night crept in, a small knot of Deaf Smith's partners spoke to one another and laughed softly.

Hoping to hear the child's voice stand out, Trezevant suppressed a groan in order to better listen. He decided to find a rock to sit against as soon as he could. His arm ached. Pain in his injured toes still jabbed. Surely every man who'd fought alongside Houston that day felt pangs and might soon experience debilitating soreness. He'd certainly strained his own limbs into use he would not have thought possible. Battalion men recently escaped from Victoria swamps could not yet know full stamina.

His left arm throbbed—the one he'd used to reach for the bridle of Sherman's horse twenty-four hours earlier. He was judging a mound of shale to be solid enough for stretching against, when a soldier lit a pipe nearby and the flicker helped him identify a familiar horse. The towheaded boy was slumped in the saddle, and he'd let the reins fall loose from Harper's neck. Only the older soldier's right arm would work to give the youngster's knee a nudge.

"Ned?"

"I'm sleepin' right here. I'm stayin' in the saddle."

The Dove Shall Fly

"You all right? I've been looking for you." The boy nodded, but he seemed not to identify the person asking.

"I don't know how many I kilt."

"Last I saw, you were being dragged off your horse," Jamie said. "But you took care of yourself. You proved yourself a soldier." The youth came out of his daze and looked with some recognition at Trezevant.

"I got the ones that came after me direct," he said. "I don't guess you heard how my daddy fared."

"Tomorrow and the next day, there will be a better accounting."

"I hope my daddy fared as well," Ned repeated, "or if he got shot, he's still on his feet and feelin' neighborly like you." He pointed at Jamie's aching arm. "It looks worse than it is, I expect, on account of your white shirt."

From the quivering light of a small campfire, a dark patch below Jamie's shoulder first looked to be a shadow. When he inspected, he found oozing blood only partly dried. His shirt was ripped and the gash from a pistol shot exposed. The pang sharpened. He now remembered the shock of a late encounter, how a frantic soldier had come at him with a saber before drawing his firearm. Jamie had been letting his own rifle rest as the worst frays eased up. Moments before the surprise assault, his horse had stepped back and allowed him to take aim.

Initially, he'd felt no pain from the flesh wound. He now understood why a throb in his upper arm grew steadily pronounced. He was thinking it best to locate that mound of shale again and rest while others were doing the same.

"I don't wanna leave you like I done Mr. Erlich," Ned said while tying their horses to a scrub oak.

"This won't kill me, I don't think."

"Promise you won't die if I go find a doctor."

"Tomorrow and the next day, they'll likely set up medical tents. You won't find anyone tonight."

"Don't let some Santa Anna devil murder the horses." The child disappeared into the dark before Jamie could answer.

An hour later, the boy was tugging at his good arm. A muscular man at his side had the appearance of a blacksmith who'd been dragged away from an intense chore.

"I got a poker here hot enough for another cauterize or two," he said. "If you don't want it, I'll move on to those that do. The little fella says it went clear through so, like as not, it won't do you in. Unless you favor festering."

"My sleeve is torn on the other side, too. There's nothing to dig out."

"Well, say if you want this poker while it's still glowing." Jamie wasn't at all sure what he wanted, but he nodded while the man withdrew a flask from inside his coat. "Take two swigs. It'll have some effect while the boy helps your shirt off from there. I need to get at it quick while this iron has some red in it."

By the first hint of morning gray, the wounded private had come to a decision about Mrs. Wainwright's son. Not having slept, Jamie had found time to plan his last exchange with the eleven-year-old. In dire circumstances, the two had latched onto one another. If they survived in the same circles another day or two, brotherly impulses might outweigh a soldier's duty. The man with the hot poker had ripped Jamie's shirt into a sling and handed him a ragged coat to slip on when he was able.

"How's your arm feel?" the youngster asked upon opening his eyes.

"It's better already." He'd practiced the lie during the long night. "I've been waiting for you to wake up. Some orders came my way while you were sleeping." He told Ned Wainwright that a soldier with Captain Karnes had come to find him. Private Trezevant was to ride clear on to Vince's Bridge before the sun rose much. Escapees still hid and ambushed Texans up that way. Every cavalryman in that direction and off toward the Brazos was on the lookout for General Santa Anna.

"I'll put a knife in him."

"Houston wants him alive."

"I'll go get the horses."

"The Karnes officer said Captain Mosely could be looking for you," Jamie went on. "Maybe you can tell some of my battalion friends where I ended up, if you hear anyone asking." Ned would likely forget the name Hardaway, though he'd heard more mention of that Macon man than about Andrews or Moses. "Over east of us, your daddy is probably worried on your behalf. You ought to check with Burleson and Hockley's men, too, if you don't find him right away. They want everyone to head back where they were mustered so an account can be made."

"Last word was…we didn't lose many." The boy's voice pinched off. Hoping for reassurance, he looked over at their horses and then back at Jamie's sling.

The Dove Shall Fly

"I imagine Mr. Wainwright's worst suffering this morning is not knowing your whereabouts." During the long, miserable night, he'd thought of another reason for their parting. "Your daddy will probably have the best ideas how to get the Harpers' horse back to them. Don't forget that your mama and everyone traveling with her will be as happy to have another ride in their mix as they are jubilant over Santa Anna's defeat."

"You think he'll get his just desserts today?" The two privates stood up and nodded at one another.

"Just take Harper at a walk directly toward the sun. There's no way to miss the thickest gathering with Sam Houston." To Jamie's relief, the boy hoisted himself into the saddle without help.

"You ought to keep my daddy's boots. Your toes should mend even if the leather there never smooths out." Ned's voice rose and quavered. He blinked and the corners of his mouth went tight. "I'll let him know, and my mama too, it was you shooed me away from snakes and cutthroats at Harrisburg." Jamie had forgotten whose footwear he'd pulled on. His arm was screaming for him to finish with the exchange.

He was relieved that morning darkness stretched out for several more minutes. Wainwright's pale hair caught the early light for a while after he rode off, but then the young rider disappeared into the gray landscape. Jamie let his own mount amble. Lifting a sleeve of the thin, hand-off coat, he dabbed at his eyes. An odd recollection surfaced, and he was grateful for the subdued dawn. Long ago, when news first broke that his own father was dead, he and Charles had gone on fingering the pages of their books. In the house on Stoll's Alley, they'd taken a seat at the children's table when the next meal was served. They'd unfolded their pajamas at bedtime, in their usual habit. It wasn't until the second or third day after tragedy that the Trezevant house went awash in tears.

Fifteen years later, Jamie thought the Wainwright son might have prompted in him yet more delayed grief over the separation of fathers from their children. More likely, the agonizing throb in his shoulder was forcing an admission of pain. Or the previous day was already beginning to haunt. *Me no Alamo! Me no Goliad!*

The main scouting group under Henry Wax Karnes paused to let Trezevant catch up. Seven scouts with the officer relaxed in their saddles, and another man sat driver of a small cart. The captain averted his eyes from the private listing in the saddle.

"Boys, this is one of Fannin's men," he explained calmly. "He's already come back from hell once. He can take a little more."

The officer's soothing tone did not assuage his men's astonishment.

"He looks more pale than crushed shell."

"He's had to run halfway across God's forgotten desert. Probably fought panthers between throwing off some Urrea patrol this side of Victoria and the next close call." Jamie accepted a gulp from one soldier's water gourd and slipped a wedge of dried beef into a pocket of the cast-off coat. Karnes waited before addressing him. "If you can stay upright, you should ride with us, Trezevant." Eight soldiers pausing to let the Goliad man join up soothed their horses. "He has more reason than the rest of us to want Santa Anna hauled in," Karnes said. His regulars had difficulty hiding their doubt that such an emaciated specimen could ride and fight. "Don't let me forget to spell his name right in my ledger."

"It's a flesh wound, likely not to fester," Jamie spoke up, as if answering their stares. "I won't slow down the hunt."

The first two Mexican soldiers they overtook looked of equal low rank and rattled mind. The pair darted out from a large bread oven a quarter mile from the narrowing Sim's. Running at first in the direction of a scraggly oak, they soon fell to their knees, clasping their hands over their heads. Without a word, they let themselves get bound and directed to the rough cart. Both prisoners cast their eyes to the ground, and their gray leggings suggested they'd been too surprised by the attack the day before to pull on trousers.

"Any we find up ahead could know where Santa Anna has headed," Karnes reminded them all. One captive in the cart looked up briefly and then studied the ground again.

"It might be that General Filisola turned back in our direction before making it to Nacogdoches."

"Might could be Santa Anna hopes to join with him just up north."

"We know who we're looking for," the captain broke in, stopping the conjecture. "Houston wants the head of the snake—alive." He'd seen a miniature portrait of Filisola and knew to beware of a husky, somewhat graying man, but he'd been told that Mexico's supreme leader had a darker complexion, was lean with no tinge of aging in his hair. Scrutinizing the two in the cart again, he doubted that scouts could easily distinguish Santa Anna from others on the run. "We'll soon be up around what's left of Vince's Bridge. Stay on guard for anything that moves. Most on the run are figuring to die and won't mind blasting one of us to the hereafter first." He held up a spyglass and scoured their surroundings for a minute. "Don't forget Captain Sylvester has his patrol in these parts, too. Let's not dispatch any of our own men to their final reward."

Jamie was still shaking off the captain's earlier mention of hell. In his four months of serving in Texas, he'd thought more than once of a stairway winding down into Hades. Ward's valiant companies had marched back to Refugio for a rescue mission, only to find themselves pitifully outnumbered by Urrea's ranks. A week later, after taking a wrong turn in their retreat toward Victoria, the desperate battalion had retraced their steps and then become trapped in the town's outlying swamp. Afterward, he and a handful of escapees had sometimes gone in circles in their attempt to distance themselves from Goliad's gray walls.

Now, the private closed in once more on the bayous by smoldering Harrisburg. Was it just the previous morning that he'd ridden here with Seguin's courier? He shook from his mind the image of Erlich's corpse and the twisted face of the snake-bitten messenger. He couldn't let himself picture the distraught Wainwright boy frantically searching for his father. Jamie prayed that if he were to get shot from the saddle, his last thoughts would not be of these deadly Texas bayous, much less of the panicked *soldados* he'd sent to eternity in the last twenty-four hours.

Captain Karnes warned them to keep their weapons at the ready. The patrol was approaching a mound of logs, a primitive domicile ruined by abandonment and time. If there had been an oleander blooming red, Jamie might have thought he'd circled back all the way to the banks of the Brazos and the shaky start of his own recovery. But these hewn logs, though in disarray, had not yet sunk into the wet muck of the prairie. Having been overlooked as Vince's Bridge was torched, the timbers still rested high enough to obscure a handful of assailants.

Captain Sylvester's unit suddenly boiled out from cover and overtook the hideout from behind. By the time the men with Karnes came within range, the runaways were already shouting, "No Goliad! No Alamo!" The capture of four more Mexican privates was mostly anti-climactic. Whatever firearms they'd fled with the day before were harmless without fresh powder and shot. These prisoners, also in torn leggings, were on their knees before their hands were secured with rope. Karnes shook his head at their general description—underdressed even for conscripted privates, all somewhat slender, and all with black hair untouched by gray. It wasn't until one of Sylvester's men marched them closer to the cart that the significance of the round-up grew apparent.

The new captives balked at climbing in alongside the first two. A sergeant nudged them forward with the tip of his rifle, but the bound men only stiffened where they stood. One seated captive was groaning and bowing his head.

"*El Presidente!*" he exclaimed at last, as an apology for not saluting.

"*El Pre-si-den-te!* The other prisoners were slow to recognize their commander. The captive standing closest to the cart raised his eyes to look directly at Captain Sylvester and Karnes. With shock seeming to squelch his captors' immediate retaliation, Santa Anna let a thin smile cross his lips.

"Your general Señor Houston, he will want to speak with me, no?"

The Hum of Elegies

Chapter 12   A Hard Path Home

Not far from the banks of the upper Brazos River, Yarico kept her evening watch. A fortnight after Houston's victory, the two families still traveled together. With Ned returned to them, they now made use of three horses. Moving homeward with a thousand other survivors, they'd struggled away from the stench of the burnt-out camp at the bend, but they were in no hurry to see more ruin farther north in San Felipe. Pieces of Aunt Maggie's mind lay strewn along the Texas prairie, and Yarico was more than a little worried about her own limits.

Like water flowing from the river to the ocean to unknowable ravines and back to deepest origins, her thoughts coursed round and round. Freedom had been won on the 21st of April. It was all the Texas families finding one another and heading back to their homesteads could talk about. The woman who'd belonged with the Pagnols and then with the Harpers kept her own counsel about liberty. At night, she felt that prize leaking away between her fingers.

She'd known for years how to keep a lantern wick down to its dimmest nub at night, and since arriving in Texas she'd trained herself to fend off drowsiness. At the start of her watch, she set the glowing tin-ware just a few feet from where the Wainwrights clumped together and Adeline lay near Maggie. Displaced and exhausted, they kept each other hopeful. Not one of them, though, could dismiss recent trauma as one might shoo a grackle from a vegetable patch.

In sensing a greater and greater distance between daily life and the garden called freedom, Yarico was alone.

When the older Wainwright boy stirred, she wasn't surprised. In the first days of their reunion, he'd chatted steadily, but lately he was mute from sunup to nightfall. Yarico thought it might have taken some time for the death of Wendell, the family's newborn, to register as final. His worry over Mr. Wainwright's fate was surely mounting, too—as well as memories of the worst in close-up battle. As families made slow work of their return home, the solemn youngster would smile if his mother or sisters hugged him, and he sometimes took Little Abel by the hand. By the time several clans made it back to the Brazos trail, the boy soldier wasn't opening his mouth during daylight except to take a bite of greens or griddle bread.

Yarico moved the lantern to a spot a little farther from the others, as she had other nights. In the relative dark, she stretched out her shawl and sat at one edge. Her own emotions didn't fit easily with words, and she felt an odd kinship with the blond boy who hadn't even nodded in her direction before the revolution called him and his father away. She couldn't make out Ned's turning on all fours to get his balance, but she sensed he was managing the maneuver. While the others sank into dreams, she'd come to expect a confidential exchange with the boy. Afterward, the child would return to his blanket. Silence would suit him until the next watch.

"We got enough lamp oil?"

"If it starts flickering before sunrise, maybe you'll fill it again." Ned was nodding. His thick blond eyelashes had drawn Aunt Maggie from her stupor several mornings ago to pay a compliment. Yarico felt it was better to let him speak first.

"How many days now since I first rode up at the Trinity?"

"Eleven."

"Same as my age."

"I didn't know that," she said. "You surely act all grown." Neither of them needed to say it was Mrs. Wainwright having the hardest time treating him like a young man who'd seen war.

"That afternoon I rode up, Mama and you all couldn't hardly believe we'd walloped the Mexicans."

"Such news came to us shortly before, but we stayed in doubt until we heard it from you."

"We were wrong about Santa Anna gettin' caught right off." His whisper was hoarse. Both hushed for a moment while Cassandra rolled over in her sleep.

"They must have found him the day after you set out our way. People don't always hear right," Yarico went on, "or pass word along exactly as it was first told." The oldest Wainwright child cupped his hands in the dark. She wondered if he might be deciding which recollections to keep and which to let go.

The Dove Shall Fly

"I wish I hadn't done like Baker's men told me. I wish I hadn't moved on without first bein' sure where my daddy was at. They said to go ride out and look for the rest of the family." Most of the Wainwrights hadn't seen Big Abel since mid-March when General Houston called rebels to amass at the Colorado. Ned had last been at his father's side the day before the Texans' decisive win.

"He was right to have you help the cavalry. Otherwise, you wouldn't have met up with that Goliad fellow who borrowed Adeline's horse." She could see he was accepting the observation. "And without your coming across us out by the Trinity, your mama and the children might have traipsed all the way to Louisiana swamps." Breathing through his mouth, the boy turned to the woman on watch.

"They could have been snake-bit over there or suffercated in a sink hole." Yarico fended off the memory haunting her—an arm in the current where she'd drawn water barely weeks ago.

"Everyone knows this trail we're on. I don't doubt your daddy will track us down."

"If I had me a spyglass, I'd keep better watch on the path behind us."

"Not much gets past your steady eye, Ned. I see how you do." She sensed he was studying her, and she was tempted to let her arm drift up around the child's shoulder as she would have comforted Adeline. Instead, she turned aside as if assessing the lantern flame.

"Houston had two Indians close by most times. And I seen a black boy ready with his fife before I was sent off to find the horseback companies. And riding with all them, just as plain as anyone speaking English, it was a whole company of Mexicans. All of 'em on our side, if you could let your mind believe it." She didn't need the youngster to explain why these facts made it easier for him to talk with her than it was for the other Wainwrights.

"We met up with that company's captain," she reminded him. "And you've heard us recollect the same Goliad soldier you rode with a while." She paused for a moment. "We were almost past our last energy, but we found it easy to do swapping with the recovering private and Señor Seguin. Both were clearly our friends."

The boy's blond eyebrows moved together over the bridge of his freckled nose. His head moved from side to side and he sucked in breath more noisily. Remembering where Mr. Wainwright's boots went, she was sorry she'd referred a second time to the battalion survivor.

"I was slow to see Seguin's messenger as helping our side. At first sighting, I figured him a Santa Anna man. Then he got kilt. The one with them boots Mama gave over, like you said, him and me went on a ways together."

"I'm so sorry. The battles you saw are likely to perch in your thoughts for a long spell."

"Can't never forget it was a snake got the messenger," Ned agreed. His voice rose above a whisper, but the others wouldn't rouse easily. "Later that day, I took down four on my own. Two with a bayonet and them other two with an axe just a layin' on the ground. I never did get my rifle powdered right."

Ned Wainwright didn't utter another word that night. He sat next to Yarico for an hour, before stealing into the shadows and crawling back where his sisters slept. He was silent the next day except for shrieking once with the girls, loud enough to startle a hawk into releasing a dead squirrel. The women came running from the riverbank where they'd been rinsing out discarded clothing collected from the muddy trail. Mrs. Wainwright's girls were more skilled at skinning small animals than at needlework, and their mother set out a pail for boiling meat scraps into a broth. Swapping needles and salvaged thread, the Harper women busied themselves with garments already spread out and dried.

In the first days since halting the exodus, scattered families treated the dumped possessions of strangers with the same deference they'd have given altar artifacts. Reality soon nudged them from such civility. No one was going to claim the warped cedar trunk filled with special occasion apparel—a christening gown, a dress coat suitable for a funeral, a multi-tiered dancing skirt, two embroidered vests, and an eyelet pinafore. If not gathered up by the Harpers, the items would be purveyed and put to use by other scavengers, torn by foraging animals, or left to desiccate in the scorching Texas sun.

Adeline, Aunt Maggie, and Yarico had begun collecting anything made of cloth. Many items, once washed, were mendable, and those that weren't could be torn into strips for pieced coverlets and sitting mats. They'd heard from others along the Brazos banks that San Felipe, though left in cinders, was already coming back to life. There, two coats might be traded for a kettle, clothing for a family of four swapped for a small cart or plow. The dried ruts and worn stretches of sod were as likely to yield an almanac and *The Last of the Mohicans* as a set of hair combs, mustache scissors, and sleeping cap. A butter churn minus its dash stick might lie in crevice. A fire grate and a bellows could turn up next. Though the rainy season was far from over, the Harper women turned their capes into saddle sacks. Both families harbored one thought without putting it to heartbreaking words. There would be no trading a feed bag full of recovered tools and housewares for any life lost in the revolution.

"I reckon Ned sat with you again last night." As Mrs. Wainwright spoke, the woman still on watch stood and pulled her shawl up around her brown arms.

"Yes'm. He seems not to sleep well." It was first light. Yarico wondered after glancing at the brunette woman if she'd been blond in her youth. The boy did take after her otherwise.

"How long since he went off to find a latrine spot?"

"I couldn't say. My last recollection is when he took a place next to your girls. Such has been his habit. But that was some time ago."

"He didn't head over to the tall grasses?"

"No ma'am. He did a turn again at the watch, and then—" Yarico had not seen the boy leave, and Mrs. Wainwright might have let anger about that oversight flare if worry hadn't taken over. General hysteria among the shifting throngs hadn't really lessened since the San Jacinto battle. If Texas colonists had been mostly fit though terrified at the start of their flight, they were now joyful but teetering on the brink of survival.

"Some along these banks would just as soon roast a lost boy as let him sit by a fire."

"Last night…lately…he's been talking by lantern light about his daddy. I wonder if he might have wandered down trail to look for Mr. Wainwright."

There was no chance that Ned's mother would leave her youngest three to search for her eleven-year-old. Adeline jumped up as soon as she learned of the boy's absence, but there was no greater likelihood Yarico would let the Harper girl navigate the clogged path on her own to find him.

"I'm officially a woman since two weeks ago," she pointed out. None of the older females traveling together wished to explain how the roughest men along the paths might respond to that information. Even Margaret Linder stayed clear-headed as Yarico readied herself to accompany Adeline.

"You and Addy just stick to one another," Maggie said. They'd all agreed they couldn't again risk a horse snapping its leg in the deeply rutted path. "This riverside trail looks no better than what a cyclone leaves behind. You two could lose each other if you don't stay close." Aunt Maggie—not a blood relative after all—found no further language to underscore the horror of that possibility. Yarico retied her apron strings to secure the family's hatchet and tried to shift the older woman's concern.

"I know you'll let Little Abel cling to you, if he frets."

As the two younger Harper women edged away, they assured Mrs. Wainwright they'd find her son. But after a day of hiking against the current of returning refugees, neither felt so hopeful. They stopped to comfort a grandmother who'd twisted an ankle in a rabbit hole. Several children were making her a pallet that their burro could pull. Not long after that encounter, they went off trail together to find privacy bushes for relieving themselves. When they made their way back to the riverbank, people were giving wide berth to several youths in a fistfight over who'd first found a small parcel of sour pinto beans.

Yarico and Adeline could have missed Ned many times in the mix of people and distractions. Finding him seemed unlikely, but they could not imagine facing Mrs. Wainwright without being able to honestly say they'd tried. Besides their growing sense of futility, the pair shared another mounting worry over retracing their original escape path.

"We knew it was no kind of travel for his mother to embark on with a new baby," Adeline finally spoke up. "But what else was there for any of us to do?"

They sat resting on a grassy patch. Within arm's reach, they'd noticed too late, was a cross formed from a whip handle and a back scratcher. With chaos all around, the tragedy marker drew no more attention than a hoof print.

"We should turn back before we get anywhere near where little Wendell was buried."

"My stomach cramps up when I wonder if it wasn't much farther down the trail," the Harper girl confided. Over the baby's shallow grave, they'd set two wet sticks down flat and edged the cross with river rocks. "It could be just downriver a ways. Remember? Sometimes it took eight hours to go a mile with all that rain and everyone in a panic."

"It was far from here," Yarico said, not at all sure. "We'll turn back before we come across that sorrowful sight."

"You think that's what Ned set out to find? Or to meet his daddy?"

"He likely had both on his mind." When Yarico stood, she bent to scoop up a pouch of men's handkerchiefs that she'd spotted. Adeline flicked the dirt off a teacup missing its saucer. There was no telling what could be swapped in San Felipe. They were both thinking they'd suggest to Mrs. Wainwright that her son might have taken that northerly direction himself and could already be upriver. Neither put the unrealistic idea into speech, and they moved again against the flow of trudging Texans.

They had not progressed more than a half mile the next morning when the aroma of roasting pork brought them to a halt. Three soldiers who had to be siblings were nearly dancing by a spit where a succulent carcass turned. Around the reunion of families and their menfolk, a ring of bystanders grew. A watchful child younger than the Wainwright girls was bold enough to approach the revelers as soon as they'd served the last of their own relatives.

"Here, little miss," one of the men said, putting a strip of pork into a cloth wrap she held out. "One more day, and the pig we were hauling would have gone bad anyways. It won't do us any use to be stingy with our extra." The families allowed themselves full jubilation over the independence of Texas, and their joy sustained the two Harper women as much as the pork slice they handed off to Adeline.

"It was a double blessing coming across them." Yarico nodded at the girl, as they approached a knot of people sidestepping impossible ruts.

"Families do find each other."

"I'm wondering if some so full of celebration will want to call this country by a new name altogether."

"*Texas* will suit most people, I expect."

"But blessedly free to name it what we want!" Adeline was carried away with the thought. Her recent passage into adulthood had not completely stanched her childlike exuberance. Somewhere far along the trail, Yarico thought, a sobering discussion might unfold with the girl about living life as a "blessedly free" individual. For now, the thirteen-year-old's joy was contagious.

"Hello," she said quietly to an older black couple walking alongside their owners' wagon. The entire family they were with had red hair, and Yarico wished she and the Harper girl had white flags with a single blue star to hand them.

"We're a country now!" Adeline's pronouncement, as if she'd just received a news transmission at sea, made them all laugh. People before and behind the rocking wagon smiled. Subdued laughter lifted them briefly from exhaustion.

"Hello."

"Hello, everyone in Texas!"

"Hello," a small voice came again from a matted spot next to the scarred trail. "I made it to letter J, without getting fooled by its having no dot. But I got mixed up after that. I don't know why there has to be so many." Ned Wainwright sat on a cypress stump and held up a leather volume, keeping four others like it close to his shoes. His lips moved but his body appeared as fixed as the stump. "My sisters told me I was near too old to get lettered, but I recollected all the way to J without lessons. You can swear it wasn't you that taught me." Adeline tiptoed in his direction as she might have approached a broken bird.

"You found an encyclopedia. That's good, Ned." She held out her water gourd and his pale eyelashes fluttered. Then she pressed the uncorked spout to his lips. "Whenever you want, Susannah and Cassandra will show you how to read, and you can learn anything."

"These are for a real teacher, I reckon. Someone like you," he said. He lifted his sleeve to his nose, and the Harper women realized that a sharp dank odor was cutting through the general smell of unwashed humans and river sludge. Adeline gestured toward a sparsely covered mound near some saplings, and the boy bit his lip. "I thought maybe that was where you all put Wendell, but I looked close enough to see it was…it was…"

"Let's make another shoulder bag from my apron. I can carry two volumes or three." Yarico tried to keep the hatchet close while she formed a sling. "Maybe if you each take another, we'll make it back up the trail with all five."

"Is every letter here? Some dang fool mighta took one book to use for a fire starter." He smiled, but his eyes seemed to fit a different expression. "My mama will worry if it goes past sunset." Both Adeline and Yarico let pass Ned's assumption that he hadn't yet caused his mother any anxiety.

A steady flow of people streamed past, and most travelers looked their way as a brief distraction. When one bedraggled man on horseback came to a halt, Yarico stiffened to make sure the stranger knew she was fully an adult and accustomed to working the sharp blade now in her hand. The beard of the gaunt rider went as far as his missing collar button. His lips parted and closed before he found his voice.

The Dove Shall Fly

"I mostly thought I'd never find you," Abel Wainwright said to his son.

Ned dropped the volume he'd been clutching and ran to the man, who was too stiff to dismount. He hugged his father's ankle and leg, before breaking into wild sobs. Mr. Wainwright hadn't given much attention to the women nearby, but his son's breakdown made him look their way and then pat the boy's head.

"All right now," he said. "We don't want to become a spectacle. What if General Houston was to ride by just now, expectin' us to salute?" His unlikely suggestion seemed not to soothe the eleven-year-old, and he shifted in his saddle before trying another tactic. "Your mama and the children will sit amazed while we swap stories, don't you think? Even the new baby will hush its cryin' when you tell everyone our hardships and battle scrapes. Is little Wendell lettin' your mama sleep any during the night? Is he calmed any when your sisters take him for a spell?"

Half a minute went by with the Harper women remaining mute and Ned crying more softly. Yarico didn't feel free to speak, but her own tears started as soon as Adeline broke the silence.

"Mr. Wainwright," she began, "it was cruel beyond imagining on this trail when we were all running for our lives." The father started pulling at his beard and stroking Ned's hair gently. "There were old folks who couldn't make it. More than one baby just couldn't survive all the…all the—"

"Is the missus farin' all right?" His voice was deeper. His words seemed to have pushed up from a low place in his chest nearer his heart. None in the exchange could find utterances to lessen the loss. He finally slid awkwardly from his saddle. "Let's get you up here, son, where your feet can rest. I have the opposite problem, so it'll do me some good to see if my legs can give orders to these old shoes. If your mama still has my boots, I might talk her into swapping me." He was trying to smile, but the Harper women were shaking their heads.

"Your boots went to another Texas private, Daddy." That news shocked the man very little, and he nodded to see the boy's tears end. "They're gone for good, but the soldier was deserving. He likely lived, on account of wearing them."

The youngster's expression appeared frozen as the four began returning to their families' camp. Ned's eyes couldn't seem to catch up to his mouth—corners upturned and ready for laughter. His eyes watered as his father told how he'd gone looking for him right after the firing stopped at the south bayou. When he said it took courage to fight alongside the cavalry, the boy squinted and his tears flowed. Mr. Wainwright rushed on to explain about managing a Spanish pony, his own ride having broken its forelegs sliding down a riverbank nearly a month ago. Ned could only get through parts of his own story about trying to help "ole Mr. Erlich," about the blow that brought Nickel down, and the snake that "kilt Seguin's messenger like Satan's cannon shot."

It was two days before members of both families reunited. More tearful than talkative, they knew to keep moving on. Susannah and Cassandra were still slight enough to share their father's pony with their older brother. Adeline took to humming a tune she'd learned at a last campfire out on the sodden prairie. Yarico kept watch on the girl, who possessed enough sense to reacquaint herself with their tan horse. With her servant apron in use for bundling, Yarico winced to imagine her own increased peril if the other white women she traveled with were to lose their minds, as Maggie had.

A half month later, just north of San Felipe, she was still reciting a silent prayer when the Wainwrights finished packing a large open cart they'd gained by barter. The Harper women managed to keep their three horses at the swapping center, and their scavenged goods and mending skills earned them two wheeled vehicles. The roomier wagon went to the reunited family of six once enough vegetables were gathered and field peas dried to sustain them. Mr. Groce, whose plantation had provided supplies for Houston's men before the victory, now permitted returning colonists to forage for any crops they could consume or carry with them. Mrs. Wainwright wouldn't let Adeline's two refusals put an end to the argument for all of them to travel together on to Nacogdoches.

"At least don't start right off in the opposite direction," Annabel repeated. "Set up a while in that blackened San Felipe inn. What I mean to say is, set up you all's cart right in front of the place. That inn don't look much now, but its stink is no worse than any other ruined domicile there. That free negress in the center of town, she never did stop puttin' out bread loaves, and I won't dispute the tastiness of what her and her daughter's ovens cook up." Adeline stayed firm in her long-range intent.

"We do figure on backtracking through San Felipe on our way to Mina—Bastrop if that's what they're calling it now." Yarico believed the girl might breathe better when the three Harpers were following only their own inclinations, but Mrs. Wainwright nudged her once more.

The Dove Shall Fly

"All's I'm thinkin' is you ought go back to San Felipe and stay there a while. That-a-way if you have regrets you can find the Old San Antone Road, like we're fixin' to do, and it'll take you straight on northeast to Nacogdoches. We'll likely make it our home a while." The woman's appreciation of Yarico had cooled since the San Jacinto win, but not her attachment to the youngest Harper. "If Big Abel can come across Ned in this knot of strangers, you ladies could track us again for certain." When her older son sprinted from the pack to hug Yarico's arm, those witnessing went silent. The revolution had used up their power to express surprise.

Adeline couldn't be budged from her plans, even as she watched the family's wagon pull away. It seemed a criminal omission that no fife and drums memorialized the parting. The girl dabbed her eyes with a pale blue handkerchief, a reminder of the cloth bolt Mrs. Bedeford had bought for her Sunday dress back in Macon. She knew they were likely never to see the Wainwrights again. Little Abel was too old for sucking either thumb, but he put both hands to his mouth as their vehicle rocked away from Aunt Maggie, who'd lately mothered him most. Adeline had no more chance of crossing paths with these neighbors than she had of sitting next to Mrs. Bedeford again by a window at a yellow porch. Never would she tell the cousins who'd marched from Macon to Goliad that she'd posted their letters home, as asked. The seasons of life did not repeat themselves.

But imagination rekindled hope. When the caravan heading west came at last within sight of Mina's tree line, the women who'd left central Georgia with a battalion the previous November fancied they smelled evergreens well before the wind could carry such fragrance.

Here was a feature to remind them of home, no matter which calendar month—a dense expanse of pine trees.

Bastrop, as the majority of folks began to call the town being resurrected, exuded a friendliness as extraordinary as its scenery. The Mexican army passing through near the war's end had burned municipal buildings and habitats, but had given up trying to torch the remarkable swath of evergreens. The wet winter explained the forest's resistance to flames, but no one ventured to guess how the expanse of straight timber ever sprouted in a location hundreds of miles from the nearest pines.

"It was a miracle!"

The Harper women heard this declaration several times a day upon their arrival among Bastrop's campers. All returning and new residents were treated with the same affability, as if their choosing to make the woodlands home were another sign of divine intervention.

"What a blessing!" Tabitha Ellinger exclaimed when Maggie assured her Adeline was an experienced teacher.

"Our darling ran a primer school on the outskirts of Brazoria," she said before clapping her hands. "The day we moved on, families hardly allowed us to pull away from the main thoroughfare. There's at least one young man who all but proposed her, but she held to her own ideas about the future. Bastrop won't be taking on a young female with any frivolous notions, that's what I'm saying."

Yarico squeezed the girl's hand, and they both silently marveled that Aunt Maggie could piece together so many words into clear conversation. They wondered if pungent pine fragrance might have the same restorative powers as smelling salts.

In the middle of June, an afternoon shower drew comments as familiar to the Harper women as to the long-term residents of the Texas town.

"I'm puttin' my money we don't see another drop 'til the end of October."

"Best thing about the heat a-comin' is that the savages will feel a tight hot lid on their atrocities." Nearly every day, the three from Macon heard reminders of where to retreat if a bell rang out or if a cannon from the stockade blasted off. When the town was set afire, the outlying structure had gone unnoticed.

"Won't get hot enough to halt Comanche raids until the first of August. Cutthroats stay cool longer than we do, what with their covering up in nuthin' but paint."

"It could be redskins don't even know white folks have run the Mexicans off. The heathens mostly stayed clear of these parts. During which all of us and every brown person north of the Rio Grande kept busy murdering each other."

The Harpers sat near Tabitha Ellinger and her children. At the edge of the Main Street gathering, her husband stood rubbing oil on a rifle barrel. Every evening after vittles and advice passed around, families lingered until fading sunlight gave them only enough time to scatter to nearby campsites. Mr. Ellinger was usually as reserved as his wife was gregarious, but he stepped calmly into a conversation when he sensed the next exaggeration might go unchecked.

"I don't know about the rest of you, but I'm plum content with Mr. Zavala as Vice President for as long as he pleases. Burnet holds him in complete trust. Anyhow, we ought not let ourselves joke about Spanish people being our natural enemies." No one countered the town's burly gun-shop owner. "Plenty in this meeting right here know what the good man risked putting his name on our Declaration of Independence."

"Yessir, that's right, I can vouch there was more than a handful of Spanish in San Antone that went against Santa Anna from the start."

"So, Ernest Ellinger. I suppose now you're gonna preach we should stick our town with the name Mina again because of some great Mexican patriot who founded the place."

"I voted for Bastrop," Tabitha's husband reminded him, "same as you did. My meaning is we got new American settlers coming over our way regular again, and the only talk they hear some days is how every Mexican was takin' orders from the devil himself."

"As long as you men are talkin' fair treatment," Mrs. Ellinger said, letting a ladle clang against a washed kettle, "I'll vote for as high as deputy any Lipan Apache willing to keep warning us about Comanche raids." There was no cascade of response after the woman's declaration, and suddenly everyone was stretching and mumbling about how fast the sun comes hugging the horizon in the last minutes before dusk.

Guiding their cart away from the eastern edge of town, Yarico kept her attention on the dim path. She'd have been happy never to stray from the evergreen clearing that Adeline and Maggie had claimed as their own. Simply returning to that peaceful spot each evening, gave her gratitude enough to tamp down objections. It was not the time to speak up, as Tabitha Ellinger had. The inner voice nagged, though. She couldn't forget Adeline's recent recognition of *the blessed freedom to name ourselves whatever we want!*

"Walk Far wasn't any kind of savage," the girl said suddenly. She'd not taken the talk in town lightly either.

"Our Indian friend knows we won't forget his help." Their horse was slowing down without any guidance from Yarico. "I don't know how else we would have made it back across the Colorado. Panic nearly did us in."

"I almost spoke up for our Tonkawa guide after Mrs. Ellinger said her piece. It got so quiet though. I was afraid my voice might wabble." Maggie was snoring in the bed of the cart. "I worried I'd show up at my encyclopedia shelf tomorrow and have no students, or find everyone with arms folded in protest."

"I expect people need to face whatever scares them," Yarico said. "Mr. Ellinger's talk likely shamed a few into braver thinking."

"I could have told everyone that an Indian cooked us a good meal after bad news in Gonzales turned us around. And weeks later a soldier born Mexican gave us more beef than we'd eaten in days." The wheels stopped rolling. Near their fire pit, the family's lantern and lighting tools were just visible. Next to a sitting log, several flint stones lay in a pile. *Home* had been whittled down to the simplest of possessions.

By August, the stifling daytime heat left the women no choice but to sleep in the open. Their rough lean-to, draped with skins and soiled coverlets, was just too stifling for rest. Yarico took up night-watch habits again. Rustling armadillos and possums kept her alert for snakes, though reptiles posed a more deadly threat in daylight. In the hottest month, the Harper women, like the other residents of Bastrop, resorted to eating mostly blackberries and peppers and pecans. None of them could bear to sit by a fire long enough for rabbit meat to cook tender.

The blistering weather did make tempers flare. Inside Ernest Ellinger's rebuilt gun shop was a large storage room with a lockable latch. Ever since its completion on the Fourth of July, it had served as the city jail. Two or three men were confined in the small space some nights, at times swinging fists until they passed out.

"God dernit!" Tabitha's husband swore one brutally hot day near dusk. Two carpenters not usually inclined to drink themselves into a rage wrestled one another in the Main Street dust. "We got a pair already under lock and key in my cell. You figure Bastrop citizens will put you two up in the hotel? Maybe serve you sweet chocolate and teacakes come mornin'?" Both builders he scolded were Refugio Irishmen who'd fled before Urrea's takeover. Shocked townspeople had expected the men's shared escape to make them fast friends.

"It's his fault! You can string me up alongside seed pods if I'm tellin' a lie." Several sober men helped Mr. Ellinger restrain the two, while mothers corralled their children, ushering them away from the fracas. Yarico adjusted the cart reins conspicuously to let Adeline and Maggie know it was time to drift away to their campsite.

"The hell you say. All right, all right—my apologies to the ladies present and the wee ones." Mr. Ellinger and the hotel owner held firm to the fellow's arms, but he bent from the middle in an attempt to retrieve his hat. "Don't be tellin' me he didn't have his bloody chance last evening. 'Twas only yesterday, he took his fair turn with yet a different Santa Anna spy!"

"You don't even know what day it is, ye damned drunkard!"

"What spy are you two bellowing about?" Mr. Ellinger wanted to know. With San Antonio less than a hundred miles to the west, residents fretted over a renewed Mexican threat as often as they worried about Comanche raids.

"The two of us put ourselves to volunteer patrol each night—"

"And pitiful poor thanks we get for our effort, isn't that right, lad—"

"Don't be callin' me *laddie*, all grovelin' and nice as you please." Mr. Ellinger let loose of the man long enough to let him point where the Colorado River wound through town. "It was me own turn to pound a Mexican into the bleedin' ground. At the moment, there's another villain tied to a tree 'tuther side of the hotel. He'll crawl away like the filthy snake he is if you don't bring him to justice before nightfall."

His rival still muttered his case as Tabitha's husband and two other citizens marched off to inspect the woods in that direction. When they returned, the street was enveloped in shadow, and buildings in town were nearly indistinguishable from the night sky. Those lingering in the main street watched with eyes that had adjusted to the fading light. Several families witnessed the return of town officials, with a fourth man hanging onto Mr. Ellinger's shoulder. The dark figure sank down as he struggled to keep his balance. By torchlight at the hotel, bystanders could discern the captive's brown skin and black hair. The stranger's torn soldier jacket and military boots gave him away as someone used to orders. But the apprehended man mumbled in Spanish, and those still sweltering in the dusty road at dusk seemed to agree about his identity.

"A Mexican, that's for sure."

"No doubt a treasonous spy."

"I say let the two Irish swing at him with their sledge hammers."

"Shame on all of you!" one woman objected. "I'm taking the children out of range from hearing any such talk."

Yarico managed to help Aunt Maggie into the cart seat and to coax Adeline up onto the driver's ledge with her. The three had just enough time to head away from Main Street before dark closed in completely. They had learned to distance themselves from knots of ill-tempered people, but the beaten man called in their direction.

"Señoritas, por favor, por favor...Miss West? No, Mademoiselle Yarico, por favor, por favor..." The Harper woman handling the reins raised one hand to cover her mouth.

Tabitha Ellinger had the sense to wave her arms at gawkers and send them on their way into the dark. Her husband handed his keys to the other constable. If the gun-shop owner felt wary of the stranger, he was at least willing to hear what the school teacher's family knew of him.

"It's Captain Seguin," Yarico said, before pulling back on her impulse to explain.

"He's one of us!" Adeline jumped down from the cart and let Tabitha steady her. "What have they done to him? Don't those fools know he's one of us? He was with Travis at the Alamo! He's with us!" Seguin's right eye was swollen and his jaw bloodied, but she recognized his distinctive forehead. "We gave him our horse when he was on his way to join General Houston! He rescued some Goliad men!" Adeline gulped in air as if she'd been held under water. "He's one of us—good Lord!"

Mr. Ellinger waited a minute for the deputy to disappear into his shop with the Irishmen. His wife stared down the last of the onlookers until they turned and dissolved into the night. Then husband and wife helped the injured soldier to the Harpers' cart as if their next course of action were a forgone conclusion.

"He's beat up, but I wouldn't say he's broke anywhere." When her husband spoke, Mrs. Ellinger nodded in agreement.

"If you can tend to him tonight, I'll ride out your way in the morning with some salve and whatever Doc Robertson stashes at the hotel for when he's in town."

"We've done enough mending to learn some medical care, too."

"He'll feel better knowing there's no greater harm coming." Tabitha scrutinized the three Macon women. Torchlight from the hotel gave everything sinister shadows, and she looked gravely from the girl to Yarico as if she had second thoughts about leaving any man stretched out by Aunt Maggie's feet. "Ernest could ride along with you to make sure you reach your spot safely."

"We'll be safe with the captain," Yarico spoke up again.

"He comported himself as nothing but gentlemanly when we first met him," Adeline said. "I don't know why he'd be approaching Bastrop at dusk, but we won't press him until he gets some sleep."

"God dern those hotheads."

"He's best kept from the center of town. Out of sight, he'll mend more quickly. I'll come on in and teach tomorrow morning as usual." Hearing the girl's optimism, Tabitha Ellinger bit her lip.

"I suppose the gossips will latch onto some new topic soon enough."

"Me or my wife can ride out your way tomorrow with whatever Doc Robertson can spare." They all hushed in an attempt to comprehend the injured man's mutterings.

"Gertie? Dónde está Antonia? Tu Juan… está aquí." His good eye opened, and he shook his head until he rolled enough in the bed of the rough transport to stare at the back of Adeline's shawl and her braids. "Antonia? Where is your sister? Where are the others? Papá está aquí."

Chapter 13   Long Shadows

Yarico couldn't help thinking of the evening she and Walk Far had stayed alert by a campfire after Aunt Maggie and Adeline yielded to exhaustion. They'd communicated using short English phrases and gestures, but their understanding was clear. Home was a long way off for the black woman traveling with her Georgia people. The Tonkawa man's family lived days away from the ferry he sometimes ran.

With Juan Seguin stretched out on the other side of a low fire, she couldn't believe it fewer than four months since she'd come to and found this officer watching over her and the frail Goliad survivor. In daylight, treeless coastland out from the Brazos looked nothing like this forested swath by the Colorado. At night, campfires were the same. Shadows evoked memories more than they accentuated landscape. Life shrank to keeping guard, a task made somewhat less lonely by the presence of a stranger.

When the Tejano soldier groaned, Yarico walked to his side of the fire and squatted to see if he would take the water ladle. He put his lips to the edge, but she didn't hear him swallow. She dampened her kerchief, waved the cloth to cool it, and then laid it over the man's swollen brow.

"There's nothing broken, we don't think. Whatever's hurting you will slowly heal."

"My wife," he murmured. "Gertie and our niños…"

"It took weeks for families to scatter, señor. You might need even longer to find your children and Mrs. Seguin." He closed his eyes for a moment, and when he looked up again he seemed to have visited a different concern.

"I think by now Miss Emily West is at her home. Connecticut, possibly. *El norte,* it is a beautiful green this time of year, no?"

"Don't try to talk," Yarico said, dabbing at his forehead. "You can tell me tomorrow after you've had some rest."

The Dove Shall Fly

"When they finally let her go, my men and I could feel only happiness. She was so far from the northern trees and birds of her first dreams. Perhaps the old ones among your own people have told bright colors from memory." The woman tending him looked into the flames as if a flicker of purple might be plucked from the fire. One slender log broke into halves, and sparks spiraled upward. Shadows whirled on the dirt clearing swept of its pine needle carpet. "There was a fight for Miss West until the officer gave orders. All the ugly arguments were made to stop… all the talk about how much ransom might be offered for her—"

"Tell me in the morning."

"It was Major Moreland's command. He had no heart to enclose a fine lady of any color in a strange land. At last, he told the guards let her take a ship home is she wished. The major's pistol was most convincing."

"Drink some water, *por favor*." She let him sip slowly, after he raised himself on an elbow. "She must have aided the Texas cause in some way—"

"*Si*, perhaps. We may never know. The ones calling her Mr. Morgan's slave did not care. They would not hear the truth that he simply paid her ticket from *el norte*. That he paid her way in American dollars, perhaps to keep his house. After the burning of New Washington, Miss West no longer had the proof. Her papers were ash. Those who spoke for her said she was a free woman, even without the documents. Major Moreland was persuaded of this."

"No one should have to—"

"You and the girl with braids spoke for me in the town."

"I don't like to see what some men grow capable of after dark."

"Otherwise, señorita, it is possible I am a dead man." Their conversation quickly wore Seguin out, and Yarico thought he'd fallen into a deep sleep again. He opened his good eye once more and put his hand gently on her wrist. "If Von Bastrop does not speak for your Moses Austin many years ago in the plaza near the Alamo, no colonists are coming from the states to Mexico. Texas would see no San Felipe, no fiery star like William Travis. Tomorrow, I tell you…"

The recovering man lay still until late morning, and when he woke it was not Yarico sitting near him and the low fire, but the girl he'd mistaken for his daughter the evening before. Seeing her brown braids, he'd called for *Antonia*.

"I did not yet thank you, miss."

"Don't talk, Mr. Seguin. Take some water, and I'll let the soup kettle warm." Adeline put a marking ribbon in her book. "It's good you slept so long."

"I never said *gracias* for not shooting me that first morning." The Harper girl wasn't likely to forget standing behind an oleander bush with the Wainwrights' musket. She'd thought at the time that a saddle would have been no harder to hold out straight for a quarter hour. "I don't suppose I would have fired. Any shot might have hit Yarico."

"I feared your aim to be as good as my daughter's."

"How old is she?" The man pushed his black hair from his eyes while he gave the question some thought.

"This is the year she will see ten."

"Oh. I'll be fourteen on my next birthday," Adeline said. "My aunt and Yarico wouldn't let me touch a firearm had we not come to Texas." Quiet settled in again as the girl stirred. Steam rose from a pork and field pea concoction. Her regular four students had showed up in the hotel sitting space for a short lesson, as well as two older boys, all likely hoping for a firsthand account of the Tejano's injuries. She'd remained strictly on the topic of punctuation and capitalization, though, and she asked them to write out five important Revolution dates before their next class. "You'll need some sips before you try to talk again, sir."

"I was fourteen when Mr. Austin's father first came to San Antonio. It was Miss Yarico I was going to tell—"

"She's taking her turn at rest." The lean-to was stifling, but Yarico and Maggie didn't think it proper to stretch out in sight of any man. "She waited until I got back with salve and gauze. I've heard Doc Robertson say head injuries can be—'"

"I was fourteen," Juan Seguin interrupted her. "I always thought to follow my father into politics. You would not have been pleased to see me in your English class, I do not think. Since my early schooling, the government lessons come to me quickly, but this second language is more than difficult. We also have German in Bexar, you see, and last night I was remembering the Dutch that Baron Bastrop sometimes used." Adeline watched the soldier's lips move, but she could not make out the sounds.

> Happy is a word too weak to describe my feeling, to be fourteen in San Antonio and tasked to make good order in the book shelves of Governor Martinez.

The Dove Shall Fly

Shelves in the office of Antonio Martinez are showing only a little dust in late December. The governor's housekeeper is a proud woman. A servant might dust and polish the shelves, but not rethink the order of his library. I am to put the governor's books in logical groups, as his library has grown rapidly. The alphabet system makes him impatient when he wants to consult many volumes on one subject. I am thinking to put all the books on Napoleon's rise along one shelf, but I know better than to ask Señor Martinez if he agrees with this category. To my own father, I have heard him respond with bitter voice about the ruler from Corsica.

It is one thing for my *padre* to discuss his ancestry with my mother, to tell her how—grandfathers ago— Monsieur Séguin took a ship from his home in France to the coast of Spanish Mexico. He had to see with the eyes in his head if the silver mines were truth or fantasy. It is another thing and not so wise, to speak to a man born in Spain, as was our governor, about the French emperor's success. What more our governor's native country has lost, it is not wise to wonder aloud.

On an ordinary day, no matter if my father is postmaster or mayor or along on military patrol, Martinez will say with good cheer, "Buenos días, Señor Seguin!" But not if Papa walks into the magistrate's office with his fingertips tucked under his buttons as the famous dictator was fond to do. No, I will arrange the books on Napoleon along a high shelf and let the governor tell me himself how often he wishes to consult such volumes. Winter is not perhaps the season for learning of worries brought to Spain from France.

But, oh, to open a cover and see the mark of a *librería* in Madrid or Toledo! Like a bellows, it enflames my yearning to travel the world.

One morning before Christmas, I hope to have one wall of His Excellency's collection arranged. He will surely find it a nice surprise before the holy day. I am putting my fingers on a page with a mark from Barcelona, when I hear a voice and an accent transporting me as easily to another place. In the office of Governor Martinez, I am happy to be the youngest aide and working at an edge where waves of travelers lap in and out. Of course, I have heard English many times, not only in the plaza from the lips of visitors, but from the tutor my father hired to help me understand the politics of the country to our east. Whether Napoleon should have been so quick to sell his Spanish land along the Mississippi and to the north, I dare not ask the governor or my father or even my tutor.

The leaders of Mexico grow quiet when their subject becomes the thriving and spreading of *los Estados Unidos*. Once simply thirteen colonies along the eastern ocean, the country now covers a space more than double. To hear English in the entry of our governor's office is to feel the quickened pulse and the rising expectation of an argument. And the voice speaking American is not the soft kind that sometimes washes in from New Orleans. I hear no tone made for flattery and the announcement of gifts.

"Would you just let Governor Martinez know that I've come back a second morning as I was asked to do. My arrival yesterday wasn't convenient, or so I was told. There's certainly no way to foresee precise travel and meeting times."

"No, si, of course, Señor Austin," the governor's secretary answers. "You were saying only last morning that you were delayed on the Camino Real. But in winter, you at least did not have the impediment of Indian attack, I hope."

"Yesterday, you couldn't allow me to interrupt the governor," this visitor says again. He is speaking English more than I comprehend. He stands straight but cannot shield his impatience. His fierce eyes have put to inventory everything before him— the haughty secretary, the polished floor tiles, the library off to the side where I stand on a ladder, the bound pages in my hand, the title, and perhaps my fingernails. He has, as my tutor explained, *sized us up*. This is an American I would not care to have as judge of my labor. "Will his highness the governor *today* perhaps favor me with an audience?"

"I believe he can offer you ten minutes," the secretary says, giving only half a respectful bow. "It is, of course, but two days before the birthday of our savior Lord Jesus. Governor Martinez has many singular duties which demand his attention."

"Let's see if he can fathom how bringing three hundred colonists to the Texas territory will be a boon to Mexico's northern economy. Texas will prosper for every family I bring in to establish home and commerce. Let's see if that prospect comes across as a gift worthy of the season."

Into my recollection I am carving these words, because I know I will tell my father and my mother what I have heard. It is for their ears alone, as I understand even at fourteen years that anyone working in a place of government must honor privacy. Otherwise is to be considered a spy.

But I memorize this conversation while Mr. Moses Austin, from the American territory of Missouri, takes his chance to speak with our governor. Their discussion does not require as much as ten minutes. The secretary of Señor Martinez has a look of satisfaction when he escorts Mr. Austin from the grand office that I seldom enter myself. The traveler from Missouri does not seem happy, and his wide forehead is now red and creased with anger. Still in the entryway, he puts his hat back on his head, and I feel myself breathe with relief, because it was my fear he might use it to strike the proud secretary and demand a duel.

I cannot like the stranger from Missouri, but I feel myself drawn away from my library work, drawn to follow him out into the plaza. I brush the dust from my velveteen jacket as my parents have taught. It is my opportunity to practice some English, I tell the governor's assistant. This man shrugs as is his way.

"Excuse me, Mr. Austin!" I am pleased with the small sentence that makes the Missouri man turn around. "May I accompany you, sir?" The American looks at me still with such judgment, and I wonder if I will suffer his stiff hat across my cheek, but something calms the worst of his frustration.

"You can lead all the way to the Red River if you want. I damn near got killed a dozen times riding this far west of the Mexico border." A fire comes into his eyes again, before he goes on. "And all for nothing, it appears!"

"The river to the north, as well as the Sabine—my father too has traveled almost that far, sir."

"Well, maybe your father will talk some forward sense into that brooding Spanish governor of yours. Who knows how that secretary translated my proposal! It's sure that nothing grand ever came about without men owning a vision of the future."

"The far future is a vision, of course. I understand your meaning, Señor Austin. Yet it is almost Christmas. Perhaps his excellency is remembering how short is his time to find a gift for his wife."

"I can't stay but another few days…"

Soon, the two of us are standing at the edge of the grand plaza. It is a spot I cannot help but remember, because ten years before, it is where I waited and waited for my father to return from one of his travels. Somehow it makes me smile, even in the presence of this angry foreigner, to think how I cried at seeing my own Papá. I could not run to him or even stand until he came across the wide stretch of tiles to embrace me. I could only fall on my knees until he came to dry my tears and tell me to be always a man. It is easy to believe in the power of your own words when you are fourteen, so I begin again talking as if this stranger longs to hear the turnings of my mind.

"Surely your family will want you to stay for festivities of *Nochebuena*, after Christmas Eve mass, then to enjoy the day of our Lord's birthday, sir."

I am proud that my English is forming into sentences, but I see that Mr. Austin is giving his attention to possibilities in the plaza. Perhaps he has already left his luggage in the lobby of an inn. Perhaps he grew so sure of success that he paid his note and expected to be on his way home immediately with the good news of permission to bring colonists. The Camino Real can easily take two weeks to ride in any season, but the American looks as if impatience has made a home on his brow from the day he was born. If Our Holy Savoir arrived with virtue glowing over his head, I am thinking ambition is this man's natural crown.

"Moses!" A voice suddenly comes from across the plaza. "Am I in New Orleans? Or do my eyes deceive me?" The accent we hear cannot be mistaken, and a new expression struggles to bloom on the San Antonio stranger.

"Can it be Mr. Bastrop?"

Until the moment these two greet each other, I stay calm and this makes me proud. But there is no doubt my mouth goes open to hear English pour fluently from the lips of Baron Von Bastrop. This is how San Antonio calls the distinguished resident. His Spanish is admirable, and I have heard his German, and his native Dutch as well. But I did not know how much better his English is than mine. The baron is wearing his winter cape even though the day is mild. He is as straight as Mr. Austin and some inches his superior in height. Such a square jaw he has. He tosses the cape folds over his shoulder, and one cannot help admiring his style.

"You can't pester ordinary people, much less government officials, two days before Christmas, my good man!" His laugh brings a smile to Mr. Austin's face. It is the first sign of light heart I have seen from the Missouri man.

"I was turned down flat, even before I could unfurl my sketch of the starting colony."

"After Christmas, my good amigo, let's try it again the day after Christmas." When the baron takes Mr. Austin by the arm to lead him across the way, I want to go along, but I know it is not my place. "What in merciful God's name have you been up to in these last twenty years?

The Dove Shall Fly

Come along now, we'll swap stories for the next three days. It'll take that long to find out what happened since we met in New Orleans. Two decades ago!" Then Señor Bastrop notices me and I breathe again. "Juan, *buenos días!*" He turns to the visitor while he shakes my hand. I feel like a man among men. "Moses, have you met Erasmo Seguin's first son? Fine future leader. Too bad his father hasn't yet risen to governor. We'd have an easier time with your colony request."

Three days later, I am again on my ladder outside the governor's private office. The baron walks out with the Missouri diplomat, but Governor Martinez is standing at the doorway, too, after shaking hands with both men. Bastrop and Austin are two amigos looking confident, but they do not let wide smiles pass their lips until they reach the foyer. I can see it is good news, and I want to try my English once more before our visitor rushes for the road home.

"Until next time, Mr. Austin. Safe travels," I say. I am holding a new edition of *Don Quixote,* and I feel happy that this man has seen better luck with his dream than the knight who took his fight to windmills.

Happy is a word too weak to describe my feeling, to be fourteen in San Antonio, to have met an American with a vision to bring settlers to our territory.

"I never…never saw…him…again."

"Who is he talking about?" Yarico asked Adeline. Only Maggie continued napping in the heat.

"I'm not sure. He's been mumbling about his father some and about San Antonio." They'd dragged the officer gently into steady shade of the nearest pines. Since he seemed unable still to sit up, they were left wondering about the extent of his emotional and physical suffering.

"He surely knew many men among those who died at the Alamo."

Adeline nodded, but the officer's new pain worried her more.

"I'm afraid his tormentors did serious violence to his brain," she said. "Even these bigger bruises will heal, but I've heard the doctor discuss unseen wounds inside the skull."

"We'd best not forget your Aunt Maggie's tenderness on the topic of Alamo losses."

Yarico feared there would be no comforting the woman if Seguin began murmuring about recent burials at the mission. Margaret Linder's nephew was likely among the Gonzales volunteers who'd arrived just one day before complete destruction of the Texas army there. Dr. Robertson had heard it was this Tejano's particular duty to organize and oversee official Alamo funerals.

"I don't doubt Mr. Seguin was suffering a battered outlook well before this needless assault…" Yarico shook her head in sympathy.

"He's not yet found his own family in all the chaos coming after, if I understand much of his rambling talk."

At that moment, it was impossible to tell if the injured officer overheard the two tending him, but when Maggie emerged from the hot tent to join the others later, Seguin appeared ready to deflect any allusion to the lost nephew. When he managed to sit up in the shade as the girl's aunt approached, they marveled at his ability to remain upright.

"You all seem to have revived our soldier friend," Maggie said, waiting for Adeline to roll another log into the seating arrangement. "I wasn't asleep this last hour. I admit I was listening somewhat to the captain. It was hard to tell which survivors he might have come across in San Antonio. I don't doubt my nephew has stories to tell anyone left in Gonzales."

"People quick at learning languages make friends in every direction," Seguin said evasively. No one had the heart to correct Maggie's use of the present tense with respect to her nephew.

"I wonder who all you came to know inside the Alamo before its last days," she began. "Maybe you were in Gonzales yourself before…at the time a goodly number of grown men and their sons, and other young men, saddled up to ride that way and—"

"Cristo!" The three women thought the soldier's exclamation a response to sudden pain in the head. "I am remembering who came riding in south of here at Velasco, when there was great trouble to calm an angry crowd there. Excuse me, Mrs. Linder, but I must tell you all before it disappears from my mind. The same poor soldier who was with me on the day you let us have your worthy tan horse—this is the young man I speak of. I am feeling much better, *gracias* to you good ladies, and I wish you to know that your generosity helped to save the Goliad man, too. He was, however, on a different horse after San Jacinto and on that later day at the mouth of the Brazos. He rode into Velasco with Karnes. Like me, the captain was raised to colonel. Still, it is a rare thing to see such obedience to an absent general's orders. Houston, you see, was not present."

"I sent a letter to the fort at Velasco," Adeline rushed to add. "I wrote to our neighbor from Macon shortly after the three of us made it to Brazoria last January. We knew at New Orleans that the volunteer companies would sail for Colonel Fannin's camp. My neighbor and his cousins had left the coast before my envelope arrived, I suppose, and gone on to Refugio. There was nothing but confusion before...spring events..."

"Si, when I spoke to the soldier Trezevant, after some calm was restored outside the stockade, he said he could not recognize the place as it was when the battalion from Georgia first landed. This is certain—no fort in Texas today could keep the prisoner Santa Anna from crowds wishing to see the tyrant's limbs strung from different trees."

The Harper women shuddered, but he had at least shifted the topic from the loss of family men to the fate of a villain. He tilted his head without flinching, an indication he was feeling much better. Some mildness in his expression convinced them he understood Aunt Maggie's fragile state.

"After we met, you and Private Trezevant went on together to San Jacinto?" Adeline asked. She was pleased Seguin could reach for the cup she held out.

"And he is now a lieutenant, but the pages of our stories turned as one for only a handful of days." Sipping water that she'd laced with a bit of the doctor's brandy, he spoke with regained vigor. "It was a surprise to see the young battalion man again after the great victory. Perhaps merely a month later at Velasco, he came riding in as if he'd never been a wandering fistful of rags. When my men and I found him, Trezevant and three others were only inching along toward the Brazos."

> Without the injury to his foot, General Houston also would be at the fort holding Santa Anna. But after the great battle, the victor of San Jacinto is taken swiftly to a surgeon in New Orleans. The wound at his ankle is a danger, you see.
>
> It is our President Burnet, on Houston's recommendation, who signs the treaty at the fort. So who are we, the triumphant, not to welcome peace. But imagine five hundred vengeful ghosts drifting from the Alamo and Goliad to the mouth of the Brazos on the day a passenger ship drops its anchor.
>
> At first we judge what we hear as rumor. General Houston's wish is to allow Santa Anna safe passage to Vera Cruz? This cannot be, all the soldiers of the republic are thinking. No matter how the tyrant promises to allow the new country of Texas its peaceful independence, surely the

infamous butcher cannot be taken at his word. Therefore, we believe it is rumor, changing shape like a fast cloud. We cannot but judge it worst gossip, like the story that Miss Emily West took possession of the despot's bed to distract him before battle—pardon my admitting such whispers. Like the fantasy that Señors Crockett and Bowie were seen proudly riding patrol together days after the Alamo fell, like the tale that there are boxes of gold coins under the ruins of Harrisburg. This fortune, as the story finds shape, was hidden safely and is waiting to be given out to all who fought for the revolution. We no more readily accept that Santa Anna, after all his cruelty, shall return to his own home in safety.

We believe it is surely a rumor, until we are read our formal orders in Velasco at the very fort where Mexico's tyrant is held. At the stockade once under Fannin and visited by Stephen Austin before the battles of spring, a nervous lieutenant shows us the treaty, as well as the special letter signed by General Houston. My men are more hungry than tired from many patrols along the coast. Nor have they found time to recover strength after the glorious victory. They are now very hungry, but they do not eat. They have no appetite. How can they eat, after digesting such a truth? Santa Anna is to be given safe escort back to his home? Jesús-Maria!

But the Tejanos of the new republic are not the only ones to think scorn of the signed paper that frees such a cruel generalissimo. Reports about how much Miss West helped win our battle at San Jacinto, these may be fiction, but I testify as direct witness that the widow of Colonel James Fannin could not be persuaded to forget grief and vengeance. You perhaps never met Señora Minerva Fannin in your Texas travels. Perhaps, ladies, your purposes here took you no farther toward the coast than the river town of Brazoria. No Mexican soldier would have dared carry out the slaughter at Goliad, I think, had the colonel's wife been there to protest.

In her black dress and cloak and veil, the widow Minerva Fannin appears. Never mind the hot damp air of May in the seaside town. She is more fierce than any upright Comanche before battle. This day, crowds are growing between the fort and the anchored schooner. As on the afternoons before, the ship is ready for its run to Vera Cruz. Every day the crowds shout their anger, and though our orders are to hold them back from violence, we cannot keep our own thoughts from mutiny.

The people of Texas want to see Santa Anna come to a cruel end. They would wish his last minutes to be slow and most painful. The day

The Dove Shall Fly

that two of my corporals lead the Mexican dictator from his comfortable cell, the Widow Fannin is already pointing from a platform. Her little daughters stare at her side. Like sad dolls, they are pale. Two hundred people would cheer to see her beckon the executioner from where she stands. Everyone glowers as the famous prisoner is directed forward. Señora Fannin is already screaming for bloody justice, but we soldiers have orders to protect the prisoner, and we surround His-Most Cruel-Excellency—the Butcher. We shield him from flung pebbles and sand and at least one drawn knife.

I do not know how the Mexican general makes it to the plank of the schooner, but when he moves up the walkway, the ship captain shows no sign of welcome.

Please, ladies, I can see from your faces that you would not feel surprise to learn there was murder on this day. Let me tell you now that it was almost the case. The sailors have muskets, and I am thinking they will not hold fire if their captain fears for the safety of the vessel. You Harper women, perhaps you have never seen or smelled a ship in flames. You have been witness to enough peril in the prairie, and unexpected death. The possibility of Texans firing on Texans is in our mind, and I see even our prisoner the great Santa Anna perspires with fear that he will be set free to suffer the angry mob.

But help to our side comes riding into this scene. Captain Karnes—no, he is now a colonel, as am I—he comes into the dusty road along the channel. Three pistol shots break through the noise of the crowd. The pistols bring to silence even the widow in her streaming black sleeves and wild hair.

At first, I do not recognize the slender man among the spy patrol with Karnes. The young man rides a prancing roan, and this day he is wearing the uniform of an officer. He is only of slight build, and somewhere after San Jacinto, he must have taken a long bath, like most of us, because his hair is curly under his officer hat and not matted down as it was the day we found him and the other poor few who escaped before Goliad's dark hour.

It is the soldier Trezevant, now a lieutenant with Colonel Karnes. The tyrant is part way up the plank, and the worst in the crowd surge in his direction, so much that the ship captain fears perhaps his ship will go down. Did you know, ladies, that a great ship from the fleet of LaSalle lies at the bottom of the gulf for these one hundred and fifty years? Perhaps the captain does not wish to drown along with Santa Anna and sink down to the bones of the lost French vessel.

I am possibly putting the kind Harpers to sleep with the long tale of a past afternoon, but I will end with the truth that the crowd disappears like salt grains in a pot of beans. The patrol of spies coming in from the southwest prairies, they are the same men of some fame for driving Mexico's General Woll back across the Rio Grande to carry news of his country's defeat. No one will challenge this spy company. Their leader is said to have escaped a Matamoros prison one day, only to find his men the next afternoon and lead them again on patrol. No one cares to question this impressive company or the official command of Karnes. The villain Santa Anna is taken back to his cell inside the fort, and the crowd dissolves like seasoning in a soup pot.

Without the injury to his foot, as I have said, General Houston himself also could be at the fort holding Santa Anna. After San Jacinto, no soldiers dare to challenge an order from his lips, but it is Colonel Karnes holding the reins that day. And I share with you a memory of the Goliad survivor, for you Harper women and I are among few, I think, witness to the light sack of bones young Trezevant looked, just days after the pitiful battalion wanderers were found.

The wind had died down during Juan Seguin's account. After his final words, a faint rustling of pines intruded on the silence. Aunt Maggie's heavy breathing was the other distinct noise, and the three awake in the clearing knew better than to jar her from her slumber. Neither Yarico nor Adeline regretted her having missed details about Minerva Fannin's grief. Seguin looked relieved, too, that she'd fallen asleep by the time he spoke of the survivor Trezevant. A lieutenant now, he was likely only a year or two older than her nephew from Gonzales.

Juan Seguin and the three Harpers dozed in the afternoon heat, but when Adeline stirred she was amazed to find the recovering man on his feet. He was brushing grit from his military jacket and pressing Yarico's damp kerchief to its creases. After the officer hung his coat from a branch stub, he practiced wobbly steps in the deeper shade. Moments after the young woman encouraged him to take her left arm for support, Yarico appeared at his other side.

Shadows already stretched back toward the fire pit. The pines in Bastrop rose up less densely than in most Georgia forests or the evergreen woods of eastern Texas. The space between trunks offered inviting trails in every direction. Adeline and Yarico allowed their military guest to take any steps he wished. They were pleased when he spoke again, and his breathing came easily. He likely whispered from consideration of Aunt Maggie's distress and not his own suffering.

In the last days of the Alamo, when Colonel Travis asks me to go and find help, a voice in my heart says I may never see him again.

He has written two letters already which my men and I have delivered. We watch from the ledge up high inside the mission walls. No army under General Houston is approaching. Lookout is posted in every direction. We sent spies to the south and the east. No help is coming, so the colonel asks me one more time to ride out. Once more, my friend Travis gives me a page from his small leather notebook. Gonzales is not so far away as forty miles. I am to ride and implore the good men of the town to join those at the Alamo for her defense. The despot, we must tell them, is on his way with thousands.

I will not grieve you with details about the streets of Gonzales when the men and boys readied themselves in their saddles. Your hearts are also tender. I cannot tell you about the mothers and the children reaching for the boots and ankles of their men.

I do not take time to ask the names of these volunteers, for Travis has asked me to next ride in the direction of Columbia and then toward Brazoria if my company and I can make it, to see if General Houston's army might be stationed that close by. When I notice a young Gonzales volunteer without a woman crying at his side, without any niños reaching up toward the stirrups, I do not wonder his name. I only ask myself where his family can be...

"If that volunteer," Yarico said, "happened to be Mrs. Linder's nephew—"

"We can't bear to hear more," Adeline broke in. "We never had the chance to meet him, but even after our own difficult escape, I don't think..."

"The long shadows reach out for us," Seguin said, taking the next few steps without any support. "This Gonzales youth had taken upon himself a jacket of my culture, though, much like the one I put on in my proud days of sorting the governor's books. Perhaps it is the same in America, the pride a grown boy feels when wearing a man's jacket for the first time. This memory finds me every day. Some shadows never shrink back. I cannot forget how proud the fellow looked to be among other volunteers, proud to join them on their dangerous ride."

Adeline stooped to pick up a pine cone, and Yarico worried that other dark memories might clutch at the girl if she let the wooded hills of her childhood come to mind. How many Macon families must be grieving the loss of sons and brothers! How solemn those neighboring farmlands must be the summer after San Jacinto and Goliad.

"We cannot imagine the difficulties you faced," Yarico said, "accounting for everyone lost at the Alamo, and all the while wondering if your own family had escaped worst peril."

"My men and I took two weeks with those who had not been buried, and another three weeks searching the shallow graves and seeing that the holy words were spoken." Juan Seguin had halted and was taking in deep breaths. He seemed to waiver about going on with his recollection. "The ones from Gonzales, they were found mostly together one day... close, I can only suppose, to where they fell."

"They stayed together," Adeline murmured.

"When I saw a familiar jacket pulled loose from the grave...One sleeve was not burned, and dirt from the shallow hole had not spoiled one side. Do you know the type jacket I speak of, señoritas? Black velveteen like the kind I was so proud to wear in the library of Governor Martinez."

"Mrs. Linder's nephew was likely no more than sixteen or seventeen."

"I did not ask names, Miss Yarico. The young one from town was without family in his home streets, but he did not meet his death alone."

Colonel Seguin could not be persuaded to recuperate another few days before continuing east of the Harpers' clearing. He took time the next morning to gingerly scrape the stubble from his chin and trim his mustache. His horse and tack had been found near the Irishmen's dugout, and no curious townspeople were given satisfaction regarding the Tejano's next course of action. He gratefully allowed the women to restock his satchels, but he took only coffee before pulling himself into an ornate saddle.

"I knew by my second week at the damaged Alamo that my family no longer resided anywhere in San Antonio." In the moment he let his gaze fall on Yarico, she sensed his grief for any persons cut off from natural kin.

"If you found their note saying they'd take the Camino Real to Nacogdoches, you'll surely find them there."

The Dove Shall Fly

"No Mexican generals made it that far before San Jacinto," Adeline added. Maggie had regressed to silent hand-wringing again.

"I did not know how terrible an empty hacienda could be, or how tender my hope had grown that Gertie and the little ones had returned to my father's home."

"They're all together in Nacogdoches, sir, you'll see."

"Perhaps we shall meet again in Columbia," the officer said tipping his hat a final time. "It is there, they say, that a new president will swear to lead the republic."

"Not Velasco?"

"Too many towns with bitter memories. The capital cannot seem to rest in one location."

"You'll likely have no need, but here's a letter vouching for your identification," Adeline said with some embarrassment. "I've met plenty of Irish who greet strangers with friendliness, so I wouldn't fear that accent from now on." The man's expression was half smile and half grimace as he read the page handed him.

"A list of many places I have served during the revolution and in the republic since."

"We could only put our own signatures as residents of Bastrop, Colonel Seguin, but if you'll stay another day the Ellingers and the other constable will sign to witness as well."

"It is a shame to have to keep such papers," the officer said solemnly. "One hopes good people can judge the truth in others."

"Nobody should have to…" Yarico began, without finishing the thought.

"The forest comes to an end not more than five miles east of here," the girl went on. "You know how to keep a northeasterly direction. I don't doubt you'll find the Brazos again and a trail as distinct as the Camino Real. Think of us when you fill your water gourd along the way." As the soldier smoothing his hat brim seemed ready to part, she looked to Yarico.

"We pray you'll stop in the shadows to cool down, Colonel Seguin, but please don't stay long enough to draw the attention of ignorant lurkers."

Early the next day, seven school children squeezed into the lobby of the Bastrop inn. There was some disagreement about whether the date of San Jacinto ought to top their lists or the date of the Alamo tragedy.

At least, most were amending their abbreviations and punctuation even before Miss Harper showed up with her correction pen.

A friendly debate was developing about the significance of March 2, and most agreed that the deaths of Jim Bowie and Davy Crockett at the Alamo four days later were more memorable than the day independence was formally declared. Not one student could recall the precise date of Goliad's executions when Adeline asked. Their pencils went still when she reminded them how beautiful Palm Sunday morning had otherwise been that spring. Their hands and minds went still, as if they had no will to memorize the callous destruction of Fannin's volunteers.

Chapter 14   Remains of a Battalion

No matter where James Peter Trezevant rode along the western bank of the Brazos, the lost Georgia Battalion shadowed him. At first, he thought there was no evidence that volunteer companies had bivouacked on the outer edge of Velasco just a half year earlier. By the light of a full moon, he'd looked back regularly at the fort to keep his horse ambling due east. He knew when he reached the stretch along the river where Colonel Fannin had directed Ward's two hundred recruits to pitch their tents. Nothing now indicated the impact of humans on the land, except a single half-buried horseshoe. Jamie was hardly expecting a moonlight search to turn up his better boots, the pair stolen by an early deserter. He could detect no evidence that the American reinforcements had ever been there.

Then a glint in the rough ground made him dismount again and crouch. His shoulder still ached sometimes when he reached. It was a shaving blade. Next to it lay a brush and a small framed mirror tied with a leather shoelace. Some Georgia private broke camp in too much haste, he supposed. Coming back to him was the army's rushed departure and transport by schooner down the coast to Copano. A knot tightened in Jamie's stomach when he recalled the cold rainy march inland from there to Refugio.

A darker possibility crossed his mind. Maybe the shaving tools had been discarded by an early runaway. He was practiced at forgetting the faces of those who never trudged deeper into Texas that harsh January. Several who'd enjoyed formations in Lafayette Square, and relished its beignets, never sailed farther than Velasco with Ward. By the first winter nights of camping outside its stockade, everyone's enthusiasm was declining, yet most adhered to their muster commitment. The least stoic, though, trickled away before shipping to the next port or drifted off during the initial wait inside Refugio's sanctuary. In the cruel, beginning weeks at Goliad, a name was scratched at every other roll call. Jamie

Trezevant didn't want to calculate how many of the original volunteers had eventually abandoned their posts.

The recently promoted lieutenant had survived many direct shocks since his arrival in Texas, but he was still recovering from the first. How could even the weakest brother-in-arms have stolen another soldier's boots? The pair he'd broken in during militia practice back at Columbia College—the ones he'd worn when first stepping onto Mexican soil—vanished before the last sunrise in Velasco. How could any man too fearful to stand for morning attention have fled in boots crafted for battle? Was there no code of honor in the wild Texas territory? And then he recalled the empty hiding spot in a cramped New Orleans inn and his roommate's sheepish apology for the missing cash. The battalion survivor didn't know whose shaving items he was holding, but he was glad they couldn't have been Pleasant Goodnight's.

"You find somethin'?" It was Karnes carrying a small torch and riding toward him. Jamie's immediate superior had achieved the rank of colonel, but he and members of his spy unit still went by last names. "You find what you were lookin' for, Trezevant?"

"A razor blade and a shaving brush, not much more."

"I forget where Deaf and I were heading the day Ward's schooners anchored here. Didn't it take four to hold all his companies? I do recall learnin' General Austin was on the dock to greet you boys. Your battalion must have camped along this stretch somewhat more than a month, is that right?" While Karnes spoke, the younger man appeared fixated on his find and in doubt as to whether he should let the artifacts fall to the ground again. "Someone might make use of that blade if the rust can be cleaned off." Jamie closed the razor and slipped it into a pocket. "We didn't judge Stephen F. to be cut out for much soldiering," Karnes went on, "but we did have hopes he could round up more American help in a hurry."

"We never saw more recruits. I wasn't told whether it was that or the sleet or the measles case that made Fannin move us on to Copano." Now adjusting to the season of dry heat, neither man wore a hat after sundown. "My boots were stolen the night before we broke this camp."

At this, the colonel squinted. Despite all the threats uttered against Santa Anna since his capture, no less contempt flared for any who'd deserted Texas ranks.

"Deaf and Seguin and I oughta find that low coward and…" Neither he nor Trezevant wanted to reminisce about the Mexican courier they'd seen killed for possessing a William Travis souvenir. The colonel struggled to suppress his rage. "Well, I'd say it's not all bad luck that General Rusk has you sometimes takin' charge of supplies." He was studying the younger man's footwear. "That's a new pair you've got now. Am I right?"

"They're almost broken in, but I don't plan to mention them in my next letter home."

"Time for composing letters," Karnes said, smiling again. "There's another reason not to curse a week or two in the quartermaster's office."

"If I ever get back home for a spell, my mother will look for those boots she had especially made for me and—"

"If we start imagining a mother's welcome or a pappy's handshake, we'll be cryin' like the little Fannin girls before the moon peaks. We'll be flailing the ground." Jamie had seen Karnes and Deaf Smith together, and he thought the two redheads must miss each other's needling during separate missions. The battalion soldier couldn't respond with another joke.

"The Fannins haven't made any spectacle lately."

"The widow likely latches onto one tale or another about Santa Anna's whereabouts—that he slipped away to Vera Cruz after all, that he died at the hands of soldiers welcoming a court martial, that he grew ashamed and hanged himself." Colonel Karnes slid from his horse finally so he could get close enough to Jamie to whisper. "Can't trust any second-hand news these days. That's why the hell I rode out here from the stockade, Trezevant. You decide whether to head up to the Phelps plantation with us? We're leavin' before midnight."

"I thought I'd take the other assignment, if that's all right, sir. Unless you think Santa Anna is fool enough to make a run for it? Or if you're worried about ambush by outraged townspeople along the way."

"As long as we get well beyond Velasco before daybreak, we won't stir up any attention. The Phelps place is back a ways from the riverbank. As secure a place for the bastard's detention as any. A handful of guards can keep him alive until his fate is certain. The president-elect must be torn up tryin' to decide this time."

"It didn't seem like anything could dampen the victory," Jamie admitted. "We all expected the villain would be gone and good riddance. News of our breaking up a lynch mob here must have reached General Houston as a shock."

"I'd as soon walk hot coals than admit in public to rescuing that Mexican butcher." Karnes kicked at a pile of dried horse dung. "Well, it wouldn't have spoke well of Texas law if vigilantes had drawn and quartered its first prisoner."

The aftermath of San Jacinto was almost as whirl-wind as the battle itself. Newspapers everywhere reported the Velasco treaties were to have been followed by Sana Anna's deportation. Few citizens of the new republic, though, wished the dictator any mercy he'd not allowed Fannin's army. For months, the infamous general had been locked up at the same stockade for his own safety.

"Until our new president assesses the tyrant's barter value…until Sam Houston …" Jamie wasn't done shaking his head about election results. Most Texans understood David Burnet's tenure to be temporary, but the upcoming inauguration in Columbia had more than a few people wondering how a President Houston could possibly work with Mirabeau Lamar as second in power. The two leaders seemed to have been the inspiration for the adage about oil and water.

"Politics will drive a soldier crazy faster than a pair of lace pantaloons," Karnes said, making them both laugh. "Go on and take up the Refugio assignment then."

"I'll embrace most any missions that don't require desks," Jamie Trezevant confided. A windowless office in the Velasco fort made him itch for some other duty, but he couldn't see himself escorting Santa Anna out of danger again. He worked to overcome qualms about revisiting his original battalion's circuit of catastrophe. During the most brutal winter in a decade, the Georgia volunteers had traipsed from Refugio to Goliad and back, only to get imprisoned finally at the big fort on a false promise of deportation. Over three hundred ragged men had been marched out and shot. "I don't doubt General Rusk did the Goliad burials justice," he was able to say. "And he made quick work of securing Victoria. I wouldn't think an assault is likely from farther southwest." The Karnes unit was credited for hounding the last active Mexican general back south of the Rio Grande. The two men patted their impatient horses.

"Whatever you said to ole Adrian Woll in French that day, that's what convinced me you were due a lieutenant's stripe. You told me how you knew his native tongue pretty well, but I forget—"

"The South Carolina professor I took for French also taught military leadership. We'd heard about the language mix among Mexico's elite. I believe there was also a German general under Santa Anna's orders."

"I'd already told Woll in simple English," the colonel recalled, "that he and his army could crowd onto an island with Napoleon and sink into oblivion. I don't think he took my meaning."

"*Monsieur* understood it was victory making us bold enough to even approach his ranks." Jamie had thought it odd how quickly the required French came back to him. *Votre général Santa Anna a perdu la guerre. Lui, il est notre prisonnier. Presque tous ses soldats sont morts.* Even the subjunctive had come easily. *Il faut que vous partiez le Texas immédiatement.* General Woll had taken time to inspect Santa Anna's signature, but his expression showed that he knew the young American with curly hair and textbook French to be speaking the truth.

"You're right," Karnes said. "You oughta go on to Refugio. You'll judge better than anyone else if the place could stand up to attack again. It looks like you're the only one who even knows what went on there last March. The odds you men faced, I'd say that's what made Fannin finally make a run from Goliad. Anyway, if you figure out where Amon King's company was shot and disposed of, write up a report."

"Should a courier take it back to you or Rusk?" Jamie asked. They'd mounted again and for a moment he wished he were joining those transferring Santa Anna in secret.

"Hell, just hang onto it until you get back here later this month. I'll read your account soon enough. Anyhow, you lead the way to Refugio. You know the terrain."

"Which captain is going?"

"That's the other reason I rode out here, Trezevant. You are. I just moved you up another notch. A letter changing your rank will have Rusk's stamp on it by the time you get back with your men. Too much dang paperwork around here, can't argue with you on that point." Since the promotion of nearly every San Jacinto soldier with officer training or leadership experience, Jamie had grown accustomed to lieutenant duties. Still, he was dumbstruck by this next rise in authority, and it was Colonel Karnes finding words for their parting, "Remember Goliad! Remember Refugio!"

Jamie's patrol waited until well after sunrise to begin their mission. Six Texas soldiers rode behind him single file down toward Velasco's inlet before tacking northwest. Any civilian conjecture about a clandestine party following the Brazos banks upriver would be countered by accounts of military movement off in the direction of Refugio.

The man riding lead didn't mind consulting his own thoughts. As a member of the Karnes unit that expelled Woll from the region, he'd already revisited the spring escape route once. He and a few other battalion survivors would never forget. His horse trotted easily along the flat and inhospitable expanse past Velasco. He ordered himself not to think of their grueling escape—one Macon private no more than a boy. Another, with three children of his own, wandered off from those fleeing Victoria and was presumed recaptured. Jamie couldn't tamp down some details of their suffering. He'd eventually come close to preferring death over ingesting any more scavenged, unwashed onion bulbs. He recalled how his stomach had rebelled when young Sam Hardaway had guessed General Houston's army was close enough to smell.

C'mon boys! We're surely not far from Houston's regiment! I just caught their stink on the last breeze. We can make it! We'll join up and give the Mexicans bloody hell if it's the last thing we do!

Captain Trezevant kept leading his men across a patch of withered summer grass, and he tried to push from memory the morning Hardaway had stumbled ahead and been sighted by Juan Seguin's unit. Word of the rescue was passed back among the remaining handful. When Jamie went to relay the news, he'd found one battalion man on his belly in a patch of vegetation. The straggler wasn't even using his hands to put green strands to his mouth. He was tearing at the tufts with his teeth. He seemed not to comprehend their turn of fortune. Then, he growled and cursed the idea of going on to rejoin the fight.

"Go drink the filthy Tejano water! Have yourselves a *fiesta* or a *siesta* before he drops you at Sam Houston's feet."

"Some of their horses can take two riders. He's offering food." Neither fact calmed the distraught man. "They know Houston's camp can't be more than a day's ride from here. They want to help us get to—"

"To where we can die another ten ways before it's over?"

"We have to move on. We—"

"Damn you and the boy soldier! Damn this Seguin son-of-a-bitch, William Ward and his rich family! Damnation to all the other fine talkers that—"

"We made it this far. You're feet are in better shape than most. If I can—"

"Do what you want. I've got grazing to do."

The two emaciated privates had stood awkwardly, fending off dizziness but preparing to continue the argument by fistfight. On a borrowed mount, Sam Hardaway reappeared to fetch back anyone unable to make legs function. If he knew he'd thwarted a mutiny, he didn't let on. At the time, Jamie marveled how quickly the sixteen-year-old sprang back into action. Just four years older than the energetic youth, Trezevant couldn't have sworn that he too would be fit to charge at the enemy anytime soon. The other man grumbled, but let the youngest Macon soldier give him a ride to Seguin's band. Even then Jamie worked to erase the hostile exchange from mind. At least, the other American recruit was not wearing boots Mrs. Trezevant had purchased for her son. Wherever that early deserter was, he'd not even suffered first privations at Goliad, much less faced the assault from Urrea's infantry at Refugio. Every escapee helped along by Juan Seguin's company had witnessed hell from more than one angle.

His new issue boots feeling less stiff, Captain Trezevant found himself fording back across the familiar San Bernardo River. Splashing along out in front, he was relieved the men under his command wouldn't ask about his wry smile. So many places in the inhospitable territory—the Republic of Texas!—were named for saints. Most expanses this far west looked forsaken by God. It would take saints, he thought, to forgive all the wrongs done in 1836. He was working on compassion for crass thieves and deserters and executioners. He would be at it a while.

Upon reaching Goliad again, he let his lieutenant go on inside the walled compound with another man who'd never laid eyes on the grim fortress. Karnes had asked for a round of formal signatures, and Jamie believed the next in rank equal to the task of turning pages as the compound's commander dipped his pen. The required stayover was painful enough, even though General Rusk had cleared the premises of its grisly troughs and pyres before departing for Victoria. Jamie preferred helping the others pitch tents beyond the gloomy hill. He chose a meadow outside the north wall, the only side out of which Fannin volunteers had not been marched minutes before their slaughter.

Still, the north side reminded him of Fannin's earlier disaster, the regiment's failed attempt to aid William Travis at the Alamo. After brutal weather in February, the army had been unable to budge artillery beyond the immediate banks of the freezing San Antonio River.

Goliad's northern slope played no part the next month in Palm Sunday executions, but ghosts surely wandered in every direction. Jamie picked up a belt buckle and recalled how many ragged men had taken to securing their breeches with twine well before the debacles of spring. Nearly five hundred soldiers, exhausted even upon first reaching Goliad, had nevertheless been put to the task of refortifying its walls. He didn't wish to spend unnecessary time near ravines where he'd collected flat, icy stones. He imagined his fingers throbbing again. Goliad's chapel tower must have loomed as a nightmare to Fannin men defeated later that March and herded back to the fortress. Captain Trezevant wanted to move on to Refugio, where William Ward's battalion had at least withstood an attack for two days.

The smaller town was twenty-six miles away. The next day, Jamie could have led his men toward the village's main path, but he rode up instead from a side where he hoped a corral remained intact. If anything cheered him during the army's initial winter weeks in Refugio, it was his interaction with wild mustangs brought from the southern range. About half eventually tolerated riders and reins. He'd proved himself among the battalion's most adept at sweet-talking the wild creatures into taking a bridle. He was a natural in the saddle and Ward asked him to tame as many as he could handle. Spirited horses reminded him of the Trezevant summer home in Darien and of the silent friend who mastered glorious jumps. Each time Jamie won over a horse, he felt uplifted.

Leading his group toward the weathered fencing, he remembered that Refugio's cemetery also stretched out from that side of the sanctuary. The somber space appeared enlarged and more crowded since he'd last seen it, but a familiar woman stooping near one headstone stood up and faced him. The closer he rode, the more she looked just as she had inside the church when Ward's companies, facing imminent defeat, readied for retreat into the night.

"Ma'am," Jamie said, touching the brim of his hat.

"It's me, Mrs. Malloy. Fiona. Oh, my..." She used a corner of her apron to dry her eyes, and the new captain now remembered he'd seen her make that gesture several times as wounded men were dragged inside from a low perimeter wall. The Irish woman had been among the first in town to rush out and greet the rescue companies marching back in from Goliad. "I didn't think there were any more volunteer soldiers still alive. Such a man rode in with Captain Eberly two months previous, but he'd been out with Colonel Fannin at Coleto. A few were killed there before

The Dove Shall Fly

the surrender, but most drew their last breath at the Sunday executions. Neither of them knew much about what you lads went through here. It was a Mr. Holliday with the captain—did you know him? He wasn't certain how many other survivors could be tallied."

"A few of us made it as far as San Jacinto battle lines."

"Merciful heavens!" She was dabbing at tears again and Jamie looked away, but his gaze rested on a newly set headstone for Amon King. A grimace settled into his expression. "Mr. Holliday looked too wobbly from drink to stay in the saddle, but our Captain E. was letting the poor soul ride along. Said the man couldn't join up anew until he could stay away from the bottle. If I was a tippler who'd lived through Goliad, I'd have a whiskey in hand before sunup every day." She rambled on about Refugio's worst night. "That last evening you gallant men were pinned down here, I tended to young Thomas Weeks. Do you recall, sir?" She took in a deep breath. "I gave him what comfort I could until the Mexicans stormed inside. 'Twas only minutes after you Georgia fighters filed out into the night. Poor Mr. Spillers had only just exited out the rear door with another boy, the Macon lad."

"Sam Hardaway," Jamie said, reliving those horrifying last minutes of the siege. He steadied himself by letting his knees hug the horse's flanks. "Hardaway made it all the way to San Jacinto, ma'am."

"God bless him! And Sam Houston!"

"Sir?" One of the men behind Trezevant now was wondering the significance of some tombstone names. "If this is where King was finally buried, does that mean we won't need to stay long?" Judging his question to be disrespectful, the others fidgeted in their saddles.

"Maybe two or three nights. Make it an easy camp again, just beyond the last row of domiciles." The new captain didn't think anyone signed up since San Jacinto had heard of mustangs running wild to the far southwest of those dwellings. They might shrug if told Amon King had served in San Patricio out that way. Trezevant's men would lose concentration if he gestured broadly toward the region and began a lecture. None knew of the friction between King and Ward over authority during the shared Refugio assignment. The deadly assault that the Georgia Battalion resisted was hardly sketched in any recruit's memory. William Ward's effort to rescue Irish colonists trapped in the village church appeared mostly forgotten.

Later that evening, a two-man patrol rode watch out from their bivouac, braced to alert the outlying camp to any Comanche activity.

Two sentries stayed on guard just outside their captain's tent. The others slept until their duty hour ticked around. Trezevant expected no trouble, but he could not sleep. He turned up a lantern wick every few minutes and dipped his pen into a dark bottle. A blank page lay before him. Words wouldn't yet come.

The report on Amon King, deceased at Refugio, Texas, had only taken a few lines. The fiery officer and his company, as well as a handful just arriving with Ward, had defied the Georgia commander's advice and ridden into the dark to deliver vengeance to Mexican soldiers. King's men ambushed a band relaxing by a fire, but a hellish reversal took place. Arousing the fury of Urrea's army, Captain King's company could not outrun Mexican front lines or find cover. Most were shot as they fled. Fiona Malloy testified that their bodies were properly interred only after sure word of the San Jacinto victory.

Since his service in the revolution, James Trezevant had seen more than one military lesson prove true. Certainly, too much information could stymie action as effectively as too little. Flooding back to him were facts from those final Refugio hours, the Georgia Battalion's desperate efforts to repel General Urrea's attack. But alongside details of the Refugio assault, images from his worst childhood loss also swept in. He dipped his pen and waited for clearer thinking. Trying to concentrate, he breathed through his mouth as Mrs. Malloy had done. She and a few Irish settlers would never forget the night the sanctuary fell to a greater Mexican force. As an officer, Jamie comprehended the relative insignificance of battle in the tiny town, and he knew that triumph at San Jacinto had set a new standard for glory. When he remembered surviving Refugio, though, his heart pounded.

He would not address any official document to Karnes or General Rusk. No battle report had been requested. Yet the young officer felt compelled to witness on behalf of so many volunteers corralled and dispatched on Palm Sunday. He felt obliged to recall the Georgia Battalion's valiant stand earlier in Refugio, all but erased from revolution accounts. Why he was steadily reminded, as well, of his father's death, he wasn't sure, except for the magnitude of the two shocks. Scouting for safe passage at the perimeter of the besieged church—and years before when a tearful mother relayed the tragedy to her children—he'd heard his inner voice crying, "This can't be! This can't be!"

He couldn't start a personal letter to his mother or even his sister Charlotte. Grateful for their affectionate interest in his life, he declined

The Dove Shall Fly

to burden them. Only the long-dead, he reasoned, could tolerate the secrets of recent, worst sacrifice. He moved the ink bottle closer to the blank page. A gnat disintegrated in the lantern wick. One sentry just outside the tent door coughed and spat. Some deep, wild smell was mixing in with drought dust, and Jamie thought a rare summer storm might have forced a downpour not far west. Mustangs might be pounding the dirt off that way in a race for shelter. He reminded himself that he was in no rush. Pleasant Goodnight was not going to barge in and interrupt his thoughts. He promised himself to keep his penmanship neat, if only to preserve memory as he wrote…

My dearest father, so long departed, it is only to you I hope these words fly,

When we meet again, Papa, you might say you don't remember riding scout with me those two nights in Refugio, but I felt your presence. I could testify. You were there.

General Urrea's army kept firing on the little church. The other men in my company knelt without relief at an outside wall. Their marksmanship forestalled our flight. Our sergeants, no older than I, were left in charge. The lieutenants had gone as couriers in search of Sam Houston, and command fell to our next in rank. Only three months before, they too had been but youths enjoying work or study and leisure in equal measure. I often think of the stirring news that made me hasten from Columbia to meet the battalion in New Orleans. Speeches in Macon surely had the same effect on others mustered in my company. God knows how many of us were still in this world when the sun rose on Easter a few weeks after Refugio.

In our rudderless group, we made each other proud. Was Captain Bulloch, afflicted with the measles and waylaid at Velasco, ever apprised of his men's quiet valor? If we ever cross paths again, I will tell him how they battled past exhaustion at the low rock wall. Lieutenant-Colonel Ward, our battalion leader, guided us as an officer but with a fatherly touch. We in Bulloch's Company took comfort from his strength, but it was you who rode with me during those terrifying nights. You spoke to me, Papa, and I was not alone.

One night when I stole back into the church, plaster was drifting down from the ceiling. Candles at the altar made the dust glow as it sifted down. Ward listened to my report as if the assault were not deafening. He told me I was doing dangerous work bravely, that the battalion would follow the route I'd found if we were forced to slip away at night. If we ran out of shot, my mapping would help the companies find their way to Victoria.

"Surely Colonel Fannin has already made it there," he said to me. I remember how his words gave me hope. He reminded me to take all caution down in the dark and difficult creek beds, to let my horse feel its way over tree roots and sharp rocks. I had already learned such advice in militia, and well before from Deefy, a boy you never knew, but I nodded because Ward had finished shaking my hand and was looking at my swaddled feet.

He asked how I could ride without boots. I did have a mismatched pair of shoes I used for marching. When I told him my horse had shoes for the both of us, he patted my shoulder, like you did sometimes, Papa. Remember when you heard I'd let Charlotte have the last water from my sojourn canteen? Even Charles was proud. William Ward was part brother, part father. I think you'll understand my sorrow in learning how his last minutes at Goliad went by.

During the siege in Refugio, so many ticking minutes felt like my own last. My feet were numb, even though I had wrapped them in burlap strips. The chill could not dull my thoughts, and I kept hearing the voice, "This cannot be! This cannot be!" I listened for your words, too. Remembering your kind touch gave me comfort. Still, I could not stop aching for my comrades, bent at the mission's perimeter wall.

For two days I nudged my horse and searched for escape routes only after sundown. You might shake your head and swear you don't recall hearing my heart beat in my throat. But you were there with me. Did you know that a soldier can whisper a whistle? I could never purse my lips the way you did when Charles and I were little. No matter how hard I tried, no sound came out strong enough to resemble the old songs passed down to you.

And then fifteen years after you were gone from this world, all those melodies sang in my ears. During those nights in Refugio, I found I could whistle every French ballad and Huguenot hymn, but can you imagine how softly? General Urrea had his patrols everywhere. Twice, a musket fired and lethal pellets brushed past me. They'd fired blindly at some noise in the dark ravine, but death off in the dusty road drew away their attention. I needed to whistle to soothe my horse and to keep my heart from pounding too loud. You will say you don't remember, Papa, but both those nights, I gave thanks to God that you stayed close by.

The Dove Shall Fly

The first night, after getting shot at, my horse appeared to understand our limitations, and its hooves moved more and more discreetly down at the edge of the shallow creek. A sharp smell made my mount shake its mane, and I tried to hold my breath as we moved along past a latrine somewhere above. Whether it was American or Mexican excrement I could not tell, but not far beyond that stinking bend, I heard low voices and the beginning of laughter that made someone hush all the others in the gathering. The soldier in charge easily put a halt to lightheartedness. Their laughter had been the nervous kind, and though I could understand no Spanish, I surmised what any officer might say to his men. He surely told them to keep their wits and not to underestimate the foreigners pinned down at the church perimeter.

He could not know our numbers already engaged inside the sanctuary, but any attempt had to first break defense at the deadly little enclosure. He surely told them that the first units sent to the unimpressive main road had sunk not far from the wall into the silence of the dead. Their laughing stopped that quickly, Papa. He could not tell them how many Georgia boys and men fired fiercely from behind the rock barrier. The stench of mortal combat had not diminished their aim.

For two nights, I'd been on lookout for any Mexican patrols moving in from the west, but I sensed that this quieted unit was trailing others in the fray. They would soon take their turn in the dusty road before the church. All their survivors would then sweep on with the greater army across Texas. I tethered and calmed my horse, and I crawled up the embankment to verify my judgement. It was true. Five men were gathering their weapons and dousing a small fire as if they would not return to the site.

Their graying leader, perhaps a captain, was the last to depart. I wondered if, like our Mr. Spillers, he had three children back at home. It may be that the Mexican knew one wise reason for keeping watch at the rear. Santa Anna's armies could not afford desertion any more than we could. The officer was alone in the clearing, and had he not lit a cigar I would likely not have seen. He made the sign of the cross, and an odd sense blew into my mind like a leaf sent aloft by a sudden gust. This mortal enemy might have lightly touched his most fearful man on the shoulder. To any of his men hearing the cry, "This cannot be! This cannot be," he might have said, "Your father would be proud. Not every man can do this difficult job so bravely."

When I could believe that he and his patrol were gone, I went back to my horse and led him up the ravine. From there, I discerned a flickering of lights from the back of the church. Sporadic firing had begun again, I assumed from the road in front where my company squeezed up against the wall. I made mental notes of my whereabouts and imagined an exodus to take place that night or the next. I felt we might make it to Victoria, and I was aware that Travis and Crockett and the martyred Gonzales men would have been heartened by any such chances.

I hope our ancestors will not judge me harshly if they learn this last thing, Papa. You were with me. Perhaps you will explain. I do remember the Huguenot hymns and the persecution that forced our first people from France, but I believe our forefathers might forgive an odd impulse I freely indulged.

When I imagined showing our battalion a route for slipping away in the direction of Victoria, I said my own silent prayer of thanks. We had made it that far. I said my thanks in silence, and before turning to report back to Lieutenant-Colonel Ward, I made the sign of the cross. It was as strange to me as any other Protestant would have found it. But will you help me explain to the first Trezevants when we meet again, Papa? I felt very close to death, but I also felt free. I believe they will understand.

"Excuse me, captain." A guard had stepped inside the tent, and Jamie was not sure how long he'd quietly waited before interrupting.

"Your duty about to end?"

"In a half hour, sir. I just wanted you to know that it doesn't look like the storm will make it over this far. Everything seems quiet to the west, though. If there are any savages out there, they probably looked for shelter."

"We need to call at a couple homes tomorrow. The Finissees and another family besides the Malloys remember us. They may have further knowledge of Amon King's presence in town before Ward brought us over from Goliad."

"Is Mrs. Malloy the one who stayed with your friend? Private Weeks was his name?"

"She was hoping he'd appear to be her son, and that Mexicans storming in would pass him by."

"Was she trying to help the other man, too, the one from Macon who came along with his cousins?"

The Dove Shall Fly

"He'd already died as we were spilling out from the back of the church. But we were all like family. It tore us all up to leave some boys behind." The private hesitated to speak again, and he almost edged toward the tent flap without saying anything else.

"Jenkins and I can go on and ride courier back to Velasco with that document tomorrow morning, sir, if it's something they need right away at the fort."

"No, it's nothing official," Jamie said, putting a cork in the ink bottle. "I need to stretch my legs." He was surprised by how many sheets of stationery he'd used compiling his thoughts. He'd originally meant to write about making it back to the church in time to help drag a wounded friend from the courtyard into the sanctuary. He'd expected to recall the battalion's nightmare retreat toward Victoria, about losing track of Mr. Spillers days later as a handful managed to escape Urrea's patrols, about the only other fighters he felt sure had made it to San Jacinto, Andrews and Moses and the boy Sam Hardaway. "Is the fire still going? Has the wind died completely?"

"Uh, both, sir."

"Then I'll be out in a minute." Captain James Trezevant was alone again. He couldn't make himself believe that any relatives back home would fully understand what his battalion had gone through in Texas, no matter how much time he spent explaining. He didn't suppose he'd ever tell his family how the boots he'd worn to Velasco had suddenly disappeared. He didn't feel like whistling any melodies at all, and he knew he was whispering to no one in particular. "Then, it won't hurt to lay these pages in the flames."

He took time to fasten his holster and make sure his pistol slipped in and out at a light touch. Wherever those three others were—those first comrades who'd also survived to reach Houston's army—they'd surely made themselves the same promise. Never again make contact with the ground except in sturdy footwear. Never again set out on a journey without water, dried beef, and a firearm at the ready. When he stepped outside, Private Jenkins had already risen and approached the campfire. Both guards at the shift change kept their voices low after saluting their captain. He would remind them at the end of a short walk that such deference was unnecessary for soldiers already traveling together. They were new recruits, one older than Jamie by several years, both thrilled by formality and the possibility of a clash.

He let himself follow only the line where light from the fire fell off into untouched dark. There was no way to teach an inexperienced volunteer how quickly a peaceful maneuver could turn deadly. He had been realizing lately that the reverse was true. It was going to be difficult to eventually accept tranquility as the natural disposition of a day. This man Holliday, the survivor Fiona Malloy spoke of, had bowed to the power of a bottle. Jamie was thankful to remember his father as a whistler rather than a drinker. The circulation in his legs was picking up, but the ache in his shoulder intensified, too. In three months, he would turn just twenty-one. Jamie Trezevant had come to understand how any man might lose his bearings and his way after stepping into the lightless tangle of combat.

Joshua Jenkins had taken his post by the time Jamie made it back around to the crackling flames. Orange fingers of heat rose straight up but stayed low. The chance of a wind gust had passed, and the captain grasped the bundle of pages inside his jacket. As his subordinate moved up closer to the fire, Jamie could tell the soldier had something on his mind.

"You were already in your tent, captain, when Sullivan and I came back from town patrol and turned in."

"I don't think Refugio will ever be much of a town."

"No, sir. I know what you mean. I'm from Biloxi."

"That's a ways off," Jamie said, noticing for the first time that this recruit was probably not much older than Sam Hardaway. "The original companies stopped over there after coming down the Alabama."

"My mother didn't let me muster." The youth shifted a rifle across his arms. "But my daddy wouldn't either, not until I had one more birthday. So I guess they both ended up saving my life."

Jamie felt he could have composed a few more sentences about the mixture of pride and anguish any parents feel when their sons march off with an army. He was done taking up a pen about it, though. He'd realized his reflections on it all would keep coming and coming. His memory of Texas action was not dependent on pages of handwriting. It didn't seem the right time to tutor the private about all the lethal foes still within the republic's boundaries.

"I think you had something you wanted to tell me, Jenkins."

"Oh, yessir. We were riding patrol in town, and we stopped in the street right outside that rock wall."

"The church was an easy target. But the worst of the siege was out there beyond the sanctuary door."

"That's why me and Sullivan stopped in the road. In town, everything was already mostly asleep. There was an old man, though, wearing one of them striped blankets. He'd been sitting, in front of a bakery I think, but he came right up to us when we brought our horses to a stop."

"I'm glad the people have come back somewhat."

"He switched over from Spanish right quick. We could understand his English easy enough."

"The Irish accent is sometimes even harder to understand. We found that out in our early weeks here."

"What the ole Mexican was telling us is that a lot of the soldiers with General Urrea, the ones who kept firing on you all…" Jamie unfolded his pages and set them on a glowing chunk of charred wood at the outer edge of the fire. "He said a bunch of them was brought up from the Yucatan… that's way down on the coast in Mexico, near the Hispaniola islands."

"I don't calculate that's too much farther away than Biloxi. Not as far as Savannah or Charleston." Whatever he'd missed in geography or French or military tactics in college, Jamie thought he'd take up some entirely new lines of study in the future. "Most of my company was pinned down at the wall for the whole siege," he went on. "Our youngest, about your age, crawled out with water sometimes, but he had orders to help inside the church as much as he could. Ward pulled me, too, and sent me scouting for an escape route."

"But what this ole man said was that most from the Yucatan got forced into Santa Anna's army."

Jamie had heard such conscription facts before. Both soldiers stayed quiet for a minute. The pages closest to the ember had already ignited and the top sheets of paper were smoking.

"Captain," the younger man started up again, "do you think the ones who never meant to come…the ones who wouldn't have been set on killin' us if they'd had a choice…you think any of those had a fair chance of making it to heaven?"

"I'm the officer leading this patrol, private, not a pastor guiding a religious flock." His answer would have met approval from military instructors, but Jamie felt a tug of guilt for his abrupt dismissal of a sincere question. There were no other men awake, and he didn't think the recruit would be dwelling on the subject when the sun came up. "How old are you, Jenkins?"

"Sixteen, sir." The same age as Hardaway, the fellow was lagging by miles in experience.

"I wouldn't listen to anyone twenty-six, or even sixty, who claims to know the certain answer to questions like that." The top layers of Jamie's abbreviated memoir darkened and curled. A single lit corner of paper wafted up above the fire and expanded into a full flame before disappearing. "I can't make myself believe it matters much whether we spent time inside or outside a particular building. I know enough French to believe it's just as good a language for prayer as English or Spanish or German."

"That's the same I was thinking, captain." If the youth had more to say, he seemed unable to formulate words. Only a far-off coyote and the campfire crackle intruded on the silence.

"If every soul has a quiet, free center where heaven hears its honest purpose," Jamie went on, "it doesn't seem to me to matter much how deeds were reported or judged in the earthly landscape." The guard on duty was nodding, but he looked as if his interest in the discussion was also curling up and disappearing.

"Sir, do you want me to go find another dry limb?"

"I'll wait here until you get back with a thin log or two."

No evidence of pages remained, but the newly promoted officer felt an odd reassurance about how valor at Refugio might be remembered. Riding those nights in March alongside deadly peril, he'd taken heart from his father's warmth and his ancestors' perseverance. Who could predict how far today's ardent endeavor might ripple on tomorrow? Jamie Trezevant thought, for the first time in many weeks, that he would sleep soundly until a calm hand nudged him in the morning.

Chapter 15   Word of Mouth

Juan Seguin felt he would never tire of watching his three children tend to their grandparents. In the first minutes after *siesta*, Antonia had turned Papi Erasmo's sombrero just so, while Teresa gently waved a fan near her grandmother's cheek and neck. Little José was helping to move blankets out by the fire where family elders might sit once the sun angled down further. The afternoon was warmer than what one expected during the second week of October. Sweat and hot leather overpowered the aroma of roasting peppers. The Texas heat stretch, though, had been broken.

In the visitor camps encircling Columbia, hope stirred over the republic's first inauguration a week away. Mixed in with confirmation of what dignitaries had registered in town and which family members accompanied them, were reminders to dig into trunks and have ponchos ready for a cooler spell.

Of the men who'd fought under his command at San Jacinto, Colonel Seguin tallied few to have joined visitor bivouacs on the outskirts of Columbia. Within his campsite, where Spanish was the language bandied most, conjecture about acquaintances hummed. There was no telling how long some in his company went searching for scattered relatives after April's decisive battle. Months later, repairs to a charred fence might well take priority over attendance at a civic ceremony. Juan knew he'd been fortunate to have his leave request granted and to find his entire family safe among old friends in Nacogdoches. When the battalions stationed there under Sam Houston and Hugh McLeod moved out toward Columbia a fortnight ago, the Seguin family enjoyed safe passage for that part of their trek homeward.

In spite of the sun's warmth, Juan slipped his arm around his wife's waist and she leaned closer to his side. After all these years, his own parents still moved somewhat formally around each other, but Juan and Gertie didn't try to hide their affection. He'd met her during his second year aiding the governor in San Antonio. At thirteen, she'd been a shy beauty, and he still loved her for the direct gaze she offered exclusively to him. As her eyes followed their son José, Juan thought she might be weighing what name to give the next baby already on its way.

"See how his mouth tightens, how serious he is at work?" Their four-year-old boy was moving the fringe of a red and turquoise blanket farther from the kindling flames. "My oldest brother has the same little frown. But look when he laughs. Then, *Juanito*, I am seeing you as a child."

Besides her angelic profile and tender disposition, he loved her resolve to share secrets only with him. It would be another two months before his mother and father learned they'd be grandparents again.

The younger Seguin couple rose to greet Señora Ruiz as she strolled toward them. Wife of San Antonio's representative, she and her family maintained tents not far from the Seguin wagons. Juan didn't need Gertie's gentle nudge to remind him that the regal woman had tried to dissuade her husband from even running for office. Opposing politicians found it far too convenient to target natives of Mexico as potential spies, and the lady was wary of large crowds.

"It is certain now," she said speaking first to Señora Seguin. "Our Zavala is not well enough to attend." Juan groaned and Gertie clasped her shawl more tightly.

"But we heard Lorenzo was improving."

"We thought simply that he had to withdraw as acting vice-president," Juan said. "His grown son did all translating at the San Jacinto surrender, so Zavala's family is surely able to inquire for the best doctor. Advanced physicians practice nearby in Galveston." When no encouraging response came, he looked away absently at the fire where his son played. The Ruiz woman stepped close enough to prevent being overheard.

"Oh *si*, Zavala has been under dedicated care. His second wife and the eldest son make every effort on his behalf." She was whispering. "Children from the first marriage still call their father's wife Miss West, as does Zavala himself, a term of endearment. The señora now has papers if ever her return to New York or Connecticut is questioned. Yet she stays while the papa of her three small *niños* is ill. I will speak this fact to anyone painting her as having no more loyalty than a slave."

"Miss West?" The conversation had taken a turn in Juan's mind. "Before the great battle, we were advised to keep watch for an Emily West, a striking woman of color who—"

"Lorenzo's falling into the bayou," Gertie broke in, "it is an accident a young man might have recovered from more quickly." Juan was so affected by her interruption that he took up her prompting as if he'd never nudged the conversation in another direction.

"*Si, si,* I had not considered his vulnerability as an older person."

"I will testify that his family has taken every care." Señora Ruiz nodded gravely while leaning in yet closer to the Seguins. "If the great man succumbs, we shall all be much grieved for those who love him, but also for the republic." Her pause allowed that statement its solemnity. "I am more than a little disquiet knowing my husband alone is to represent our people on the podium next week." The lady strode on toward the Ruiz tents. Juan waited until she disappeared behind a canvas flap to reprise the topic of Emily West.

"Perhaps you will just nod, *mi corazón,* if I am right in thinking that—"

"Ayeeee! Mama!" Over by the fire, José was flailing about. The wispy boy favored one hand, and a glowing stick rolled where he'd let it fly.

"*La sábila!*" Juan shouted to their older daughter.

"Antonia! In the trunk," Gertie called as she swept up the injured child. "There's a jar of aloe vera! Oh, *pobrecito!*" she said cradling him.

When the Seguin's eleven-year-old emerged from their largest wagon with a bright blue jar, they were dismayed to find the burn unguent dried past usefulness. A teacher from Brazoria, Rosalia Mendez, rushed over and offered a paste of corn starch and soothing herbs, but it seemed not to assuage the boy's pain. Juan and Gertie felt only a doctor could adequately treat the wound. If misjudged, the injury might fester and eventually limit flexibility in that hand.

"There is a physician at the crossroads," the teacher told them, pointing past the Ruiz tents. A fixture just downriver in Brazoria, Señorita Mendez had come along with families of her students. "We thought we had a case of measles last week, but a kind doctor said it was only poor healing from the work of blister bugs." José could not stop crying. "Do you know the Peyton *cocina* table right on the way into town? I can't remember the doctor's name, but he's staying where meals are served, where he's easy to find." With his son in his arms, Juan was already starting off in the direction of the crossroads "I think he's the representative from Bastrop!" she called after him.

Señora Seguin and their little daughter stayed behind to calm the grandparents. Antonia, her thick braids swinging, trotted close to her father's side as he marched the short distance to a merging of two paths. A friendly woman managed a wagon arrangement there. Kettle beans that she and her crew offered every day were as familiar to English speakers as self-rule. When visiting with Captain Eberly at the Peyton food line, Juan had found the main dish lacking cilantro and *comino*, but the widow from San Felipe managed the enterprise with genuine friendliness. Juan was relieved to see the dark-haired proprietress standing with her hands on her hips. Customers who'd begun to spread out from the dusty line sidled back out of her view. Juan judged he could be heard over his son's subsiding moans.

"Mrs. Peyton! Does a doctor stay with you now?" Behind her, a fellow with graying hair but a young face rose from a stool where he'd been sharpening a carving knife. Juan kept scanning the assembly for another newcomer, since this man lacked the air of a professional. "My boy is hurting from a burn, señora! Is the physician here?"

"Shelby, go see if the doc left his regular medical bag! Delilah, ask the captain's girls to keep an eye on Mag!" Angelina Peyton also passed her servant the ladle before dipping her hands in an earthenware washbowl and drying them on her gray apron. She reached out to José, who let her gently inspect his blistering hand. "Poor baby! My boy Alex did the same thing to his wrist not two months ago. It'll all quit hurting soon," she said, before turning anxiously to the father. "But your daddy was right to seek help. Let's go over to Dr. Robertson's wagon and get you fixed up."

Proud of his son's stoicism among strangers, Juan also respected women who managed crisis. His own Gertie had known when to calmly lead the family beyond Santa Anna's reach. His admiration swelled for Angelina Peyton, Ruiz's wife, and the Brazoria teacher, as well as the Harper women, and the mysterious "Miss West." These females might have shown as much fury against the tyrant's army as the toughest men. He was less sure, though, that anyone but a trained medic could adequately treat his son.

"The physician is not here?"

"Dr. Robertson rushed into town last night for a delivery. The lady's husband had secured no lodging except a tent by the stables. But unless it was Jesus born again, the doctor should be back any minute." She'd been patting José's ankle, but the commotion had already put a stop to his tears. "Shelby! Did you find a big tapestry satchel?" The child was transfixed by her rapid English and imposing air. "You'll have to elbow your own way into town, Colonel Seguin, if Robertson needs fetching, My hired man would rather pry seeds from a thousand jalapeños than lend a hand at one nativity scene."

The Dove Shall Fly

The civilian emerging from behind the wagon flap looked as unlikely to take charge as his employer was natural with the reins of command. He held a roll of gauze and an ointment jar, though, as if prepared to use them. Sitting on a log where his father had set him down, the boy extended his reddening hand to Shelby Whitmire.

"Does it hurt bad?" the man with the jar asked. Juan rephrased the question in Spanish.

"Si."

"Will you let me patch you up?"

"Si," José said again, interpreting the handyman's gesture.

"My friend here looked out for little ones when he was but a child himself," Angelina explained to the colonel. "I wouldn't be surprised to see him wrap a bandage as secure as any expert's work." Her smile softened as she observed his touch with the salve. "Shelby, I doubt the doctor just delivered another immortal, but I'll testify your turning up again in my life proves resurrection of some type."

"*Señora?*" Her meaning had escaped Juan Seguin, who hoped no debate over religion was about to heat up. He was relieved to read only warm appreciation in her expression.

"In Natchez, Mississippi, this dear fellow was just turning twelve when we met. Then Mr. Peyton and I rushed on to Texas, and young Shelby was gone from my own world." The injured four-year-old gave rapt attention to bandaging that left his thumb in use. "A decade and a half later, right here in my Columbia dinner line, this familiar man appears like a miracle. He's searching for a friend likely lost at Goliad."

"Ah," Juan said, nodding, but rubbing his chin thoughtfully.

"When my Mr. Peyton passed away suddenly, I feared all of our shared experiences would depart from mind. Yet Shelby Whitmire sits before me now, graying but reviving memory of a Natchez family that showed us all special kindness."

Juan Seguin's son seemed rather pleased with his wrapped hand. He stood up and stepped timidly toward a molasses barrel where curiosity had led the widow's two children. Antonia ushered her brother in their direction.

"Mr. Whitmire," the Tejano officer said. "Do you come to Texas, I wonder, by way of Louisiana's Fort Jessup?"

"He most surely did." Angelina answered for her quiet handyman. They were watching the youngsters communicate through gestures and smiles. "Never even sat on a horse until he saddled up at the Mississippi and rode west to find his life-long friend."

"In Nacogdoches," Juan went on, "my wife was hearing of a man at the stockade across the border." Shelby Whitmire grew fascinated by a green beetle struggling on its back. "A woman sheltering there was suddenly in need of a birthing doctor, and there was a man, a civilian, who took charge and—"

"Don't mistake my Shelby for possessing any such skill," Angelina said laughing. "He's got enough sand to ride alone from Natchez and risk Indian attack, but I'll bet all my wagons and my entire crew he wouldn't take up the first task of a midwife!" Throwing her head back, she laughed again heartily and Juan Seguin thought such an appealing lady would not long remain unmarried. "Isn't that right, Dr. Robertson?" The approaching physician looked haggard but happy. The maternity call appeared to have ended well for all. "I was saying Mr. Whitmire would have been useless as an assistant to you last night."

The tall Bastrop representative tugging at his mustache shook his head, but he seemed less interested in the current discussion than he was in recalling his previous encounter with Seguin.

"You were delirious, colonel, the last time I saw you. I only rode out to the Harpers' clearing to make sure no more could be done." Juan stood to shake the doctor's outstretched hand. "Miss Adeline has a gift for medical care, and Yarico, too. Already friends of yours, I hear. You were in good company. Town folks were mighty sorry you'd been treated as a spy by those drifters."

"I recognize only your voice. A little out of one eye, doctor, it was all I could see."

"Ignorant newcomers!" Angelina Peyton knew from Captain Eberly about the attack Seguin suffered in Bastrop. "Likely half the gawkers lining up at my kettle don't know one fact about who walloped Santa Anna!"

"Oh, most are hoping for a glimpse of Houston and Lamar during the festivities. You can bet their speeches will remind folks who won what, ma'am. And your Stephen Austin arrived yesterday," Dr. Robertson went on, "though he may be too weak to participate."

"Mexican prisons inflict damage long after a captive is released," Juan agreed. The doctor sighed, but nodded vigorously when the Tejano made his next comment about the boy with the fresh bandage.

"Come back and let me see your son after the swearing in. Once the blisters subside, his fingers are best exposed to the air." He smiled again to see the officer entirely recovered. "You did mumble about San Antonio the last time I saw you. You and your boy headed home after President Houston gives his huzzah?"

"And my daughters, my wife Gertrude, and my parents."

"Well," Dr. Robertson marveled. "It'll be a while before many of my house calls involve three generations or more." He moved off toward the bunk wagon as if already imagining the pillow. "How wonderful to think of families staying put from now on, the fresh born and the aged sharing a roof like in the old days."

"Go on and get some rest while you can, sir. Your Bastrop constituents will be up in arms if you nap through next week's doings." Mrs. Peyton looked down the path toward town but didn't say who might be approaching. "Delilah will come rap my knuckles with the ladle if I lollygag here any longer. Let your wife know we'll swap corn bread for tortillas, colonel, if any in your camp have acquired the taste."

Both Juan Seguin and Shelby Whitmire were left gazing at a growing group of children. Captain Eberly's five, who'd been without a mother for a year, joined the Peytons and the Seguins in a translation game. The oldest daughters handily managed their siblings. It was no more necessary for either man to step in than it was wise for Juan to revisit Shelby's midwife expertise. During the revolution, few escaped daunting responsibilities. It was good to see children embracing their natural roles.

"I wouldn't have recognized Dr. Robertson if I'd just seen him passing," Juan said. "Do you still hope to see your Natchez friend in a crowd like this one day?"

"As time passes, that hope grows smaller."

"My men and I did come across a scattering of Fannin's volunteers. One wounded man and an older fellow, we sent on to the Galveston hospital. But another four came along with us to San Jacinto."

"Thomas Weeks of Mississippi is the friend I came looking for." The Whitmire man spoke slowly, as if he'd just moved a stone slab from a vault. "My friend had straight dark hair and a changeable manner. He was only twenty—"

"Ah, *si*, there were so many away from their parents for the first time." Finding the name unfamiliar, Seguin shook his head. "It was not possible to learn every muster roll." He wished he'd been able to pass on some comforting word. "There was such a private by the name *Trezevant*. He was so wasted away, I do not think his own mother would have known him at a glance. But he survived to be promoted and is often posted in Velasco." Angelina Peyton's handyman had no familiarity with that surname.

"In his one letter home, Thomas only mentioned a Sam Hardaway, a boy from the Georgia town where speeches…" Juan Seguin's eyebrows rose in reaction.

"*Ah si! Si*, Hardaway, this is a survivor I know! He was the first ready to fight again. Yes, he and some of the others were in the battalion of Colonel Ward and the company that—"

"Oh," Shelby interrupted. Both took in a distraction some distance yet down the crowded path. "General McLeod is riding our way along with Captain Eberly. I suppose he'll press me again about taking a message to Brazoria. The captain comes to check on his children and to offer the widow Peyton another compliment."

"I have heard from my wife about courtship at this *cocina*…" Off duty for another two days, Seguin nevertheless thought better of the topic and brushed off his sleeves. On leave in Nacogdoches, he'd been introduced to McLeod once, but simply as head of a Tejano clan. He wondered how close Gertie was to final mending of his officer jacket. "He asks someone outside the military to take a courier's assignment?"

"I witnessed an accident that a Brazoria family needs to know about, but I'm not keen to ride off from the Peytons. We only just crossed paths again." Seguin was listening, though he also saw that Antonia had placed her hands in her apron pockets as her mother often did when it was time to end a visit. He could read his daughter's thoughts.

"José! Antonia! *Tu mamá*, she will worry!" The owner of the wagon arrangement waved before untying her work smock as the soldiers rode nearer. The children dispersed. "Tell me, señor, what is this accident you saw?"

"Up in Nacogdoches, a private serving Sam Houston was killed during a misunderstanding. Chief Bowles punished the hothead who let an arrow fly. I'd only just met the youthful recruit, but he was from the next town downriver."

"Cristo! You are the man who was with General Houston's messenger! Of course, even on our side of Nacogdoches, we learned of this tragedy. But this means you are the same rider who came to Texas with McLeod, after passing through Fort Jessup where there was a woman in need of—"

"The private's people are in Brazoria," the Peyton handyman repeated, "and possibly a schoolteacher he was sweet on."

"You must walk with us, Mr. Whitmire. A Brazoria teacher stays in our camp."

○

A week and a half later, Rosalia Mendez and one of her students spotted the majestic oak that marked Brazoria at its northeast edge. Having heard multiple accounts of the Columbia swearing in from those who'd squeezed close enough to see, the teacher doubted her patience to pass reports to even one more Texan hungry for news. According to every witness, Sam Houston went on way too long and loud after his oath of office, whereas Vice-President Mirabeau Lamar's brief delivery was barely audible.

Señorita Mendez and her students did manage to view the entire parade. In the Tejano gathering, observations about Representative Ruiz and Colonel Seguin included greater detail. The teacher burst with pride at descriptions of Juan Seguin riding in full uniform as head of the procession. She was tempted to apprise her pupils of the day she'd spent polishing the officer's brass while his wife Gertie repaired button holes. It was better, she concluded, to let such small accomplishments remain anonymous. Otherwise, her lessons about shunning braggarts would ring hollow.

She was relieved to see it was the young Velasco captain, Trezevant, at the northern post with three others. An armed ship docked at the mouth of the Brazos had been expected to deter any aggression there during the ceremonies upriver. Riding up as far as Brazoria, a full contingent from the stockade patrolled the perimeter as long as crowds and dignitaries a bit to the north remained vulnerable.

Rosalia had promised herself to prepare a discreet lecture about what to expect from San Jacinto veterans. She would tell her boys and girls to cease their laughter and keep their eyes on the ground as any military patrols passed by. Civilians were likely, they already knew, to harbor deep resentment about the Alamo. But those who'd avenged that disaster at San Jacinto, included some perhaps haunted by retaliatory slaughter in the bayous. Who knew whether a drunk soldier's vow to "kill every Mexican on the continent" could shift to sober appreciation of a brown child's innocence. She would comfort her pupils with a reminder that many in uniform, no matter the color of their hair or their language or manner of worship, were raised as gentlemen.

"*Buenas tardes,* Captain Trezevant."

Looking only at his countenance, one might judge the officer to be no older than her senior student, Alberto. The talented pupil sat next to her on the wagon seat, enjoying his first turn at managing reins. Clearly accustomed to adult civilities, the man in charge tipped his hat. He carried himself with a dignity belying his age. She had wondered whether this soldier stationed periodically near Brazoria might speak to her students about his role in the war for independence. But a gravity in his manner convinced her that his reflections should remain his own.

"That's quite a string of wagons coming along behind you."

"Yes, captain. The first inauguration for The Republic of Texas! These children will talk of nothing else for the rest of the year." Two privates with Trezevant stretched in their saddles, and the teacher predicted his special patrol would ride back to Velasco as early as the next morning. "Do you mind to talk with me as we head toward town? I'm afraid I have sorrowful news for a certain soldier's kin. If you come with me when I call on them, your condolences will give comfort."

The parents of Private Zeke Moreland had been bracing for bad news. Even in half-tamed Texas, nine months was a long time to hear no report from a family member. They were proud that the fifteen-year-old had made it to San Jacinto, even if only to serve by carrying a banner. It was some consolation that their boy hadn't fallen as one of the rare casualties there.

"Young Zeke was taking a message to McLeod. Do you know of this general who was given the star flag to take to Texas?"

"Your son was taking him a peace document," Jamie added. In just the last day, he'd learned this fact from the teacher.

"This is the leader famous for speeches in Macon. So many volunteers came to Texas because of McLeod, and your son was on his way to meet him." As she explained further, Señorita Mendez nodded to the captain, who seemed relieved she wasn't emphasizing the tragic encounter with Chief Bowles' band. "I have heard also of an officer named Isaac Moreland, with special duties at the last battle."

"It's a wide world," Zeke's father said, his eyes glistening. "We don't recall an Isaac among our relatives, but my kin came from Arkansas. Might could be some of our name put their roots in Georgia long before.

I reckon my boy's being buried up near Nacogdoches lets him lie closer to where he was born." His wife couldn't stem her tears.

"According to the Good Book," she sobbed, "we're all family when it comes down to it."

○

Two miles south of the last Brazoria outcropping, the emotional scene was still affecting Captain Trezevant. The Brazoria teacher, familiar with occasional displays of affection from her students, had recovered quickly from Mrs. Moreland's surprise hug. Jamie found it harder to regain his composure. The grief-stricken woman didn't look anything like his own mother back in Darien, and the little sister he doted on would not grow to resemble the Brazoria teacher. Yet, on the ride back to Velasco, he couldn't help recalling other encounters inspiring an embrace.

"Captain?" Private Jenkins had been slowly gaining on the officer, and he finally pulled up alongside. "Are you laughing?"

"I suppose I am."

"I just never heard you laugh before."

"It's finally hit me," he said evasively, "that we've really all lived to see the birth of a new country."

"Yessir."

"Less than a year ago, this was all Mexico's territory."

"It don't hardly seem possible," the recent recruit said, not at all sure the chuckling had been explained.

Jamie's recollections evoked equal parts pain and mirth. A thankful Santa Anna, after being rescued from an angry mob on Velasco's docks, had greeted every stockade guard with a kiss on the cheek. As gratifying as it was to see a brute humbled, Jamie admitted to nearly throwing his own arms around native Texan Juan Seguin for pausing generously to assist him and other desperate escapees.

The captain pulled ahead of the men in his patrol, and he shrugged off the impulse to explain his state of mind to anyone of lower rank. He set aside family memories that Mrs. Moreland's show of affection elicited. Instead, as he rode, he peered with his lookout piece to the west and east and south. His example would remind the others to wind down their disappointment about leaving Brazoria just before its *Día de los Muertos* diversions.

"Captain?" Private Jenkins startled him. "Do you think a *señorita*, I mean a mature woman who's not married..." The youngest patrol member was risking one more stray question. "Is it your opinion she's never been courted, or she just doesn't want to be?" Jamie kept the lookout piece at his eye.

"I think school teachers have their hands full once the academic year starts."

In the extended quiet, Jamie considered his own misgivings about ending the Brazoria mission. Unlike Refugio and Goliad, the larger town was a more potent reminder of bounty than of sacrifice. Mexican ranks rushing north of there in April had been so determined to make the ferries at Fort Bend that they took little interest in destroying river-town structures. Residents dodged enemy forces for a week or two as best they could and then returned to find their dwellings and belongings mostly intact. Brazoria's quaint cabins, whitewashed cottages, well-stocked mercantile, familiar wooden steeples, and cheerful citizens might now interfere with any soldier's concentration. If Jamie had any more dull assignments in the quartermaster office at Velasco, he too would have to chase off daydreams. He resolved to put a frank request to Colonel Karnes next time he saw him. Any duty with a serious spy unit out in Comancheria or near the Rio Grande would suit him.

"*La Toussaint*," he said to himself. The French name for the first of November, a day for remembering the dead, came back to him. He smiled without any impulse to laugh as he and his patrol moved down alongside the banks of the Brazos. To the west, five hundred men had perished at the Alamo and Refugio and Goliad that spring. To the east, five times that many women and children and old folks had scattered in terror ahead of Santa Anna's armies. The soldiers with him might fall asleep that evening imagining candlelight gatherings in Brazoria's main avenue. If he were free to follow his impulses, Jamie felt he'd cross the river on his own and search to the north for a lone oleander bush that had blazed blood red in April.

"It looks like Sullivan, captain." The youth who'd borrowed the lookout piece from him had been scanning south for any Velasco patrol.

By the time the rider from the fort reached them, everyone with Trezevant was eager for news and relaxed again about protocol.

"That there Huston general, or whatever he is, he's an ornery son'bitch."

"President Houston?"

The Dove Shall Fly

"Naw, spelled different. General Felix Huston—general or adjutant or, well Rusk and Lamar have opinions that run counter, and there's already been durn near a duel over it all. Up some place yonder wherever they're now callin' headquarters, all the higher-ups argued about who's in charge."

"Slow down, Sullivan," their leader said calmly. "You're talking about an officer we'll all answer to, it sounds like. Have you met him, or are you just repeating what you heard?"

"Oh, he barged in yesterday on me and another private sweeping up in dining hall like you said we should do if there was no trouble." The four soldiers tasked to scout Brazoria's perimeter stopped to let their horses nibble grass tufts. "First, he says he's gonna shoot the next Texas soldier he sees touching a broom handle. Then he wants to know *where's this baby-face captain said to be good with orders and receipts?* I'm sorry, sir, I was trying to figure who he meant, but he went on and mentioned you by name."

"This is the general from that fully anchored vessel? He finally came ashore?"

"That's the one, Captain Trezevant. It looks like he charged in just to get us riled and tell us he's got a plan to line the Rio Grande with a dozen new stockades and men ready to swoop down on Mexican renegades that cross over. He said he's gonna have *this Juan Seguin fella* earn his keep by shouting ultimatums across the border. He swears he's gonna *light hell-fire under this fort's college-boy quartermaster*—I'm sorry, sir, I think he meant you again. He's going to have you do the paperwork on new buttons and new rifles, in that order, because he's seen—I'm quotin' again here—*how snap can scare the daylights out of a heathen enemy even before the firing starts.*"

"He surely must know!" Jenkins said in a rare flare of temper. "He ain't proved his soldiering any more than Sullivan's cat has. I can't brag either, but I wager he didn't make it to Texas any sooner than I did, not until Santa Anna had put his signature on the surrender."

"My pappy would say that the fool's breathing a scab on the end of his nose!"

"All right, men," Jamie broke in. "That's enough rumor and conjecture. Plans and ranks are forever changing in the military. You all know that by now." His voice, if not his face at first glance, conveyed authority. "I'm calling for a silent ride the rest of the way to the stockade.

Use the time to reflect on what is not hearsay in the Republic of Texas—soldiers follow orders."

○

In the Tejano enclave outside Columbia, relaxed visiting continued well after the inauguration. Juan Seguin and his family were spending their last night before making the final trek on to San Antonio. They'd located more friends among the throng on swearing-in day. It felt natural, after the peak in scheduled festivities, for clans with longstanding ties to enjoy an additional week of quiet camaraderie.

Antonia and her sister were sleeping within reach of their grandparents, and in the other Seguin passenger wagon José's light snoring meant he would not be disturbed by muted talk.

"I am glad Señorita Mendez was not the teacher who broke Private Moreland's heart," Juan whispered to Gertie. Nights were turning cool, and the couple snuggled under a quilt and a blanket.

"The teacher who left Brazoria and the poor boy soldier who died, they were only children when they crossed paths. They could not have known lasting love."

"And you are the one who has told me so many times how your heart was mine only hours after we first met. You were but thirteen, *mi corazón*."

"Not every girl who is thirteen can trust such feelings."

"No one can tell me I did not marry the wisest girl in all of God's creation."

"No, husband Juan, *por favor*, it is you who must tell me one thing…"

"Are you going to ask if I can feel the new baby kicking?"

"Not yet. Perhaps in another two weeks." She laughed and patted his hand as it moved across her belly. "I ask you, from now on, if you go with your company farther away than a day's ride, to let us all go with you next time. I can watch over the children, but I cannot do again how we fled after death at the Alamo."

"Shhh," Juan said to his wife. "All that is over."

"Yet I can feel my heart break for the wife of Lorenzo Zavala." He was not sure where Gertie's worst worries lay.

"One day—God forbid it comes too soon—my father or my mother will depart this world and leave the other with loneliness that only happy couples suffer. But, you and I understand that this is life, and you are not one to feel sorrow before its time."

"I only ask myself how much can a person bear—to lose the sweetheart who gives you happiness," Gertie said, "and then to have the world regard you as a dangerous stranger." Her jaw tightened before she went on. "I do not rejoice to hear Señora Ruiz talk of *our people* as if Texas soldiers did not fight for everyone. But do you imagine where Emily West's thoughts travel as her husband Lorenzo grows weaker? She has children to protect."

"She was seen at San Jacinto." Juan stroked his wife's fragrant hair as he spoke. "There are stories that she appeared like a goddess near the officer tents of the enemy. They say she remained composed as if musket balls and war whoops could not affect her world."

"She has seen more of the world that we ever will. Did you know she went with her husband to Paris when Mexico appointed him ambassador to France? To think of the precautions she now must take, to seek signatures in case she must show papers proving she is no slave." Juan knew the subject of slavery to be thorny. In the territory just wrested from Mexico, no black people had won freedom. Not sure how those born free in the North might now fare in Texas, the officer wished to steer conversation elsewhere.

"Perhaps in France, Mrs. Zavala crossed paths with some Seguins of my sprawling ancestral tree."

There was no immediate response. Others in their campground had also doused their fires and settled in for the night. The acrid smell of damp ashes made him wince. A muted cough and a child's whimper mixed in with an occasional snort from a horse or donkey. With the larger crowds departed from Columbia, the evening calm stretched out. It was not difficult to imagine the miles now left between Juan's family and San Antonio. He could tell from the way his wife tilted her head back toward him that she had something else to say.

"I wonder if that boy in Nacogdoches ever told his parents that he crossed paths with Juan Seguin, the fearless Texas Revolution fighter."

"He made me promise not to tell anyone he had wandered into the Mexican part of town." Juan hugged Gertie and sensed she was drowsy enough to fall asleep soon. Louder snoring from José's pallet suggested he'd settled into deep dreams. "The Wainwright boy was buying sweets at the little *mercado*, when he overheard me give my name at the counter. I'm surprised he didn't insist I buy his *padre* a new pair of boots."

"And yet it was his mother who gave them over, and not to you, but to the young Goliad private."

"The boy said he'd heard the whole story from Trezevant himself. He can only pronounce it *Tressant*."

"Oh Juan, let us not forget the quiet work of God." Gertie's breathing had quickened, and her fingers brushed at one eye. "He turns wandering souls into neighbors, if only they listen to each other's stories."

"In all of Nacogdoches, perhaps no one but the boy and I can tell the escapes and battles of James Trezevant," Juan said, shaking his head. "The little white boy-soldier fought at San Jacinto, too, yet he still trembles to imagine his mother's scolding." Gertie's shoulder shook as she breathed this time, and he knew she was suppressing laughter.

"Wisdom from heaven gives mothers such power over their children." She didn't speak again for a while, and he thought his darling wife had finally drifted off. "But promise me, Juan," she said at last. He gently squeezed her hand. "Promise you will stay within reach, as long as we both shall live. Say to me you will take your family with you when you travel far again. If you had not come to find us when you did, perhaps the next white soldier in our part of town would not be a child coming to buy candy."

"Shhh," he said. "It will be all right from now on."

"But even after God lights a candle, there are some who can still look at stranded mothers and see only strangers."

"Shhh, *mi corazón*." He was pained by her final comment, but he knew she was not wrong to worry. "From now on, we will always stay together."

Celestial Fire

Chapter 16   Past Meets Prologue—New Orleans, 1839

When Jamie took out his pocket-watch for the hundredth time, he thought fate might be putting an end to his ambivalence about the soiree. One coach belonging to the Robinets—a transport at the beck and call of the family heir Theo—was expected to pick Mr. *Trezevant* up at a small inn near the French Quarter. It would whisk the two bachelors on several blocks to the annual fête that followed *Toussaint*. The carriage was nearly a half hour past due, and overcast skies made it seem even later. With each sudden breeze buffeting the inn's windows, the scent of nearby rain swept in.

A missed ride and a downpour might entirely excuse the law student from the event. He could return to the nondescript lodging he'd found perfectly adequate for serious study. Wanting to see Jamie do well, however, a colleague had advised him to begin building his clientele early, so he'd marked the soiree for the second Saturday in November. He wanted to be more resolute and cheerful about the occasion. He would turn twenty-four in another fortnight, after all, and he'd already been congratulated about his coursework. He thought he could exude congeniality for an evening.

Jamie decided to give the Robinet carriage another ten minutes, but he was already visualizing the walk to a concentration of antique buildings where the wealthy New Orleans merchant Samuel Hermann hosted the annual party. Assessing the Avignon's dim foyer and sitting room, he chastised himself for recommending the inn as a convenient stop. The little *auberge* did not suggest the welcome it had when he'd stayed there several weeks after returning from Texas. Jamie wondered if it had changed management in the last three years since he'd ventured in its direction.

"Ah oui, monsieur," said Madame Genet, the concierge he remembered. She was a freewoman, at ease in a city whose population included many black people at liberty to direct their own lives. "Ah, *mon dieu*, there was a steamboat tragedy in early '38. A great explosion on the Ohio River. The Avignon's owner was lost and hundreds more." The tall, affable woman smoothed the lace edging of one cuff. "Why he was traveling so far from home, we may never know, but I often say a little prayer for him. *Certainement*, no Toussaint will ever pass without a remembrance." She did not seem the type to indulge in secret criticism, but she'd likely guessed what sparked Jamie's inquiry. "The vines here used to be trimmed twice a year, and the door repainted almost as often. The floors were regularly stripped and polished as if for royalty. Sadly, monsieur, we see no such care under the current proprietor. It is a shame, but *c'est la vie*."

Mr. James Trezevant, as he was becoming known, nodded. He could have avoided the grim story by giving Theo his own address. Some gloom had already seeped into his mood since the day for remembrance of the dead. In his quarter of New Orleans, the old holy days commanded steadfast observance from Catholics, but the young Protestant from the East Coast was just as affected by streams of family members bearing flowers to the city's cemeteries. The occasion always reminded him that an entire burial ground could have been dedicated to the murdered Georgia Battalion. He admitted that the evening's party was more than a chance to meet prospective clients. Hosted on a Saturday evening soon after Toussaint, Mr. Hermann's annual champagne gala was said to dissipate all malaise. It was a celebration of the living.

The retired Texas officer readied for a vigorous walk. Foreseeing a dash through mud puddles, he'd chosen a somewhat worn pair of shoes to complete his formal attire. Theo would probably needle him about the footwear, whether the polished carriage stopped at the declining inn or his own dull boarding house. No matter what the Robinet heir thought of him, however, he couldn't really make himself care. Had the two not briefly shared one literature class, the wealthy Louisiana native would have been long forgotten. Whatever had become of their mutual acquaintance Pleasant Goodnight, Jamie considered himself a reasonably accomplished man. He'd completed one degree and started law studies well. He allowed the possibility that some new acquaintance made during the evening might help him decide where to conclude his professional training. Theodore Robinet, the man in that family after his father's sudden death, might never lose his adolescent demeanor.

"Madame, if a footman steps in to ask about me in the next few minutes…" He waited for the concierge to finish calculating a hotel bill.

"I will tell them you began walking in what direction?"

"Toward the Hermann house in the Vieux Carré."

"Ah oui, monsieur. What an evening you will enjoy there!"

Jamie nodded his thanks and set out along the boardwalk at a brisk pace. The scent of rain dominated, and its sweet earthiness made tolerable the rising odor of horse excrement along the cobbled street. Cafe aromas were countered by smells of dampened waste. The gray sky darkened. He hoped the deep hues overhead could be attributed to nightfall and that the rain might hold off. When a thunderclap was followed immediately by a downpour, he was too far from the Avignon to sprint back to its lobby.

The nearest shelter was the next covered entryway to a shop, closed but its windows still lit from lanterns within. A figure hunched over accounts much as Madame Genet had done. With nothing to do but wait for the deluge to subside, Jamie observed that the place was a portrait studio, specializing in miniatures. He felt he might have passed it before, but sounds held his attention as water poured off an edge of the shop's tiled roof.

When two boys ran to the same covered space, their laughter and smart clothing drew Jamie's notice. Their waistcoats were tailored as sharply as his, and he judged their cravats to be tied more fashionably. The two black youngsters were worried about having stepped in puddles, and they smiled at the man as they removed and shook one shoe at a time. All three looked from the sky to the window displays and to each other with the absentminded good will of strangers sharing a predicament. It did flit through Jamie's mind that a store owner in Columbia or Charleston might have rushed to the entryway to have the youths name their master. These two were only fretting over excuses they might make to their "Maman."

The older boy, who'd been studying the windows more carefully, suddenly dashed inside. He could be heard asking the man at the counter if he could take an ad page from a stack set with other items in the display. Jamie was surprised when the youngster with a handbill approached him.

"Monsieur? This is you, n'est-ce pas?"

He held up a paper on which a portrait sketch had been duplicated. Though reprinted by lithograph from an early pencil rendering, the abundance of curly hair was unmistakable. Jamie recognized his own large, solemn eyes, as well as the neat design of military gold trim on deep blue wool. On his mother's insistence, he had sat for the portrait just a few months after his last day of service in the Texas army.

"It was just striking me that I'd been here before," Jamie said, nodding. "This was done nearly three years ago."

"But now you have a beard, *non?*" The rhetorical question made the law student shake his head and exhale.

"I have whiskers, *c'est certain*. Perhaps we'll meet here again next year and you'll pose the same question." With their identical expressions of puzzlement, the two had to be brothers. Then, the taller youth broke into laughter.

"You are making the joke, monsieur! In the big city, except for *la famille*, people seem never to cross paths again." The rain had almost stopped, and he held out the sketch ad for Jamie to take. "If you do not tell our *maman* that we let our good suits get wet, we will not tell your *maman* that you have been trying to grow a beard. *Au revoir, monsieur! Ce n'est qu'un au revoir!*"

As the pair scampered across the street, Jamie was left clutching the advertisement, which he folded in half before walking on. In the last two years, he'd forgotten his awkwardness at sitting for the portrait. He didn't think the shopkeeper bent over accounts was the artist who'd complimented him for his ability to keep still.

"How can a soldier with the face of a boy rise to the rank of brevet major?" the painter had asked. Jamie's answer made the smiling craftsman put down his brush and palette.

"The general who promoted me to major on my very last day asked the same question, though I took his calling me 'baby face' as less tactful."

"The general's own face was perhaps the kind only a mother could love?"

The artist had commended Jamie again for his ability to sit immobile, and the young man in uniform kept his thoughts to himself for the rest of the session. He'd stayed sure he would never have felt fulfillment serving at a desk in Velasco. Now, he predicted that passing by any portrait studio would put him in a good humor.

He hadn't really noticed when the storefronts stopped halfway to his destination and the black grillwork surrounding an old cemetery started up. Expansive burial grounds had sprung up near the edges of the city over the decades, but these blocks from the French Quarter had once marked the city limits of New Orleans. A gargoyle stared from the top of one vine-covered vault. One swath of stone slabs leaned toward the street. An entire section of crypts tilted the other way as if petrified within a river of mud.

Because of La Toussaint and his remembrance of Texas, other muddy crossings came back to him. Jamie's exchange in the last hour with Madame Genet brought to mind his first encounter with the woman called Yarico and the girl Adeline, who'd been as protective of each other as any true kin. He'd heard second-hand from an acquaintance of Juan Seguin that the Harper women survived the exodus before San Jacinto and settled at last in Bastrop. That hopeful news had cheered him, but he couldn't entirely suppress his melancholy over so many lost in the spring of 1836. An old churchyard was a fair resting place, preferable to a site marked only by half-buried house timbers and a lonely oleander. An elegy had been going through his mind all week and he was sure no soul in the cemetery would be bothered by his quoting the poem aloud.

"Perhaps in this neglected spot is laid some heart once pregnant with celestial fire."

"James!" A familiar voice halted his reflections. The call might also have rattled the heavy clouds again. Though the Robinet carriage stopped just shy of the cemetery's far corner, the second downpour was enough to soak the young man hastening toward the vehicle.

"Oh—"

"François was afraid of this," Theo said as the new passenger shook water from his hair and brushed droplets from his coat. "They had to shift horses to the covered rig. That's why we were late. Sorry, old man." He'd come back from a short trip to England with a collection of expressions he spent as freely as his inheritance.

"I might be made to remain in the foyer with the dripping cloaks."

"No doubt the weather will pop into every conversation this evening," Theo agreed. "But, I say! Don't be surprised if you find yourself inspiring other conjecture, such as where men of means purchase proper dress shoes these days!"

"I'll lay odds much more will be made of what the ladies are wearing and how they've arranged their hair."

"I can't take you up on that, dear chap. I've promised Mama to abstain from bets of any kind this evening. On the other hand," he went on, "I am expressly ordered to assess the ladies in attendance—their style and their marital status, as well as their worthiness of the Robinet name."

"As I said, sir, I'll likely keep the wraps and umbrellas company." Jamie relaxed, smiling and sensing his shoes would not be brought up again. In the company of someone as self-involved as Theo, he'd at least feel prodded very seldom to share his own feelings.

"By the way, old boy, my mother asked me to cross-examine you about your own romantic prospects." He laughed at Jamie's expression. "She reminded me to be circumspect, so we'll have to disappoint her on that score."

"I'm not attending the Hermann soiree so that I can shop for a bride." Some new apprehension made the young veteran remember the handbill he still clutched, and he tried to tuck it into an inside coat pocket. "I wouldn't mind hearing advice tonight about where to finish law studies."

"Bravo, James Trezevant! I have proof that you're fully capable of parrying the topic in another direction, and I shall feel no guilt at being led away by two beauties at a time while you're engaged in debate on higher education." The carriage ceased rolling where a long line of vehicles made their way toward the only covered entry of Mr. Hermann's residence. "Anyway," Theo said offering Jamie a cigarette, which he then lit for himself. "It was just the news about Pleasant that Mother thought you might take badly. I told her you'd jolly well shrug it off, but you know how females are about such things and—"

"What happened to Pleasant?"

"Well…" Theo was smiling again, and he choked on a drag of smoke for a moment. "That's something like how I judge the prospect, but don't look so alarmed. He didn't sail off for a Waterloo on the Mexican coast like you did!" The passenger managing a cigarette could see he'd brought Jamie to the end of his patience. "Pleasant got married, that's the near sum of it. He's married, and my mother thought you might be a bit put off by the details, since it was to that flame of yours in Augusta, that Yvonne or—"

"Yvette Lachapelle?"

"Mrs. Yvette Goodnight now." Jamie was nowhere near crestfallen, but he was baffled.

"I had the impression she was interested in—probably in love with—an officer some years her senior."

"Interested in and betrothed to…wed to and widowed of, according to a letter from Pleasant last year." Looking relieved that the announcement caused no heartbreak, Theo tugged at his lower lip in an unconscious signal that he was about to speak frankly. "I know. It's just the shock of how much can happen in four years. I forget sometimes how our family first met you two Texas volunteers in Mobile. I never imagined at the time that I might have to carry on so soon without my father, much less how my mother might manage the loss."

"They grew up together, didn't they?" Jamie meant the elder Robinets, but he was also thinking that Pleasant and Yvette could entertain one another, given sufficient funds. He didn't expect much more candor from Theo, who was already taking in long puffs and watching a group of ladies scurry to the protection of an awning.

"I think my parents would have admitted quite readily that they never *fell in love*. They were just always part of one another's lives," he sighed. "Which would you choose, my good man," he asked, "a *fait accompli* or a *raison d'être?*"

Jamie had turned to take a look from his side of the carriage. A gown of deep violet stood out, and no observer would have been disappointed to note the pretty brunette with a matching tiara at the doorway.

"My parents must have shared deep affection. What I remember most is that they laughed together at little things. "

"That might be Emma MacDonald," Theo said, straining to see, "or the one in light blue. I can't make out her face. She has a younger sister and an unmarried aunt. Dash it all! Why couldn't we be in the carriage right behind theirs. You have no idea how handily I can carry a lady's parasol once she takes my arm."

"I suppose contentment is a Trezevant tradition," Jamie mused. "It might go all the way back to my great-grandparents. They were young sweethearts before coming across the Atlantic." He knew he was talking to himself, but he was trying to stay primed for convivial exchanges. Later that night, when he finally got home, he'd mull over his reaction to the wedding news. He honestly felt no loss about his first romantic fixation. And after surprise, he could feel nothing but good wishes for his former roommate.

"Tally-ho, Major James Trezevant, the rain has let up!" Theo rapped his knuckles against the coach door to alert the driver. "We can at least give these *demoiselles* an arm as they arrive, and those shoes of yours couldn't suffer further from drenching. The females will swoon that we made the sacrifice!" he laughed. "Besides," he said as they neared the group at the entryway, "I'll have Baptiste buy us each a new pair."

Jamie didn't mind being introduced that evening by his rank at retirement. The interior of Mr. Hermann's ballroom inspired formal decorum, and the aspiring attorney had no qualms about giving *Theodore* an equal nod of respect. The same ladies who'd giggled upon reaching shelter at the entryway reined in their exuberance as they entered the richly decorated salon. Three matching wool rugs covered one half of the gleaming floor, and their ornate midnight and ivory pattern denied attention to any guest's shoes. The other half of the grand room was open until a velvet rope cordoned off a small chamber orchestra. Couples gradually filled the dance floor. More than one guest holding a champagne glass whispered that only the wealthy host might dare the first waltz.

The spectacle was more entertaining than Jamie expected. If not for the violet gown, Jamie might have lost track of Theo in the mass of similarly suited gentlemen. One tan or gray waistcoat, one somewhat ruffled white shirt, one black or burgundy cravat looked much like any other suit. But the attractive brunette was often on Mr. Robinet's arm, and the youthful lady in a more muted blue was surely also eligible. The surrounding areas filled with guests too old or reticent to dance, and Jamie sensed a shift of onlookers toward one side hallway when Samuel Hermann did step conspicuously into a space nearest the music.

His companion, whose hand he held up before a lilting melody began, would doubtless be part of conversation for the rest of the evening. At least the host's age, she wore her hair in ringlets more suitable for academy girls. The top of her wine-colored gown edged close to her shoulders and dipped dangerously in front. Jamie heard a shocked woman behind him whisper, "Feathers!"

He then smiled back at a more composed lady, a guest who seemed as amused by gawkers as she was by individuals in the spotlight. Her own elegant brown dress took on a sheen in the candlelight and invited no such critique. When the aspiring lawyer looked again in her direction, she was already greeting a gray-haired matron. He was trying to remember names, having been introduced to two dozen couples and individuals since arriving with Theo.

The prospective *Mrs. Robinet* in violet was indeed Emma MacDonald, and Jamie was sure the petite guest glued to their side was her sister Fannie. He didn't now see the unmarried aunt in their family, but he recalled that woman's dismissive response to his bow. It was ill-advised to grin too much after meeting any woman, and he resolved to smile about her haughtiness, as well as Yvette's need for attention, only after he made it back home. While some revelers pressed in to get a better view of their host and his dancing partner, there was slow, opposite movement toward the wide corridors off the ballroom. Serious champagne drinkers headed that way, Jamie believed, as well as people interested in topics more weighty than the pedigree of a guest wearing too many feathers.

Out in the one hallway, another group balanced their glasses as they inched close enough to hear a grandly dressed foreigner switch back and forth from his native language to English. His brocade suitcoat suggested aristocracy, and Jamie was not surprised when a solemn gentleman identified the Frenchman as a Monsieur de Saligny, soon to represent his country in the new capital of Texas. In a disdainful voice, the dignitary held forth about lending money. The graying man who'd recognized the attaché leaned in toward those on the periphery and quietly spoke his mind.

"I don't care whether Texas fills its coffers with French money or a fortune from Timbuktu. As long as President Lamar convinces his country to make right on the land grants they owe our Georgia boys, I'll rest easy. Otherwise, even old friends won't escape lawsuit." Noise in the hallway died down, and Jamie judged from the older fellow's sorrowful expression that he'd not rest easy any time soon. "Pardon my lapse of manners," the man said. "I'm not used to these occasions in the last few years. I'm George Stovall, from outside Macon. There are still not too many attending parties out our way."

"So many in the Georgia Battalion came from there," Jamie said. What Macon had lost after executions at Goliad was well known in New Orleans and the entire South, if not the whole country. "I'm James Trezevant. Honored to meet you, sir." Still fixed on what de Saligny might be saying, the gentleman shook his hand, but he appeared not to recognize Jamie's surname.

"People who enjoy their pomp and festivities won't be faulted by me, though it was Mirabeau Lamar's nephew Basil who urged me to come tonight, since I'm passing through."

"You're on your way back to Macon?" Jamie hadn't heard the nephew's name since before battle at Refugio. Basil Lamar was one of the lieutenants who'd ridden off to inform Sam Houston about the battalion's precarious status.

"I usually have a few days stopover until there's a packet to Mobile and on back home. I probably would have kept to myself to prepare another few writs, but Hugh McLeod said he'd attend this evening. The general and I had some interest in sizing up the French diplomat but—"

"Mr. Stovall, pardon me…" It was the haughty MacDonald aunt, speaking in a much more solicitous tone. "Allow me to introduce a friend before you retire to some drawing room. This is Mrs. Mary Hicks Williams from outside Jackson." Jamie didn't mind that his own name had slipped her memory. When he presented himself, he found it natural to smile again at the pleasant woman in brown satin. "Mary's husband was a friend of a Mr. Greenleaf, a Mississippi landowner whose grandson perished along with your own son at Goliad and all those other poor boys." The Georgia man had a tired look, as if he'd survived this kind of introduction many times. Jamie knew it was not the proper moment for telling how he and a fortunate few had escaped the tragedy. After an awkward lapse, Mr. Stovall spoke.

"Mr. Williams shares in Georgia's sense of loss, I'm sure."

"My husband passed away before the year of the revolution, sir," the lady said. She had more than one type smile, Jamie noticed, and her large dark eyes conveyed sincerity as sympathy turned the corners of her mouth. "Mr. Greenleaf, though, is still residing in the Mississippi countryside. I do know that no March goes by but what he mourns his grandson Thomas Weeks."

"Oh, yes," Stovall said, "young Thomas, just a lad not much older than Sam Hardaway." Jamie could feel his cheeks flushing, and he hoped his beard was thick enough to hide the color of emotion. Thomas, at the Refugio battle, was the first in the battalion to perish. Sam had been with Jamie on the harrowing escape from Victoria. In the last two years, they had exchanged letters. Private Hardaway maintained his good cheer among Macon mourners, though in his last letter he'd spoken of his intent to try business in Montgomery. All this information, Jamie knew not to share during a champagne party. He didn't wish to inflame Mr. Stovall's grief or to elicit another dismissive response from the Mac Donald aunt.

"Surely every battalion family feels gratitude for your efforts, Mr. Stovall." Mary put her hand calmly on the gentleman's arm as she spoke.

"It's well and right to wave a 'liberty or death' banner," the bereaved father said. "So it shouldn't be hard for the living to compensate families of those who died serving. Of course, Mr. John Spillers in Knoxville was as deserving of his land grant, too, and his children have their papa back. And none in my home state wish dear Sam Hardaway anything but good outcomes in his future."

"I've heard nothing but praise in New Orleans for Ward's efforts, sir," Jamie heard himself say. His voice came from deep in his throat, and he was relieved that it didn't crack. "They had the most honorable intentions. It's certain their last days in Texas would have tested the endurance and faith of any soldier."

"God keep them, yes," Stovall murmured, his eyes moist. "Basil Lamar tells me the boys carried on without officers during that fight at Refugio. It was a nephew of mine and other sergeants commanding my boy and Sam and Thomas and the whole unit."

"Well, my goodness, bless them all." The conversation was taking far too maudlin a turn for Edith MacDonald. She'd made the most of her tenuous Goliad connection. "We shall never forget our lost Americans, of course, but I wonder," she said nodding in the direction of Saligny. "I'm curious whether our foreign friend over there knows how many conveniences he'll miss once he resides at an embassy in the wilds of Texas!"

Jamie didn't doubt she'd hear more disparaging predictions from "the count," as people were already calling him. George Stovall looked to have no stomach for the official's banter. After letting the New Orleans woman take his arm to briefly meet de Saligny, the gentleman headed on his own toward a less crowded anteroom.

Strains of a lively waltz started up from the ballroom, but Jamie kept gravitating toward a small courtyard off the grand entrance. He was thinking that he might take Theo up on a cigarette if the Robinet son were to appear near a solitary bench and tempt him again. He realized he'd missed the chance to say something more meaningful to the father of a lost comrade, as well as an occasion to offer help filing for promised compensation. His written reflections achieving greater clarity, he vowed to compose a letter to Sam Hardaway, asking him to forward belated sentiments to George Stovall.

"I'm so sorry, Mr. Trezevant." It was the Mississippi lady, and Jamie was glad he'd not yet taken the bench. "I didn't really wish Edith to bring up the loss of the Weeks family at such a lighthearted occasion. Mr. Greenleaf is one of my more jolly friends back home, except when he speaks the name Fannin and recalls his first grandson."

"And Miss MacDonald is another good friend of yours?"

"Not at all," she said. She smiled again, but she did not go on to critique the acquaintance. "The girls—Emma and Fannie—and their mother are friends of my in-laws. Mr. Williams had family in Louisiana as well as in Mississippi. They claim they invite me at this time of year because they're looking out for my social life. I am well aware that my real purpose is to chaperone their eligible daughters. I don't mind coming down the river once a year."

A cameo hung from a fine golden chain at her neck. In the shadows of the courtyard, her hair was the same hue as her gown. She was mature enough not to feel awkwardness at Jamie's shift in the topic, but they were both at ease without talk. A couple about to call for their coach appeared, and the husband asked for the time. Jamie was heartened to see that two hours had elapsed since his arrival. Mary Williams was studying him with a changed smile, but she waited to speak until the pair whisked themselves toward the entry.

"Did something fall from your pocket?"

"Oh, it's a portrait ad." He bent to pick up the folded page, and it seemed impolite not to open it momentarily as proof.

"You look so young," she said.

"So I was told at the time." It was a relief to smile at something, and he couldn't help laughing about the impression he'd once made on General Felix Huston. "I was told that my superior referred to me as *baby face*."

"West Point?"

"No," he said, "though I might have had such ambition if I hadn't felt called elsewhere."

"Another military academy?"

"In South Carolina, Columbia, until I left for Texas." He wanted to explain more. "I knew Mr. Stovall's son and nephew well. We were all in the same battalion, even the same company." Her eyes didn't leave him, and her expression grew more somber. She seemed to be assessing the recent hallway conversation in a different light, and her gaze included some new and grave conclusion. "It just didn't seem like the right time to say how I last remember them all."

"No," she said softly. "Such recollections are sacred."

A round of applause from the ballroom was followed by spirited opening measures, and moments later the younger MacDonald sister bounced into the courtyard.

"Mrs. Williams, there you are! Emma doesn't want you to miss Mr. Hermann doing a polka," Fannie said. "No one else this evening will be so bold, we're sure! Come on, James. Theodore says to find you, too, or you'll miss the spectacle!"

"Mr. Trezevant was just going to call my coach—"

"Oh, no! Sister said you might leave early, but…Oh well, you can tell Mama all about it, then. Be sure to say we witnessed Mr. Hermann do a polka with his lady-friend!"

The Dove Shall Fly

"Could you let Mr. Robinet know that I left early as well?" Jamie didn't think he could abide overhearing Count de Saligny foretell what hardships he'd endure in the new capital called Austin. He was already claiming he'd as soon set fire to a domicile made of logs as sleep in it. When the younger MacDonald daughter shrugged and dashed back to the ballroom, Jamie noticed that the stars were out and the threat of rain had entirely passed. "My state of mind will probably be improved by a long walk."

"Your friend Mr. Robinet might press you to stay and get better acquainted with more debutantes." She didn't appear wistful about having matured beyond that age. He liked her voice. Her confidence made him think of Charlotte asking him to name a flower by its fragrance. "I've known the MacDonalds since those two were little girls. I have a motherly affection for them, I suppose, not having any children of my own."

"I don't imagine you'd raise any daughters of your own to be so silly," he said. "Theo is a friend of a friend, just an acquaintance really."

Jamie didn't mind their long wait for the MacDonald's guest coach. Mary Williams asked him about his law studies and whether he'd considered returning to South Carolina to study. Accepting her offer of transportation, he didn't object to the crowded French Quarter thoroughfares, or that the lady from near Jackson insisted the driver take him beyond the Auberge Avignon to the plain boarding house closer to the wharf. She had time to ask him if he preferred Darien to New Orleans and, given the choice, if he might prefer life in a pastoral setting to the non-stop bustle of the city.

"I do try to stay in Jackson proper, during this time of year and in the spring when the windows can be opened wide, but…" Jamie rather enjoyed the seconds of quiet as she finished her thought. The polished coach came to a full stop, and he recognized the doorman, employed at the lodging only on weekends. The man began his shuffle toward the vehicle. "I suppose I prefer my small estate out closer to the Natchez Trace. It reminds me of my childhood. I never learned to ride myself, but I do love to see the horses at a gallop."

"I might come see Jackson one day," Jamie said.

"At least, come explore what our law school has to offer. Once you finish your degree, if you don't care to dive into all these dramatic disagreements over manumission and female property rights, you could inquire about a teaching post in town."

247

"I should look into that," Jamie said. "I will." He had stepped onto the cobblestone and was suffering a sudden pang about the finality of the evening.

"Major Trezevant?" The doorman, impressed by the gleam of the unfamiliar transport, had come all the way out to greet Jamie with elevated formality.

"You dropped your portrait ad again," the woman in the coach said. She leaned toward the window, and her swept-up hair changed from brown to dark blond as the gaslight quivered. She was holding out the folded page. "Don't you want your keepsake…Major?" A young lady might have posed the question as flirtation, but this woman's tone conveyed more kindness than playfulness.

"You might want your own portrait made, Mary Williams. You should keep the ad. I don't think the sketch looks much like me anymore."

"The artist got the eyes right. I'll recognize you when I see you again." She smiled in a way that no man would judge silly. James Peter Trezevant made a small bow as the carriage rolled away. He told the doorman that he needed to stretch his legs after so much standing in the ballroom and sitting in the carriage.

He couldn't look up at the moon until he'd walked a few blocks. It was a half sphere of yellow light, and he was struck by how life could play out for a man, even one just shy of his twenty-fourth birthday. Half breath-taking brightness and half deadly dark, that was how he might characterize his adult experience so far. Jamie knew the shadowy tangles of the Guadalupe River would continue haunting him without warning. He would never forget the icy ravines outside Goliad and the menacing creek-beds of Refugio where he'd scouted alone for escape routes. He would always have to brace himself for an encounter that might evoke comrades lost to their families in the hostile stretches of Texas.

But the moon above him, though partly visible, was whole. James Trezevant felt fortunate that his family had instilled in him an abiding hope. Dark as events could turn, light would come around fully as well. After the November soiree, he was less interested in what tomorrow's headlines might say about the new president of Texas than he was in finding some pamphlet about law study in Jackson. He was wondering what the Mississippi countryside near that growing town might look like in its deepest winter and in its first weeks of spring.

Chapter 17   To See What He Could See— Near Seguin, Texas, 1856

"If I had written my memoirs already, I would know how to make the story simple for Rosalia's students."

"She's a good teacher," Gertie reminded her husband. He'd been standing at the northwest window of their home in Floresville. A wagon from that quadrant of the Seguin's ranch was expected along the old Alamo Road. "Children always have questions. The morning will fly and you will wish you'd had more time."

"Tell me of grandparents who do not wish for more time." Juan hugged his wife. This visit from Señorita Mendez would be somewhat stressful because of the trip his own family intended to start the following morning—almost half the distance between San Antonio and the Rio Grande. But travel, they agreed, was now often its own reward. It was two days ride from the ranch they shared with Papi Erasmo, a widower since the year before, to a friend's cabin on the Nueces. There, they would meet with Antonia's family and see her youngest baby for the first time.

"I never thought our firstborn would live so far away, but she was already grown when we…left Texas," Gertie went on.

"You mean when I was chased out and you clung to my side."

"I should not bring up our time in Mexico, not this morning."

"I think," Juan said patting her shoulder, "if Antonia was not already a woman in her thinking that year, she grew up when we lived with hostility either side of the Rio Grande."

"And we could not have been more delighted when she found love." Lately, whenever Juan's wife spoke of happiness, she had to brush away tears. She assured him such emotions often came to older *señoras*. The three children still living with them would be their last. Seven of the Seguins' ten had survived and were flourishing. "Do you remember her letter, how many ferries she says now begin from the Nuevo Laredo side?"

"Santiago's first memories are of life across the border."

"Even to travel only halfway there, he will take in our trip more than his little sisters," Gertie agreed, brightening. "What a blessing that Teresa still dotes on Papi and wishes to stay. She easily keeps him from melancholy. We will be absent only two weeks." They could not allude to Erasmo without thinking a prayer for Juan's departed mother. "What a comfort, too, that Rosalia agrees to stay in our house and keep the candelabra lit." They'd stopped lighting candles for the dedicated teacher to find a husband. She had followed Alberto's parents from Brazoria to Floresville, where a cluster of families worked the established Seguin ranch on its perimeters. Retirement from teaching seemed never to tempt *la maestra*.

"When you live long enough, you witness many kinds of contentment." Juan was thinking of Rosalia when he spoke, but he might have made the same comment in appreciation of improved Texas trails. Regular coach transport kept paths worn smooth and easy to follow.

As he moved chairs into a circle near the fireplace, he was trying to remember a time when it could take almost a week to accomplish just the twenty miles from San Antonio to the Medina River. Now, the clear passageway that went in both directions, southwest and northeast from the city, was so well traveled that livery stations made help no farther away than an hour-long walk. A merchant could boast in 1856, that he'd gone from Laredo on the American side to Nacogdoches seven times in one calendar year. Juan still awoke sometimes feeling shock that it was now the state Texas—not the country—that people moved to from every other part of the nation.

"I will begin my memoir with my great-grandfather's adventure , what it was like in the 1700's to bring a family from Mexico's interior to the wild northern outpost called Bexar."

"You will know how to start your story," Gertie said, placing a hand on his shoulder, "but if you pace these tiles any longer, your first sentence must start with how we built our house next to your parents only two years ago. *Tu mamá*, she lived to see it take shape. This beginning will also remind you not to wear the floor down to caliche as you think and write. " They both looked to the window where Santiago had just made an odd sound.

"Who is following Miss Mendez? It's a smaller wagon that's just barely keeping pace with her—"

"More students than she expected?"

The Dove Shall Fly

"No passengers that I can see. There are two black men on the driving bench and no one else," their son said. "Is the Mc Cullochs' nephew old enough to have a beard?" He was stroking his own bare upper lip and chin when his parents came to the window.

"Perhaps she asked for an escort." Even that reason meant a troubling development of some kind. "The five youngsters she promised us are in her wagon. Their parents might have hired Sam to take the children home this afternoon. I don't see Alberto's older boy."

In the open living space of Juan's and Gertie's one-story house, adults in the gathering avoided direct inquiry about Samuel Mc Culloch's presence when the guests entered. Despite his welcome status as a neighbor, the explanation of his sudden visit was bound to be unsettling. This rancher's youngest nephew looked boyish even with facial hair, but he was as adept as the others at keeping any disturbing topic from the children. The *niños* bubbled with excitement from the excursion and detected no tension in the voice of their teacher or their host.

"With our famous neighbor Mr. Mc Culloch here, I must start my recollections this morning with the Battle of Concepción!" Juan announced. The Seguins had three good wells on their property, and spring water was served with the *polvorones* that Gertie and Teresa made the day before. Ready to retrieve cinnamon crumbs from the shiny floor, Maria and Lupe handed out napkins.

"As you should, *amigo*," Sam nodded. "Without us two and a few other independence fighters, it might be no revolution would have started." The nephew couldn't subdue his pride.

"And your participation, uncle, meant you kept your liberty rights all those years later, whilst other black people in Texas—"

"This is correct!" Juan exclaimed. "His reward was slow in coming, as it often is for those who fight for freedom." Relieved to have his misstep redirected, the younger neighbor nodded. The hardships suffered by black residents of Texas were not a topic for children. Who knew for certain how the discussion of slavery unfolded in the homes of Rosalia's students? Samuel McCulloch's recognition in the state as a *free black* was rare and precarious.

Before statehood, the republic had made its law clear—any person of African descent who possessed manumission documentation had a window of time to depart Texas altogether, or else be detained and sold like any other slave within its borders. Only Mr. McCulloch's proven participation in the first battle of the revolution eventually gave him a winning edge in his appeal. Juan would never forget that 1842 was the year he, too, had been forced to flee Texas, in his case by newcomers ill-informed about the patriotism of brown-skinned Spanish speakers.

While Señorita Mendez gave a short review of Texas history and a reminder about respectful attention, Sam quietly pulled their host aside and confirmed Juan's assumption of trouble.

"Our smallest wood shed was put to crackling flames before daybreak this morning. It woke us up. We both heard boyish laughing, so it's not likely any organized raid from the city." He wiped a bead of sweat from his brow. His hair was now grayer than Juan's.

"Just young hooligans, turning the cooler weather into cold-hearted plans."

"Still, Juan. It seemed like I oughta ride out to let y'all ponder it."

"I'll send word for Felipe to come in from the range, as well, and ride patrol over your way. If you come across him first, let him know."

"Can't these young'uns apply their minds and bodies to passable work?" Sam wondered. "Some city folk don't know a lick about how to rein in their own children."

"Too many citizens our age are the ones stirring up spiteful action," Juan pointed out. He was glad to see his neighbor. The McCullochs' land holdings were not as extensive as the expanse the Seguins owned, but they had maintained the same ranch for four generations. "I am no longer the magistrate even of Floresville, but I will talk to San Antonio's mayor when we return from the Nueces. Trouble has always found a way to bubble up on the outskirts of town."

"Not like the trouble we found brewing long ago at Concepción," Sam added. How very long ago the threat from Santa Anna's brother-in-law seemed. In that earliest clash, he and Juan could not have predicted the rapid surrender of Bexar by General Cos.

"And nothing like the terror we used to suffer from Comanche renegades." Travelers faced little risk these days along the stage coach route the Seguins would follow, but the danger of attack was not impossible. For many years, any Indians determined to roam the vast, harsh wilderness of west Texas—rather than relocate to Oklahoma—were left to their nomadic habits.

If both men were considering one final comment about the crying shame of thankless white boys, they thought better of making any statement an innocent child might quote.

As two Seguin wagons pulled out the next morning, the new layer of worry could not be turned down easily like a bedcover. It was not fair that a family of their neighbors' reputation should suffer any such indignities. In Floresville, though, and even in the town just north named for Juan, acts of hatred could occur with no provocation. He and his wife consoled themselves that the burning shed would not likely bring on further acts of enmity. A new provocation was usually followed by a breathing space. By that logic, news of the Mc Cullochs' distress gave the couple an extra measure of ease about the security of Papi Erasmo's ranch. The flare-up in hostility robbed them of some natural joy, however, and they fixed their attention on their own three children as their travel wagons made progress.

"Santiago! Stay within sight as you lead the way!" Juan had no real fear that their sixteen-year-old would wander into trouble up ahead, but he shared Gertie's need for special reassurance. "The boy reminds me of myself as a youth, all confidence and independence."

"How proud our son looks riding scout, as you soldiers say." She kept her arm linked in his as he handled the reins. "Though it is best perhaps, husband, that you and I call him a *young man* from now on." The jiggling of the wagon had lulled their daughters into an early nap, but their parents' voices awakened them. They would soon be scrambling to look out the front opening of the rocking vehicle and to wave at Pablo, in control of the *cocina* wagon behind them. "See how straight and with what dignity Santiago rides," she said. "Si, even more than José and Juan at that age, he reminds me of you."

"A young man setting out to make his mark in the world."

"At least, as you always did, setting out *to see what he can see.*"

"Shh," Juan teased. "The girls will sing that song five hundred times before we stop for the night." It was good to laugh while holding the reins. "Now you make me think of bears, *mi corazón*, but we are not likely to see any so far from the great forests. I am thankful that you have a beautiful voice, if we take up serenades as a pastime on this trip."

"Let the girls look for all the other animals we might catch sight of."

In two hours, Maria and Lupe had spotted three jackrabbits, a scurrying coyote, tan lizards that blended in at first with jagged rocks, a band of scorpions crossing the road single file, and a quick gray animal they guessed to be a large rat or a small armadillo. Santiago paused to school his siblings on the habits of the shelled creatures, which he felt certain would dwell somewhat closer to a water source and protective foliage. A friendly debate arose about whether giant mounds of fire ants could be counted. They were in scrub mesquite country, but Juan pointed out a cougar lounging on the lower limb of a live oak that marked the merging of their cross-path and the better defined Camino Real. Gertie's suggestion that her daughters sketch the animals and make the pages into a book kept the youngest Seguins occupied until a stagecoach going the same direction passed them up.

"You goin' all the way to Laredo?" the coach driver asked. He had six passengers who already appeared exhausted from the cramped quarters.

"Only as far as the Nueces," Juan called back. "We have relatives meeting us there!"

"Makin' camp tonight at the Frio water hole?"

"*Si*, if we can find it."

"It's mighty near the main path, and the trail going off to it is almost as clear as this here road."

"There used to be mustangs roaming up this far," Juan said nodding.

"Now-a-days they mostly stay south of the Nueces." The coach driver held up several strands of leather as an indication he was about to spur on the team pulling his load. "Likely they fear runnin' smack into some collision on this busy route. Times have changed, *señor!*" The coach lurched, and the speed with which the vehicle pulled away startled the Seguins.

"Don't have a collision up ahead with that young man on horseback!" Juan shouted. "He is ours! He is learning to scout!"

Juan went with Santiago to investigate a small stand of trees before stopping there for a midday meal. A patch of dense brush at some distance was a good spot for the travelers to relieve themselves, but it had to be checked for snakes that might have already claimed privacy there. Pablo was still experimenting with skillet bread that the Seguin children had acquired a taste for. He fretted that he'd put too much water in the cornmeal batter, but he'd also brought tortillas. Nothing diminished his savory rice and beans.

He wouldn't hear of accepting help from Gertie, and she was pleased to have relief from cooking duties. Out on the open range, any man who claimed expertise in meal preparation was free to take that task from her. A lone hawk practicing its gliding limits held her and the girls transfixed. The rustle of autumn brush accompanied bird calls and their conversation. During their stop, three carriages rumbled past going toward San Antonio, and a feed wagon moved more slowly in the family's direction. Behind it, four Texas Rangers directed their horses at a trot, and the last man finally touched his hat brim in response to Maria's waving.

When the Seguins started up for the second leg of the day's distance, Juan let Gertie take the reins while he dozed next to her. Creaking wheels heightened a sense that silence itself was the dominant being in these parts, a huge, authoritative creature that stretched its body to the west and south. The girls were soothed into a long siesta, and Juan's wife convinced him to recline fully in the bed of the wagon for real rest. The unusual gathering at their home the day before had worn him out, and she knew he would stay up that night to take turns at watch with Pablo and Santiago. When her husband came to and took his position on the driving bench, Gertie supposed he must have been dreaming significant passages in his memoir.

"Off to the east, is where the other road from San Antonio picks up. We at the Alamo had such hopes that Fannin's army was marching our way."

"Where the sun comes up tomorrow morning, that is the way to Goliad?"

"I knew when Colonel Travis sent me one last time to Gonzales, to ask for help…" Her reflex was to pat his leg or arm or shoulder whenever he spoke of his last conversation with Alamo defenders. "I knew even then that…though some additional men might come…enough help would not be possible."

"I am glad that you've decided to write your recollections. Your family is so proud. It will always be so."

Juan made a laugh that was not his usual kind. She wanted him to write down his understanding of the revolution, what came before and after. But she understood there would be times during the project when her husband's laughter would give her a chill, like the shiver that first hail brings on. From time to time, he might scoff like one who drinks tequila long past a wise stop. She believed, though, that putting bitterness onto paper helped to dilute its power. She would feel her own grudges disappear, she knew, when her husband grew able to think of his service to Texas without any derisive chuckle.

"They sent me from the Alamo, because they knew it would be harder for Santa Anna's patrols *to distinguish me* and my men from loyal

Mexican troops." Juan made that odd little laugh, and then he spat, a crude American custom that she knew not to disparage at the rare times her husband's reflex went so far. "And only six years after defeating the dictator at San Jacinto…" He spat a second time. "Then I am hounded south across the Rio Grande by my fellow Texans, because it is so hard *to distinguish me* and my family from traitors loyal to Mexico."

Up ahead, Santiago had turned to point to the sky. Gertie called the girls to the front of the wagon, and the children looked up in time to see a great crane flapping aloft in slow elegance, its legs extended behind as if floating on a current. They all kept their exclamations to themselves and held their breath long enough to hear the *whoosh whoosh* of its wings treading air. The bird was a sign that river water might not be too far off, and their anticipation of a hospitable campsite grew.

Only by chance, a few hours later, did Juan have his eyes already fixed on Santiago. There were occasional dips in the land where a stream turned off from a river, and his son's horse was taking on the illusion of lost height. The family scout, though, suddenly brought his mount to a halt. He was even faster at spinning the horse into a reverse and beginning a canter back toward the Seguin wagons. Anything out of the ordinary might have spurred the youth into action, but the experienced soldier handling the team in front had seen that maneuver before, in battle. He hushed the girls, and Gertie was quick to reach for a rifle that lay in the floorboard near their feet. When they singled out the word *Comanche* from whatever their son was shouting, nausea struck so quickly that they both wished they'd been fasting for a day.

"How many? How many?" Juan called out. The answer meant the difference between taking cover under the wagons or meeting the threat armed, but otherwise as they were.

"Just one that I can see!" Santiago needed to catch his breath before going on. "He's wearing a vest that shade of blue you told me to watch for. Anyone can see he's an Indian, with such long hair, but his hat looks bent out of shape on purpose, and there are blue feathers dangling from it. He looks fierce, so there could be more down by the river."

"Maybe an ambush," the man in charge said. More than one hostile tribe was known to use that tactic. If they sent a single warrior ahead calmly, he could put the victims off guard before initiating an all-out attack. Juan shuddered at the possibility that the recent posse of Rangers might be already hanging upside down by the riverbank or partly buried next to ant mounds.

The Dove Shall Fly

When the Indian came into view, they didn't take his posture as either convincing evidence of threat or comforting proof otherwise. The fearless individual brought his palomino to a stop, but the nimble horse refrained from nibbling grass. Santiago was right. The stranger's vest was a bright blue distinct to the Comanche, who prided themselves in use of wildflower dyes. The rest of his attire—leggings, homespun shirt, moccasins, *vaquero* hat—suggested alignment with no one culture.

Allowing their wagons to roll slowly forward, the Seguins readied themselves for clearer signals from the rider facing them. He was not old, Juan judged, though he had encountered many Tonkawa and Caddo whose elders never grayed. Whatever the man's age, though, his demeanor was enough to make Santiago stay by his father's side. It was perhaps Juan's consideration of history in the last few days that made him less fearful of the lone Indian than in awe of him. Comanche had become adept nomads since the year the Spanish first brought horses to the continent. The people called Comanche were fierce survivors well before any European even imagined sailing west across the ocean. The Seguins and the stranger were close enough to study one another's faces, and the stranger made a sweeping gesture with the hand not holding a rifle.

"*Buenas tardes*," the Indian said. "If you mean to stay overnight by the Little Frio, I will take you. We have only two hours before the sun goes behind the river trees."

"*Buenas tardes*."

"I am making my last watch of the road before dark," the rider went on. "The wagons I am leading already make their camp."

"Si, the Little Frio." While Juan spoke, Gertie kept the rifle perfectly still in her lap.

"My name is Youruh," the man said, placing his weapon in its sling. He allowed his eyes to follow the sound of another *whoosh whoosh* overhead. This was a small sign of trust, and Juan knew it would be an insult not to reciprocate.

"I am Juan Seguin. We are going as far as the Nueces tomorrow to visit other family, but *si*, we are ready to rest for the night."

"I know your name," the Comanche nodded. "You were once mayor of San Antonio." He backed up his horse, so that he could ride alongside the wagon seat. With duplicity looking less likely, the parents and their children began to relax again.

"Twice I was in charge of that great city," Juan said. "And my father before was an alderman and then postmaster." The man named Youruh appeared to be mulling something over, and Juan felt a prickle of apprehension again.

"We will not speak of the disaster there that killed so many chiefs. Since then, the buffalo have left these plains and more than a dozen autumns have fled into the past. " Though Juan was not in the Council House the day in 1840 when soldiers cut down Comanche leaders, the catastrophe would fill a dark page in anyone's memoir. He could not offer adequate condolence. "Instead, we will talk of your family now waiting for you near the Nueces. The Germans that I bring to the country of hills, they visited last night with travelers from Laredo. I think, Señor Seguin, those people are your daughter and your son-in-law and your grandchildren."

"You met my sister?" Santiago could not keep from asking. "They're already at the Nueces? You talked with Antonia?" The Indian guide was not exactly smiling, Juan noted, but there was a change in his eyes that showed him fully responsive to humor.

"The dark-haired *madre* from Laredo did not say her brother could form questions so quickly. She did not tell me your sentences are like the changing song of a mockingbird." The Seguins were inclined to trust the stranger who conversed so easily with Santiago. "At the Nueces, Señora Antonia did speak of you to my German friends, the Kuempels. She said her little brother was almost a grown man with far more answers than questions."

"She said that?" They all felt a surge of relief from the guide's fresh acquaintance with their daughter's people.

"She and her husband spoke of her worries about Nuevo Laredo, across the Rio Grande," Youruh elaborated. "This Mexican town is where her children breathe in freedom, but she says it needs a wise leader. Her brother should move there one day, she told my German *amigos* last night, and take the reins as mayor." Their chaperone gestured toward a string of trees now visible along the edge of the small tributary. The two wagons were ready to follow him. "Ambition is maybe in your blood," he said to Santiago.

The campfire ending that day's travel proved unforgettable to both families. None of the Kuempels spoke much Spanish or easy English. The elderly couple's two balding sons rephrased in amended German whatever Youruh used to interpret the Seguins' conversation. Their own English had improved during Rosalia's efforts to teach her students language versatility. After their guide explained that his name meant "thank you" in Comanche, he conceded that his native tongue was very rarely in demand. Instead, he sat between the heads of the two families and reshaped English or Spanish phrases into German and back.

Maria and Lupe eventually convinced their mother to join them in "The Bear Went Over the Mountain," a song Rosalia taught every year. The Kuempels clapped enthusiastically. Then, though it would be several weeks before Christmas carols ordinarily came to mind, Youruh wondered if they all might know a version of "Silent Night." The group went three rounds of the familiar strains, once in English, once in Spanish, and once in German.

When the Indian chaperone explained that there had never been a version in Comanche, he obliged them with a heartfelt rendition of a chant he remembered from his earliest days. With the firelight accentuating his smooth, wide brow, it grew clearer that he was still a young man. His fearless demeanor, Juan thought, had discouraged close scrutiny before he began his rhythmic song. The fellow's gaze, as he intoned mysterious syllables, fixed on the starry sky. Heinrich Kuempel's wife wiped away a tear at the sorrowful incantation, and the Seguin family was equally affected, especially since Youruh had mentioned his sudden separation from all relatives as of the 1840 disaster. For a time, a German doctor in San Antonio looked after him. Then he was taken to Austin by a man from Mississippi. Soon after, he found himself at home with an older Tonkawa who ferried the Colorado. He counted himself lucky to have friends "from every corner of the creation."

His comment left the entire group in a reflective mood, and the pause in conversation allowed attention to the waning fire. By its light, both Kuempel sons could be seen stifling yawns and loosening their suspenders, while their parents murmured to each other in guttural syllables. The Seguin girls leaned in toward their mother and closed their eyes. Though the Comanche appeared naturally alert, Santiago might have been digging his fingernails into the palms of his hands to stay awake. Juan was guessing that in another half hour only he and Pablo, as well as the watchful chaperone in the other family's employ, would be keeping guard.

"This reminds me of many times I have shared a campfire with friendly strangers," he quietly told his wife. "With the fighting and the burning that comes to *every corner of creation* from time to time, perhaps I should start my memoirs with just such a scene." Juan could tell she was listening well enough to be forming a response.

"Tell me of someone in Texas whose day has never started or ended with the calm of a campfire."

"Even at times when peace is nowhere in sight, talk among wanderers can be like the healing touch from above."

"*Si, mi corazón,*" Gertie said, and he was moved by the term of endearment that he used in addressing her.

"I have told you of a campfire one day, on the far bank of the Brazos, a gathering only days before the glory at San Jacinto." While Juan spoke, Youruh moved his gaze regularly from the fire to the perimeter of the resting site. No direction seemed to elicit the hired guard's concern. It had occurred to the former mayor of San Antonio that opening pages set in that city might put off many readers. Descendants of Moses and Stephen Austin would rue the early demise of both visionaries, each of whom had made trips to the mission city on behalf of potential colonists. Any Texans related to men who'd laid down their lives at the Alamo would hesitate to read much in a memoir that began with Bexar. And now, he had been reminded, any kin to the Comanche could not entirely subdue their grief over the decimation of their leaders in that city. "I could start my recollections with a fire that gave some comfort and hope to strangers in sore need. Not one of us knew who would win the revolution, only the Almighty. But spirits from the Alamo and from Goliad had surely wandered to the banks of the Brazos. I felt them asking if those of us under General Houston would bravely march into the afterlife in the great fight for freedom."

"You have told me before of this meeting among wanderers…families on the run, as well as lost soldiers." Gertie gave her husband's arm a hug. "The one private you found was skin and bones. He and the other Americans were hunted by General Urrea's scouts, no?"

"I still feel pain when I think that I almost left him at the riverbank."

"Without another horse for him, what else could you do?" she said. "In times of war, this is the question ringing every day like a sad bell. What else can a person do?"

"If the American soldier and I had not crossed paths with the woman and her family—"

"The women who gave you and the Goliad man an extra horse. I remember, Juan. This is what saved the weak soldier, *si?*"

"I thought, at first, she was possibly Emily West, because she had dark skin and she was hauling water, in a way that looked to be her own idea—" His memories infused them both with new energy, and Gertie sat up straighter, so she could see his face.

"Si, this is the part I love so, husband, and now I know how this evening made you think to start your memoir with that day near the Brazos."

"The woman was not Emily West," Juan said, though his wife knew the story. "And even before she began answering us in French—she was right to speak anything but English at first—but before her French words, I could see that no, she was no spy trying to blend in with other brown-skinned people in the fight against Santa Anna. She was only there to protect her family." He nodded again as if he were now imagining the first page of his life story. "If I start with these Georgia women, then it will be easier to write my chapter about being beaten in Bastrop. A worst thing after the revolution happened there, but it was also where I was healed at a campfire tended by the same women—Yarico and Señorita Adeline."

"Yarico—" Gertie had barely repeated the name, when Youruh sprang up from the clearing and stalked off into darkness to the east.

He departed without explanation, alarming the entire gathering. Language differences made it difficult for the grown men to decipher one another while the women and children scurried to the shelter of their wagons.

"An animal is what he hears, perhaps," Mr. Kuempel suggested. "He can kill a beast in the dark?"

"I heard *nada*, nothing," Juan said, trying to let the Indian's direction bolster his own optimism. Had the man headed west, a lurking band bent on ambush would have seemed more likely.

"Some very big cat?" one German son said to the men while his brother searched for words. "Zee wolf can eat people, yes?"

"One cat wouldn't attack, and we would have heard a wolf pack," Juan explained for his daughters' sake and Santiago's. Heinrich Kuempel shook his head as he struggled with English.

"This walking away, Mr. Youruh did this before. When we started our trip, it is open country, like this, with nothing to see…Only one time, he leads our wagons past where the cotton is growing. Suddenly, he walks off. And after we travel past, to more country with nothing, when he returns, he says…*so sorry*. He tells that he walks when he is angry or sad or… Only this brings his feet to where his mind wants to be."

"Maybe it was something I said, but I was only telling my wife about a Goliad soldier…and about a woman who spoke French at first." The German men didn't seem to understand the term Goliad, and they all shrugged from worry and frustration.

"All this is what I know," the immigrant father finally continued. "When our cousin here in Texas says to come for land to farm and for sheep, he marks a line under one name. He writes, *ask for Mr. Youruh* to bring your wagons safe, to near San Antonio. If he takes you the long way, no worries. *Das ist gut.* Wait only for Mr. Youruh. He is our honest friend."

"I wondered why he didn't take you more directly north from Velasco," Seguin said absently.

"So difficult with too many rivers. So many—how do you say?—obstacles where they are building the railroad." One son's English was surprising. His brother finally formed a comment.

"Too many cotton fields."

Mr. Kuempel's sons declared they were competent to stand guard, but there was no sign of Youruh during their watch or later when Santiago took a short turn. Juan could hear no evidence of predatory beasts nearby. The Seguins' hitching teams and their single horses rested peacefully, as did the animals the Kuempels had tethered for the night. If any band of hostile Mexicans or Indians had been creeping up on the campsite, the veteran military man heard none of the telltale chirps and clicks that preceded an attack. All was so serene that Youruh's sudden appearance on the other side of the glowing logs completely surprised Juan. He felt as if the Indian had appeared on the command of some pagan deity.

"I walked a far distance into the dark," he said. "I am very sorry."

"It's a good way to calm down, but I do it myself only in daylight if I have the choice." Juan was relieved to see the Kuempels' chaperone lower his body in one movement to a squatting position. For several minutes, both men sat silent, watching small flames and the red and orange embers.

"You spoke two names that touch my heart, Señor Seguin. There is perhaps only one Yarico known in all of Texas…in all of creation." Nothing but a slight movement from the Tejano conveyed reaction to the startling explanation. "And to speak of Adeline in the same sentence is to make their identification certain."

"You know Yarico and Adeline?"

"It is because of them that I know as much French as Spanish," Youruh said, nodding. "Languages fall on their ear like music."

"I didn't realize Señorita Adeline knew French, too, but of course—"

"Miss Adeline was, not like my mother, but a *tante* while I stayed with Grandfather Walk Far. Even though I am Comanche, the old Tonkawa makes me feel I belong with him." Juan was beginning to understand the Indian's particular revulsion at the sight of slaves in cotton fields. If Yarico had been as kind to an orphaned Indian as she'd been to an injured Tejano, Youruh would have found it impossible to stomach slavery.

"And you know of Yarico, her kindness and her knowledge."

"She is mother of the woman who has my heart." The Comanche's statement washed away all of Juan's reserve, except for his hope the man wouldn't inquire about any Tejano connection to enslaved workers. Despite universal denunciation of Santa Anna as barbaric during the revolution, the dictator had outlawed slavery in Texas before his demise. How could some Americans now, Juan wondered—even those in the North—claim no dependence at all on the cruel institution? Everyone wearing cotton clothing bore some guilt in the practice that God was bound to end one day.

"You have a betrothed? Yarico had a daughter?"

"*Ma chérie* lives with Adeline's family. It will be so until the day we can marry. Perhaps I will be as gray as you are, señor, but I will wait." Juan wished that Gertie were sitting at his side. She would be able to talk through all these facts with complete understanding and compassion.

"But, then, where is Yarico?"

"To the north, in Ohio, with her husband Gerard. My heart, Adelphine, stayed with them for ten autumns. I will always call her *Bright Hair*. Then she came back down the Mississippi with Mr. Whitmire one year." Juan Seguin heard himself make a sound of recognition. "She lives with the Whitmire family…Shelby and Adeline…and their children." Like a page from his finished book, the scene at the first inauguration replayed in Juan's mind—a widow named Angelina who prepared a daily dinner line, her handyman Shelby who'd been handy as a medic.

"Shelby Whitmire," he repeated, as if he were reciting a phrase from a pleasing dream.

"When I first came under his care, I called him *Tassel Man*. He wore gifts from a Cherokee, a life friend from his home place." Juan listened without commenting, worried that an appeal for more detail might send the Kuempels' guide off on another introspective hike.

"Twenty years ago, when so many gathered to see President Houston sworn in," he cautiously began, "I had the feeling the lady Angelina would find another husband."

"Mr. Whitmire tells me she was happy as Mrs. Eberly. So sad when the captain took a deadly spill from his new horse. That sorrow came before my time."

"Terrible. But you say Yarico does have a husband—"

"They had to slip away up to the north. Mr. Whitmire took them. It was not safe that time to take her daughter…the little girl with green eyes, hair like first light. She stayed with Adeline. A year or two later, when Shelby and Adeline had wedding rings, no one challenged them about the girl both dark and dawn, so cheerful attending to them."

Juan was hoping he could remember this whole story. Then it occurred to him that the Comanche, Youruh, might not have pieced together so many spoken sentences in years, that maybe the undulating sound of his voice had gently awakened not just Gertie but everyone in both travel groups. Juan thought maybe no one on the banks of the Little Frio that night would forget the poignant tale the extraordinary man had revealed.

"Yarico's daughter was not content to stay in the North with her parents?"

"One day on this earth…" The man in the blue vest first shook his head, and then he answered resolutely, "Bright Hair will take me as her husband. She has said these words and I have memorized the visions." Juan nodded, though he had grave doubts about the acceptance in Texas of such a marriage, the union of a woman understood to be a slave and an orphaned Comanche. Youruh seemed to wait for this much hope to sink in. "The Great Father of all creation will see that it is so."

Back on the Camino Real going southwest the following day, the Seguins made progress without conversing much. They had sung all their songs and observed a variety of animals and waved to passersby going in both directions. Juan and Gertie, along with their three youngest children, directed their thoughts as well as they could to the family reunion ahead. What continued to intervene, though, were recollections of the previous night's company. The German family made an impression, and all hoped for their safe arrival in the immigrant community just outside San Antonio. Surely the path they intended to take— around the western and northern edge of the city, before curving back around to the east—would circumvent the kind of conflict that had arisen recently near the Seguin ranch.

But the Comanche man, the individual named Youruh, left the greatest impression. Even Maria and Lupe had heard their father speak of the Harper women, his first meeting with them on the dangerous banks of the Brazos twenty years before. Even Juan's parents, while his mother still lived, had heard him tell of the beating he took after the revolution from strangers in Bastrop, followed by the restorative care that a Miss Yarico and a Miss Adeline provided him.

Whenever Juan heard Gertie sigh or move her head from side to side, he supposed she might be replaying the Comanche's parting words to their Santiago. The Indian was a grown man, serious in the way he carried himself but occasionally tipping his hand to a more playful nature.

"Your sister has said you should become the mayor of Nuevo Laredo when you make your future." Youruh had made this statement to Santiago after shaking his hand the same way he'd formalized departure with the boy's father. "But among us backwards people," he went on, waiting for the group to acknowledge his ironic tone, "only strong signs can prove any vision of the future to be true."

"What signs?" Santiago had wanted to know.

"Will you see orange clouds in the middle of the day? Will you see baby rabbits chasing a low-flying hawk? Will you see a campfire spring up from the dirt where no wood was gathered?"

"Will I?" the Seguins' son wanted to know. Ever since hearing his own name and the word *mayor* in the same sentence, the youth felt his energy and his ambition wrapped into one. "That means I will follow in the footsteps of my father and my grandfather?"

"Is it not a sign that through me you know what your sister has said, before you reach your meeting with her at the Nueces?" Youruh concluded talk with this cryptic question. He then led the Kuempels on in the direction of San Antonio, and left every member of the Seguin family with a stinging sense of his absence.

Santiago remained out in front on this next travel day, and his parents wondered when they saw his hand move up to his face, if he'd needed to erase evidence of overpowering emotion. Juan and Gertie did not need to remind each other that the trip's momentous developments could be shared later. After so many years together, they understood that each day culminated in embraces and confidential musings. Had they spoken then, they would not have been surprised by mutual recollection—how Santiago had come to a stop and done an about-face upon first sighting the Comanche.

In the afternoon of the second day, when Santiago abruptly halted up ahead, it seemed as if he had decided to enact again his initial observation of Youruh.

It took a full minute for the Seguins to conclude he was not playing out the meeting that had defined their first night away from home. With eerie stillness, the sixteen-year-old paused on a rise where the land surely dipped before him. But something had so riveted his attention that he could not even reverse his horse's direction and ride back to the wagons with a report. Juan and Gertie saw him finally remove his black felt hat, a finishing touch to his style that he ordinarily took great care to protect. They thought he might wave the finely made hat while shouting back to them, but the boy never turned. When he let the piece of apparel fall from his fingertips, his parents had no power to tamp down their apprehension. As they had done the day before, they could only allow their two wagons to move ahead, if somewhat more slowly.

Even when they rolled up behind Santiago, their son was unable to turn around and greet them. Whatever he observed held him spellbound, as if averting his gaze might extinguish existence itself. His parents' wagon and then Pablo's came to the edge of the slight rise and dip. No adults were able to utter a word. Only Maria and Lupe, whose world was still the domain of discovery, allowed themselves to shout in glee.

"Camels! Camels! It's camels, Mamá! Look!"

"Papá! Señor Pablo! Camels!"

Two dozen camels, pairs roped together in single file, lurched steadily toward the west. The shaggy animals and their guides on horseback were now equidistant from the Frio tributary and the wide Nueces. Most of the ungainly creatures bore tall bundles on their humps, though one pair enjoyed a rest from carrying supplies. Occasionally, one groaned and the others responded in raucous, wheezing grunts. Their most recent drink could have been from any river or spring back east, but there was no misjudging the scarcity of water in western Texas. Juan Seguin— retired colonel from the army of Texas, former mayor of San Antonio and Floresville, fourth generation native of Bexar territory—had never witnessed the like. As with anyone else raised in this hemisphere, he knew about the existence of such humped beasts only from books.

He knew that he and Gertie would talk long into the night about the possibility that camels might prove superior to railroads for westward transport. Investors often visualized iron track connecting Texas to the Pacific, but Juan was recalling talk years ago about testing such animals for the journey. He'd dismissed the suggestion as drunken bar talk.

Now, he was relieved that his family would reach the friendly cabin on the Nueces before nightfall, and it wouldn't really matter if excitement stole sleep from all in the reunion. It was soon clear how their son Santiago had interpreted the extraordinary sighting. The boy might not go to bed during the entire ten day visit.

"When we see Antonia, I will tell her!" he shouted. He'd finally turned to his parents. "I'll let her know I'm coming to Nuevo Laredo in a few years! We will all go across the border, so you can see me become mayor!"

"Don't shout, Santiago," his mother said. "Don't scare the desert beasts."

"This is better than an orange sky in the middle of the day! It is a new sign, Mamá. Papá, even you will agree that this is a very strong sign!"

"It is a sign both new and old," Juan Seguin mused. He was still undecided about where to start his memoir, though he was leaning toward that first campfire with the Harper women and the private named Trezevant. He had no doubt that his children would want him to conclude with the sighting of camels in 1856, en route to the Nueces. He could imagine his little daughters, grown one day, but even then asking as they read their father's pages when the part about the camels would come in. He could imagine his darling wife Gertie, *mi corazón*, reminding them that they must wait until the end.

If Youruh could wait years and years for Bright Hair, Juan Seguin told himself, his descendants could keep hope ablaze until the end of his story and the beginning of their own.

Chapter 18   Again at a Riverbank—Austin, Texas, 1869

The first two weeks of October in Austin had seemed no cooler than summer, but on this morning a deep gray to the northwest suggested seasonal change. For the short excursion, Adeline and Shelby had decided to saddle up their rig team, since the rocky creek bed west of town prevented wheel crossings. Adeline sweet-talked both of Bright Hair's little boys into keeping their shirts on for the ride across town to see their grandmother, Yarico. At their own homestead, thirty miles west near Cypressville, the three-year-old and his baby brother were used to wandering bare-chested and barefoot near the family cabin.

"Uncle Shelby and I live mostly in a city, Walker, so all the men and boys wear shirts when they go visiting. Did you know Austin is a special town for everyone in Texas?" The child looked somewhat less irritated when he watched his Aunt Adeline slip a soft shirt down over River's shoulders, too.

"You can make him do anything. He's only one," he said.

"Babies are all like that," Adeline agreed. "That's why they need good brothers and sisters. And good daddies and mamas."

"And aunts, too. And uncles and grandmothers."

"*Oui, mon cher petit.*" She gave him a kiss on the cheek, but she didn't hug him too long. Shelby was stepping stiffly onto the porch of their dogtrot just north of French Hill. Lately, his knee bothered him more than his shoulder. Her husband had been reminding her during the children's stay in Austin that the three-year-old probably shouldn't be coddled too much. Youruh and Bright Hair expected a new baby any day. The infant would be needing every attention.

Adeline was relieved, though, that her sweetheart didn't repeat his other recent claim. He'd commented that boys needed to go on and grow up, because so many old men were dying off. Her heart ached when she saw him lean against door frames to straighten himself. His sixtieth birthday was only weeks away. For the last few days, they'd been discussing the easiest morning route to Yarico's neighborhood, the sequence of paths most likely to prove uneventful.

"We could go straight to the river first and then follow the shore up to the creek." Shelby meant to avoid as many Austin inhabitants as possible, Adeline knew, by going directly down to the Colorado from their eastern side of town. Walker le Coeur Whitmire could suffer the unnecessary shirt with better understanding than he would any insults from local bystanders. He'd have to learn soon enough to expect hostility from some city folks. Brown-skinned people who spoke no Spanish were often more suspect than those with a clear Mexican heritage. The boys' "tante" also worried about how her husband and his horse would eventually manage the steep ravine, though a newly cut zig-zag trail made the descent to the creek less treacherous.

"But we'll want to show them where we used to live," she said, after some thought, "the old cabin on Pecan, Dr. Robertson's first office, the hotel the Bullocks used to run, and where Angelina's inn was for so many years." Adeline took care to speak without testiness, reminding herself of good will that townspeople usually afforded them, *the reclusive pair who know how to fix ailing bodies as well as worn furniture.* If she recalled which Austin residents withdrew hospitality once the boys were in tow, she lost patience.

"I don't suppose there'll be much tadoo about our riding up Pecan so early in the day, and on over to the creek side," Shelby said. "I'm thinkin', though, that the young'uns might not be as interested in sightings along the way as we are." He shared his wife's affection for Yarico's grandsons. He was equally proud that Youruh had taken and passed on the Whitmire surname. "You're probably right, anyhow, about showing them where the count stayed for several months and their grandmother did needlework with her French friends—"

"We're going to see Grandma," the older brother reminded River la Paix. "Don't take off your shirt," he ordered the toddler.

The early hours were gray but mild as the two horses made leisurely progress toward town. Walker sat behind Shelby with his arms hugging the man's belt. Adeline held River to her side, though he was already snugly secured with a shawl knotted into a sling. The toddler with beautiful eyelashes regularly raised an arm to point. Yarico's porch was only twenty minutes away from the Whitmire home on a fair day, no more than a half hour in chill or light rain. There was less activity at that hour on East Pecan than on a typical Wednesday, and Adeline thought the graying sky might have given people reason to sleep later than usual.

"What's Bright Hair going to name the new baby if it's a girl?" Shelby asked.

Adeline didn't think the one-year-old pressed to her side understood the question, but the little fellow wriggled against the unfamiliar restraint.

"Josephine la Joie," she said. "How happy we were to have a baby we could name Maggie." Not too many birthdays from fifty, she'd begun admitting that old age went that way, day after day marking joys which those already gone couldn't know. Adeline promised herself to let the happiness of the young stay a comfort rather than a wellspring of grief.

"I want a boy," Walker called out to her. "We're going to name him *Ever le Vent*, if we get a boy!"

"Your mother and father think of good names," she said. "Now let's be careful not to wake anyone up. Uncle Shelby and I will tell you quietly about the places we're passing. Your grandmother and I used to live on this street up a bit farther." Adeline felt sure none of her teacher or medic instincts would fade with age. "That was years and years before you were even born, Walker."

The youngster hugging Shelby's back stayed silent all the way to Congress Avenue. Even before secession, the central street was an unbroken swath of business enterprises. At the main crossroads, their horses stood side by side to let pass a long-bed wagon hauling timber. Mr. and Mrs. Whitmire smiled at one another as the boy stared and the little brother pointed. The tree trunks out near Cypressville were mostly thick and straight, though some curved like the ones near the creek bed they'd view in a few minutes. The fragrant pine logs now between them and the corner hotel had to have been felled in the Bastrop area.

Both Shelby and Adeline were contemplating trees and precarious life-spans. Often, the pair didn't need speech to be sure of understanding one another. Older couples often shared that ability, but the Georgia native and the man from Mississippi had felt that ease of comprehension even in their earliest meetings.

"I used to sit on that log over there by the hotel," Shelby said after the timber went by. "I'd look across the street where your Aunt Adeline assisted Dr. Robertson. Sometimes it would take all morning for me to figure out what in the world I could say to such a pretty girl."

The Dove Shall Fly

"Didn't you know how to talk? Were you like Grandfather Walk Far? Did you learn how to say hello in French then?" The child didn't expect his string of questions to get answers. "I would just tell her good morning, and then I would say *Bonjour*," the boy declared. His deep, musical voice had caught the ear of a lady stepping out from the hotel with her three children. She put one gloved hand on the shoulder of the younger daughter, and used her other hand to shield the girl's eyes. The older siblings, their mouths slightly open about who was crossing where, sensed their mother's concern.

Shelby and Adeline nudged their mounts, and the calm horses trotted across Austin's main intersection. The couple moved along more quickly where the street narrowed by the hotel. Bright Hair's two boys—with skin the color of pecans and thick hair glistening like wet hay at dusk—wouldn't become a gossip topic for anyone else, if their adoptive aunt and uncle could help it.

"See those two houses joined by a walkway and a roof?" Adeline continued, seeing they had the western length of Pecan to themselves. "That's where your grandma came to sew with *les dames françaises*."

"And right there," Shelby added. "That was where I worked when I brought your daddy back from San Antonio. Visitors slept there, too, but only a few at a time. Your father was still a boy then, and we slept in a little room right over there. Those days were before we met Walk Far and found out what a good grandpa he wanted to be."

"Daddy is Comanche, but Grandfather is Tonkawa."

"Walk Far is good at finding people," Adeline heard her husband explain.

"One time, he took Aunt Adeline and Grandma Yarico across a river," Walker said nodding. "Was that before you were born?"

"Not hardly," Shelby laughed, "but it was before I came to Texas."

This statement gave the boy a puzzle too big to put together in the next few blocks. Adeline could tell from his expression that he had more questions than he could formulate. When the one-year-old squealed and pointed, the older brother let go of the story parts.

"A mama pig!" Several pink creatures nuzzled up against a sow's belly in a pen across from the French count's old quarters.

"I can't believe they still keep any here." The Mississippi native shook his head. "Maybe she's the great-great granddaughter of the animal that tried to eat me one day after I fell off my horse."

271

"You are not a Comanche."

Walker made the comment sympathetically, and both adults on horseback knew it was best not to tell how an arrowhead lodged in Shelby's knee had once made him weak enough to slip from the saddle. They were about to look down on a ravine where a lone Indian and Angelina Eberly's handyman had faced off in a near fatal duel. He and his wife silently shared this thought—maybe the Comanche who sent an arrow deep into Shelby's knee years and years earlier was Walker's great-grandfather.

"Did you hear thunder?" Adeline wondered as they reached the top edge of the ravine.

"It was either a storm a ways off or some of the timber we saw a few minutes ago being dragged onto the ground."

"I've wedged one slicker underneath River, but I forgot to fold any oilcloth squares or a poncho for you."

"I remembered to fold a slicker, Addy. It's tied to the saddle horn. I still think I oughta cross with you all. I haven't seen Yarico in a couple months."

"As soon as you step inside, she thinks she needs to fuss. She'll miss seeing you this time, but I'll tell her you wanted to give her a hug." Adeline Whitmire wasn't at all sure her husband was steady enough on his horse to cross the rocky creek bed. "Did you think you might stop by the hotel on the way back to talk to Nathan about fixing a couple stairs?"

"He's countin' on showing me where there's some rot."

"Well, if rain starts coming down much, just sit a spell with him. Hold a coffee cup until it lets up." She knew she'd worry. "I suppose Francis will look for you there if he catches a ferry to report that the baby has arrived." For this news, they were counting on their son who lived across the Colorado, not too far from Youruh's family.

"He might go on downriver some to the new bridge crossing, if the dang thing is finished."

The four had arrived at the top of the wide break in land that sloped to the creek bed. After all these years, the view down to the glistening stream still took their breath away. On both sides of the water flowing on to the major river, a string of ancient live oaks stretched their limbs in every direction. Shelby's eyes always went first to the mammoth limb where that same Indian had finally climbed back up on his horse and signaled the end of rancor between the two strangers.

"Every time we pause here," Adeline said, "I say a prayer of thanks that Francis took up masonry over in New Braunfels before Custer got new orders and moved away from this spot. I was so worried when he was in a fever about joining the army." Her husband looked to be offering his own prayer of gratitude.

"He isn't attached to books the way Thomas is, that's for sure, or anything like the scholar Maggie's grown into."

"She may come back to the wilds of Texas once she finishes medical study. Hard as it is for a woman to get papers, certification might be more straightforward than gaining a circle of patients."

"We have plenty of stories between us about what official papers can and can't do to secure a future."

"Go on, Uncle Shelby!" The boy behind was kicking his moccasins against the horse's rump.

"I could walk us all down from here," Adeline said, wishing she'd already suggested it. "Tassel is so old and calm, he won't do anything but a gentle walk. River is tied on tight, and Walker will lead the way. Why don't you just keep an eye on us from right here, and stay until we make it across the water." Another rumble from the northwest seemed to counter her case. "It's not more than five minutes from the other side to Yarico's porch."

"Going on down is nothing but a lazy back-and-forth since this path was cut. If I can't direct a horse to mosey that far—just to the edge of the water and up—I might as well get a saw and hammer and put together my own six-foot box."

"What box?" Walker wanted to know, and both adults knew to turn comments elsewhere.

"I'll bet Grandfather Walk Far used to tell your daddy about Tonkawa children and this creek right here," said Shelby, whose wife was already gesturing.

"They would play in that water, while their parents gathered acorns or scooped for fishing bait."

"He doesn't say words you can hear," Walker stated. "His lips only work for smiling and eating. His ears don't work either." Adeline wanted to wait for Shelby's horse to catch up so she could give the child a kiss on the forehead.

"I'll bet Walk Far can still hold a crying baby until it falls asleep."

"I hope we get a boy."

Mr. and Mrs. Whitmire let the talking subside as their horses plodded down the path. The descent was slower but far safer than it had been in Austin's early years. With the one neighborhood on Yarico's side sustaining itself and increasing its independence, the route connecting the black population to the capital's white neighborhoods was often deserted. The garden that the boys' grandmother planted every year was admired by everyone in her community, and nearly three dozen families had learned in a few years who grew what best and when to get together for swapping produce. Since Custer finished enforcing emancipation, a livery, a tin-ware shop, and small mercantile had started up to serve the neighborhood. A person could spend weeks on the hill west of town without needing any supply from Austin proper.

Occasionally, members of Yarico's small Methodist congregation, or the Baptists, would convene at the edge of the creek for services. The pristine beauty of the place inspired individuals leaning toward any denomination. Brittle live oak leaves rustled in every season. The trees' massive limbs stretched out at supernatural angles. Adeline had commented more than once that any person not feeling spirituality down in that creek bed was more than likely to miss the ferry to heaven altogether.

"We made it," Shelby said. While Adeline waited for him to ease Walker down and then dismount to help her to the ground, she gave in to some to a wave of emotion. Only the morning before Shelby and one of the doctor's helpers came with the boys, she'd strolled to Aunt Maggie's headstone. Just now they'd talked about Walk Far's limitations, without acknowledging that he couldn't live forever. And not far across the creek, up behind the dogtrot that Shelby and their sons built for Yarico, was the simple wooden cross marking Bernard's grave.

Adeline wanted life to hold still the way the sloping landscape seemed to. She wanted Yarico, whose birth date had never been verified, to live on and on. There was no denying, though, that the elder woman had lost considerable strength since the winter before. Long ago in Macon, with ailing Delphine Pagnol and the child, Yarico had tended to the dying and then taken up care of the orphaned girl as tenderly as any mother. The woman's strength had seemed infallible.

"Are you crying?" Shelby asked as she handed him the bundled toddler. Again, the darkened sky rumbled from a distance.

"I don't know. This place always puts me in the same frame of mind a church would." She didn't say cemetery. "I'm worried about Yarico,"

The Dove Shall Fly

she admitted softly, "and all our older people. I can't help feeling apprehensive about others in the family, too. Bringing the boys into the world was pretty easy for Adelphine...*Bright Hair*, I know." She didn't want to say any more with Walker just at arm's length by the water's edge. "I can't wait to find out if she and Youruh have a baby girl or another boy."

"A boy," Walker said. He was cupping his hand at an eddy, and they supposed he'd spotted a minnow. They knew the child would get himself wet if Adeline didn't cross with them soon. The water was flowing faster than she remembered, but the flat rocks that she and Walker would use were completely dry and easy to navigate. Whatever rain might be coming down in the area, it was falling upriver for the time being.

"I'm not heading back up until I see you all have made it to the other side," Shelby said. He helped Adeline retie the shawl that secured River, and he bent with a stifled groan to the three-year-old's level. "Are you going to lead the way across those flat stones?"

"I caught one!" The wriggling specimen slipped instantly through Walker's fingers. "Yes, I'm going first!" He reached the second stone before turning to see if the others and the horse followed his lead. Frowning, he witnessed Shelby, hat in his hand, taking time to kiss Adeline on the lips. The toddler wrapped one hand around the knot in the sling and pointed with the other. Their *tante* finally stepped out, keeping the reins in her free hand, though the horse ambled at a manageable pace.

Halfway across, it grew difficult see the pebbles at the bottom as clearly as when they started, and Adeline thought there could be some runoff stirring the silt upstream. When she and the boys made it to the western bank, she turned back to Shelby.

"Give Yarico a hug for me," he called. "You'll get to her porch before I can coax this slow poke back uphill."

"Maybe you should walk him a ways." Shelby waved. It would be easier on him, too, to lead the horse to the summit before climbing back into the saddle. She could tell he wasn't even going to start back until she and the boys were on their way toward Yarico's and out of sight.

"River, look!" Walker shouted. A miniature waterfall was starting up over the edge of one flat rock, and the evidence of rain nearby made Adeline glad Shelby had a stop planned on his way home. The sky was only light gray except farther to the north, but she imagined she felt a drop, and she was relieved when they all reached dry shore.

"Don't run, Walker!"

The toddler in her sling squirmed, too, but she was determined to hang onto him until the horse was secured at Yarico's hitching post. She glanced back as she and the boys ambled on. Shelby was kicking something he'd spotted on the ground, a piece of quartz he wanted to save for the youngsters, maybe, or an arrowhead.

Adeline and the children continued up the hill, and suddenly she remembered one of her last mornings back on the outskirts of Macon. Usually, she nudged aside images of the tidy homestead tucked between modest plantations. She'd lost her father there and then her mother. She'd understood for years now that the patch of Georgia land was also where she'd enjoyed her last innocence. It had been her childhood habit to trot up the incline behind their tiny house at dawn—her mother's house and Adeline's, as well as Yarico's, and then Aunt Maggie's. Clearly coming back was a final carefree morning when she'd rushed home from her excursion, an Indian artifact in her apron pocket. How the two had marveled at a kitchen tool carved from stone!

Yarico's split log dogtrot with a wide front porch was coming into view, and the boys' tante smiled to see the hitching post, though she was surprised not to find the children's grandmother waiting for them in her rocking chair. Both women consulted their calendars carefully, and neither would have confused or forgotten the date. More skilled at seamstress work than cooking, Yarico might nevertheless be tending some baked treat.

Adeline's arms felt strained, and she couldn't brush aside memory of that long-past morning on the hilltop outside Macon. From her observation point, she'd seen a toddler below squirm from its mother's arms and slide to the ground not far from experimental tobacco rows. She'd called out to her neighbor in charge, as those brought in by slave wagon saw to the struggling mother. At the time, the girl on the precipice felt she shared the shock of onlookers. Gentlemen simply did not allow themselves to scoop up babies, yet her neighbor had rushed for the wailing infant. Adeline had not needed the intervening thirty-five years to grasp another reason for the silent reaction of observers. Not many residents of Georgia in 1835 could have testified to seeing a land owner console the distraught child of an enslaved field hand.

Adeline Harper Whitmire had never recounted the incident to Yarico. She'd told herself from time to time that the artifact find had taken priority, that an unexpected trip into town had won over her concentration as a girl, that her whirlwind weeks at an academy for the first time absorbed all attention, and then the departure to Texas under the protection of the battalion…that such upheaval had nearly erased from her memory the small, morning incident on land abutting the Harper homestead. After all these years—and the clarity of emancipation—it was not pleasant for Adeline to admit that shame, too, had kept her from fully informing Yarico. She'd held back from telling how a white man had allowed his humanity to extend to a black baby. Even a twelve-year-old understands that decency should not be noteworthy.

So many years after the loss of that Macon man and his battalion at Goliad, so many years after dire survival challenges and then the unspeakable war between North and South, whenever Shelby's wife and Bernard's widow had the chance to share an evening or two, one of the women sometimes gave voice to a memory long thought lost. Maybe on this occasion, while they all waited for news of the boys' newborn sibling, Adeline would tell her own surrogate mother about the baby who'd slipped to the ground.

"Yarico?" Walker was already scampering up the porch steps. Halfway through securing Tassel's reins, Adeline paused to loosen the boy's brother from her side so he could follow.

"We're here, Yarico! Looks like it might rain any minute! Shall I move this beast under the overhang out back?" The visitor went on and led her horse to a more sheltered post behind the compact house. Rows of turnip greens and spinach already flourished in the fall garden, and she thought of picking a handful and going in from the rear, but she approached as the boys had. The side of the house with the kitchen and sitting room was all Yarico really used these days. She had a pallet just a few steps from the stove, and she made the case that bedrooms on the other side of the breezeway were always ready for company. By the time the boys' *tante* made it to the steps, River sat spread-eagled on the smooth wooden porch planks, and Walker was dragging a heavy basket from inside.

"Grandma was going to bring these out, but she's tired."

"Is she sitting inside."

"She was lying down, but now she's sitting."

"Is your grandma all right?"

"She said it was all right for me to bring out these blocks." Walker stopped to put his hands on his hips the way his grandmother frequently did. River clapped. "She didn't know if I'm strong enough but I am!"

"I'm all right, honey," was the first thing Yarico said. "Why don't you set a chair in the doorway, so you can keep an eye on them while we chat. I mixed up a cake batter that has another fifteen minutes, but it won't be near as *délicieux* as what we ate that time out near the Place at the Bend."

"It surely smells as good as that crumb cake Mrs. Kolar made us all." Adeline wasn't used to seeing Yarico lean onto the upholstered chair's arm, made even softer by a rolled blanket. The Harpers' rosebud quilt draped over her lap and as far down as the floor. "But are you all right?"

"I expect I just tried to get up too fast. I got the sudden urge to have something baking. Then I stood too long trying to remember what all goes into a cake. Thank goodness I had eggs collected from yesterday. By the time I had the pan set in the oven, I pretty much needed to lie down." She chuckled and Adeline was relieved to hear the familiar sound. "It seems to me I must have dozed off because I heard Walker's voice and knew you all were coming. Getting up too fast…that's what made me dizzy. Maybe you can take a peek at the cake in another ten minutes."

Adeline watched the boys unpack the basket of blocks Shelby had sanded smooth for them. Walker talked about what he was going to build, and River was adept at removing smooth, squared-off shapes from the basket. He pointed at whatever his older brother began stacking up. Already, Yarico needed to catch her breath from talk spilling faster than she was used to. The two adults silently took pleasure in the brothers' animated play and the sound of light rain. Even if it started raining harder, no one in the Austin area would mark cold on a calendar for another two weeks. On such a gray, temperate day, the aroma of a baking cinnamon cake underscored tranquility. Neither of the women needed to speak for a while. They, too, relied often on wordless understanding. Both thought of Adelphine, about the woman likely in labor, whose husband called her Bright Hair.

Cloud cover kept direct sun from illuminating the older woman's face, but Adeline thought Yarico would retain her lovely, thoughtful features forever. A slight wrinkle between her eyebrows hinted at worry. Prominent veins along her hands were clearer evidence of age. Suddenly, two squeals drew attention to the porch.

"Whose yellow dog is that?" Adeline's question elicited a full-throated laugh from the lady in the soft chair.

"It'll likely take a church meeting to settle that question once and for all." She shook her head as she laughed again. "The Andrews children are trying to get their mama to claim it. Then Mr. Dearman says, no, it sleeps in *his* tool shed every night. And Jeremiah declares it must have training from somewhere as a hunting dog, because it helped him corner a coyote last week." When the hound ran up the porch steps, Adeline sprang to her feet.

"Anyone seen it bite or nip?"

"It'll lick you to pieces if you let it." The dog was rolling on its back to let Walker pat its belly, and Adeline nudged her chair a bit farther out on the porch but sat back down.

"Does it have a name?"

"Yellow dog," Yarico said, slapping her knee. "Don't ask me if I ever carry on a conversation with him when no one's around." She was sitting up straighter in her armchair, and it was clear that company had given her energy. "I know you remember how I used to have some fear of any animals except chickens, horses included."

"I still wonder how you held your nerve driving our wagon out of Macon behind the battalion." Their sighs suggested they would reminisce for a long time after the boys were asleep.

"Can that be cinnamon burning?"

"Sit and let me get it!" Adeline told her. "It doesn't smell ruined, just ready to be taken out."

"My oven mitt has a hole in it," Yarico called after her. "I should throw it out. See those two folded towels?"

"I have them! The cake is fine. I'll just set the pan on the trivet, all right?"

She was smiling at Yarico when she stepped back into the sitting room, and for a moment it seemed the wonderful aroma had brought Walker to the open doorway where her chair was positioned. The faint bark of a dog and the patter of light rain triggered no immediate alarm, but the little boy's expression didn't fit with the prospect of cake.

"River can run," he said.

"Is he out on the porch?" Adeline asked, but she was already bolting in that direction.

"The yellow dog made him run. I think they went back down to the creek."

Not until Yarico sprang up from her chair, did it become clear she was still in her socks. In an instant she laid the younger woman's hand on Walker's shoulder and flew down the front steps. She reached down and clutched the hem of her skirt so her ankles were less likely to catch a fold and make her trip. Without consulting the older brother, Adeline raised him to her hip, and trotted after the boys' grandmother. Walker made a low quivering murmur that rose and subsided with the jostle of his *tante's* rushed pace. As they neared the turn where the creek came into view, a troubling noise grew prominent.

The rain as far south as Austin had remained light, if steady, but it was clear there'd been a sustained downpour to the north. Water rushed across most of the stepping stones the visitors had taken only a half hour earlier. What Adeline saw in a flash registered like the elements of a nightmare. Waterfalls swelled steadily behind and beyond the flat, crossing rocks. On the far bank, just at the spot where Walker had dipped for a minnow, a noisy swirl battered the shore. As if he, too, had just turned to see the worst of the creek emergency, Shelby was staggering back down the ravine toward the flash flood. River la Paix, his shirt removed and his tummy poking out, stood on the last stone step nearest his grandmother's side of the creek. The yellow dog next to him barked nonstop, and the tiny boy had both arms outstretched pointing as if he'd orchestrated the current crashing around them.

From Adeline's vantage point, there was need of a rope and a steady horse, both of which were crucial minutes out of reach. It was not at all certain the tot knew to hold his footing. Clapping at the dog and pointing at the onslaught of murky water, he looked entirely capable of stepping out and of getting washed downstream. When the dog leapt into the floodwater, Adeline heard herself shout for the baby boy to stay put, and she would also have called out for the child's grandmother to wait for help, but Yarico was already charging wildy toward him. Adeline's hands went up to her ears, as though there were safety in barring the noise of the flood or anyone's screams. Walker wrapped his arms around her waist, as if anchoring himself could keep others from getting swept to oblivion.

Unfolding was a breathtaking feat, managed by Yarico Harper Giroux, beloved wife of Bernard—once a French count's footman—both free persons for all time. The little boy's grandmother held her hand to her hips and set one foot ahead of the other within the powerful current. She called out "Wait! Wait!" to the baby, but her feet kept moving toward the flat stone, one and then the other. In the rushing water, the yellow dog paddled and fought and then let itself get pitched some downstream before barking and paddling again against the flow. Walker's little brother was pointing in its direction, but Yarico's voice redirected the toddler's attention. "Wait! Grandma says wait!"

By the time she had the child in her arms, Shelby was frozen on the incline of the far bank, and Adeline stood immobilized at the edge where Yarico would head. Going back through the turbulent water, the older woman took her steps even more slowly. The tot had wrapped his arms around her neck, and she gripped him with one arm, while letting the hand at her hip assist in keeping balance. Somehow the yellow dog had scrambled ashore and darted back up to the crossing. At the moment the grandmother reached firm ground with River, the dog barked and set its muddy paws against her apron. She lost her balance and sat hard on the ground, but she kept her grip on the rescued tot.

"Are you all right?" Adeline asked breathlessly, seeing nothing clearly broken. "Hold River's hand, Walker. I need to help your grandma up." Yarico waved her away to indicate she'd get up faster if she could turn over onto all fours first. "We're all right, Shelby! Go on back up! We're safe! Go on up to the hotel before it rains any harder!" Her husband picked up his hat where it had fallen, but he didn't look as if he could budge until the women and children moved away from the flooding bank. "We're all right, darlin'! Let's all get out of this rain! Go on to the hotel!"

The two women and the little boys in their care struggled back toward Yarico's cabin. Even the muddy dog wobbled as he made progress uphill. Adeline pried River from his grandmother's arms and asked Walker to stay between them and hold hands. She was already picturing the sequence she'd follow to get everyone into dry clothing without taking her eyes off either child. Their clothes were soaked by the time they made it to the porch, and Yarico sank down on the top step, shaking her head and waving Adeline on to see about the children.

The two boys, drained of any resistance, sat meekly on the blanket that Adeline took from the armchair and spread on the center of the floor. Walker, capable of concern for his grandmother, did not question the gentle command to sit still with River.

"Just help me up," Yarico called. "Get me to the chair, and I'll see that the boys don't budge while you get bedspreads and anything dry from the guest rooms. Maybe something in Bernard's drawer will help."

Walker was patient with the number of rolls Adeline needed to put in the sleeves of a chambray shirt. He pulled on a pair of his grandfather's woolen socks to make do while his own leggings dried. The boy giggled, partly from exhaustion, when one of Bernard's undershirts had to be secured at the toddler's waist. Adeline fussed a while over tying off an odd stocking at the baby's middle.

"Don't make a bow," the three-year-old said. "River already looks like a girl."

"Now, you two sit still while your aunt brings in the blocks," Yarico said. With a crocheted shawl draped over her shoulders, she appeared to feel more like herself. She'd been watching Adeline glance toward the door, and she could read the younger woman's mind. "You all can make a fort or house to show your *tante* when she gets back. She's just going to run on back to the creek to make sure your Uncle Shelby got his horse up the hill. You can show her what you made, when she comes back. And then we'll all have cake."

As hard as it had been to trudge in wet clothes up Yarico's hill, it was nearly impossible for Adeline not to trot down. She half expected to see her husband still standing mid-way on the opposite slope. Like Yarico, he might have needed several minutes to simply catch his breath after the near catastrophe. It brought back to Adeline those floods during the revolution—the Harper women's desperate crossing of the Brazos when common sense said to stay put. In the climactic weeks of 1836, though, the greater urgency of escaping Santa Anna had sent thousands across dangerously roiled rivers. Adeline, the last of their group to cross, had witnessed Yarico starting from the far shore to meet her halfway. Each had waved at the other to wait and stay safe. Miraculously, no Harpers or Wainwrights had perished that day.

For an excruciating minute, Adeline scanned the steep ground across the rushing creek water. The ageless incline marking Austin's edge was deserted. She made herself look downstream, though she'd have been tempted to throw herself into the current had there been arms flailing somewhere near the sharp rocks closer to the Colorado.

Then, she spotted not one, but two horses, at the top of the far ridge. There were familiar men astride and both were waving their arms and calling, though the roar of the surging water made their words difficult to interpret. Gray-haired Shelby, back up on his slow horse, and their son Francis were signaling and shouting. They were safe and not far from a good fire at the hotel. Both were trying to get some message to her before she reversed course again toward Yarico's.

Heading back up the hill, Adeline lifted the hem of her skirt as she'd just seen the grandmother do. They'd learned the tactic during their earliest days in Texas, at the same time riding side-saddle was dismissed in favor of expedience. She surprised herself by trotting as easily as any girl could have. Relief energized her, and she knew the boys would be growing impatient for their taste of cinnamon cake. The news that Francis Whitmire brought from Cypressville was also pumping her blood faster, and though she was smiling broadly when she stepped into Yarico's sitting room, she had to catch her breath before making the announcement.

"Josephine la Joie!" she exclaimed. "It's a girl!"

By early evening the boys were soundly asleep. They curled together in a mound of blankets at one corner, without protest about not getting to sleep in a big bed across the breezeway. Walker's eyes had drooped first, either from his disappointment over a baby sister or in reaction to the frantic scene he'd witnessed.

"Josephine" Yarico repeated softly to Adeline. "Well, it will be a few years before my granddaughter understands that she was named after me. I wouldn't remember my real mother calling me that. Just Madame Martin at times, and even she had needed to use her maiden name right away for safety. All my life I've answered to *Yarico*."

"It's still hard for me to understand it, *belle-mère*." Both had lost their mothers early, but at least Adeline remembered hers.

"So many river crossings and name changes likely in one life," the older woman mused, "sometimes I think the young ones, if they knew what all could rush out of reach in the current, they'd just ask to be lifted up to heaven from the start." She had to take the edge of her shawl and press it to her eyes. "If that baby grandson of mine had been swept away, I might have thrown myself in after him and gone on to greater peace." Adeline knew they'd both have to fend off images of the day's near disaster, and she tried to turn the subject back to less immediate upheaval.

"There are few lives that don't include some portion of harrowing change. People forced away from their natural homes by persecutors or plots of the greedy…borders shifting this way and that over time…"

Adeline, seeing her companion nod and gaze in the children's direction, supposed the woman had gone on thinking of her own infant days on an island in the Caribbean. Probably even Madame Martin had not known the full history of the baby girl she'd brought to Georgia's shore.

"Adeline, honey," Yarico went on, almost in a whisper. "Not too many years back, when Bernard and I were on a ship that stopped in Savannah, right soon after Appomattox—"

"I can understand why you two declined to come down the Mississippi, even with officials at every port."

"Worst hatred and danger then, it seemed to me, but ships with their home harbors in the North were safe for us. Do you remember my telling you how the two of us took a few days to see some of what had been my hometown?"

"I know you wished Adelphine had still been with you, that you had as much to show her as you did Bernard. But she was already back with us, and preferring the name Bright Hair."

"My poor husband wasn't able to embrace much in those days, so soon after his rescue from illegal capture…" Adeline never knew Yarico's tone to grow bitter except when recalling Bernard's mistreatment during the war, and his inability to recover completely.

"You remember how happy we were that he took to Walk Far right away. There'd be no sound made between the two, but both those gentlemen would smile and nod and often laugh, though who knew at what."

"I remember. I remember," Yarico said, smiling again. "But I'm going to ask you something, dear Addy, and it'll sound like you have to promise, but I only mean if your life works out that way, and no storm comes along to sweep you in another direction entirely—"

"What is it Yarico? There's precious little I could refuse the only mother I can well remember."

"I do recall Walk Far dubbing you *Two Mothers*, back when Aunt Maggie was always with us. Adeline understood that there was, in fact, no request she would refuse this good woman. She, too, felt the surge of gratitude that rushes over anyone narrowly escaping grief. She let Yarico take time to find her words, though. Whatever the darling boys' grandmother requested, it would be something entirely worthy and lovely. "If Josephine and her brothers show any yearning for travel," she started at last. "If you and Shelby…or should you and their parents… have a mind to see Savannah one day—"

"I'd love to see where my mama lived with her folks, where she met her Mr. Harper, where you were brought ashore years earlier from Tybee."

The Dove Shall Fly

"Yes, it was wonderful to see the old house that had been my sanctuary, mine and your mama's. But what I'm asking about is on the other side of Savannah. There's a plaque that's gone up since I was a girl living with Pagnols and Harpers." She sat up straighter in her armchair, but she kept her voice at a firm whisper. "If you all go one day, would you take my grandchildren to see a certain historical marker. That town has dozens of parks, but you'll find the one."

"I already want to go," Adeline laughed, "but I suppose now you'll caution me to wait until these little ones reach ten or so."

"Until they can read for themselves, *mais oui, madame*," Yarico agreed. "They should be able to read about the brave volunteers from Haiti. They sailed from their island home to help America in its fight against British oppression. If you all go, you could pay a photographer to preserve the occasion. I've got some savings." She breathed in with deep satisfaction. "Nobody made them sail a foot from home," she added. "They just heard tell of human events leaning toward independence. Those men from Haiti just had to get in their ships and come help."

"I didn't know." From the kitchen came the faint sound of charred wood shifting position. No smoke filtered into the sitting room, and Adeline recalled the good Franklin stove that the Harper women had been sorry to leave behind outside Macon decades ago. "There's too much to know in just one life," she murmured.

Both women grew sleepy in the extended silence, and Adeline drew her own bundle of blankets up around her shoulders. She could hear the woman in the armchair shuffle her feet and take a more restful position.

"Dear merciful God," Yarico whispered, almost to herself, "Can't you just imagine what our precious Josephine will learn in her long, long life? I wonder what's going on in that lovely new baby's head tonight."

Chapter 19   Blessing in a Bottle—Yucatan, 1726

From his seat in the dinghy, Monsieur Guillame Séguin scanned the green coastline of a peninsula that the Mexicans called Yucatan. He'd been listening to the slosh of ocean waves for many weeks, but the pounding he heard now was his own pulse. He was minutes away from stepping onto firm earth again. A glint in the low mass of foreign vegetation kept catching his eye. Meanwhile the Spanish cargo vessel *Potencia*, its main sails furled, was waiting for the handful of men rowing ashore. Their grim task was expected to take two hours.

Before the ship's departure from Coruña, another traveler from across Spain's northern border had refused to purchase fare without the captain's signed oath. Should the French adventurer expire during the voyage to America, his body would not be discarded at sea. The only Toulouse native on the manifest had drawn his last breath in the middle of the Atlantic. Now the Yucatan shore—*mon dieu, promise me, not on an island*—was the first opportunity for a burial.

Guillaume Séguin was asked to say a few words *en français* for the deceased, and he hoped his throat would not tighten at the gravesite. He felt it such a pity that the fellow would never reach any *famille* already settled some distance up the Mississippi. The crew sent to row and dig would not likely understand Séguin's benediction, but anyone could interpret the wobble in a voice and a hand shielding the eyes.

The surviving traveler from France fought off emotion by trying to identify that glint in the tangled greenery ahead. Séguin then turned his thoughts to his own intentions. Reports of abundant silver in Mexican mines fired his imagination, and he believed himself far more determined than most young men to see his dreams through. Around the wide end of the coast before him lay the mainland proper, his destination city Veracruz, and a thousand open miles of shining possibility.

Young as he was, though, Monsieur Séguin had not needed sea travel to understand that any man's life is a tale of ebb and flow. The imminent burial would be sobering, but he'd never supposed an ocean crossing to be a sanguine affair. Having traveled from his *petit village* to the near edge of Spain that summer, he'd worked at deck chores in Coruña while waiting for the *Potencia* to pull anchor. Its voyage begun at last, the ship set out on an unexpected travel leg to Cadiz, far south on the Spanish coast. He'd thought it a poor start, adding over a week in order to pick up a small number of shackled Africans and sundry dry goods. They were to be fed better than most human cargo, the captain assured anyone asking, because of their stature or relative education or some such attributes declared by the original Portuguese handler.

There were few other passengers on the vessel meant for crates and casks, but those who'd voluntarily paid their fare felt ill at ease about the need for chains below deck, where sleeping quarters were already cramped. Once out on the open sea, however, every living soul on board shared a single ambition—to survive the crossing, to set steady feet again on land. Especially after each sunset, murmured prayer and consolation in several tongues slowly filled the hold.

After eight weeks afloat, the surviving Frenchman had fought off an impulse to briefly go ashore in Hispaniola, the island cluster they'd just navigated. At one port, a half dozen enslaved men and four women were marshalled in their irons to the plank. Their gait conveyed stiffness and sorrow and apprehension. No words were needed. The last captive, blinking from the bright light, turned back once toward the ship. His dignified stare seemed a silent pledge to survive.

Séguin winced as the group was led to the port's stucco enclosures and lost from sight. Who could say from what tribes across the *Méditerranée* they'd been stolen? He didn't know if the shackled individuals were destined for sugar cane fields or domestic tasks. A knot in his throat tightened as he wondered how the Africans compared their fortune to the fate of the Toulouse man about to be interred.

Alive and at liberty and standing on firm ground again, Guillaume Séguin thought. He moved his feet in the afternoon sun as if walking were a small miracle, and he was overcome with the sense that free movement was itself a prayer, one step translating into gratitude and the next indicating compassion.

"Non, non, Señor Séguin!" The wrapped body was being taken to a shady spot not too far from the beached dinghy, but the shipmate in charge worried to see *le monsieur* trudging away on his own. "It is not safe to walk beyond our sighting, señor! Many are the tales of savages and pirates along here!"

"I'm just going to inspect that clump of bushes," Séguin said. "I'll be back with you before your men begin earnest digging."

"A good place to relieve yourself! Of course, *mon camarade Guillaume!*"

"There's some reflection at the edge of those shrubs and vines. Something keeps catching the sun!"

"You can be sure it is not silver, Señor Séguin!" The shipmate was sympathetic, but he was laughing to think the lone man from across the Pyrenees believed he'd already discovered riches.

Gratitude and compassion, the Frenchman said to himself as he took the last few steps toward a brown bottle half buried in sand. Even at arm's length, it was partly obscured by wild growth. *May God put me to drift at sea should I fail to give thanks for good fortune. May God put me asunder should I shed no tear for suffering strangers.*

The label on the dark bottle was almost entirely worn off, but the word *Bourgogne* was still legible. Guillaume, who was already planning to introduce himself as *Guillermo* once in Mexico, was nevertheless gratified to find an artifact from his own country. Ships and people and possessions from every earthly corner were finding their way to the vast western hemisphere, yet discovering an object from home remained a comfort.

Monsieur Séguin brushed sand from the glass and from the cork pressed snugly into the neck of the bottle. He could tell from its weight that no wine remained, but the tightly folded page inside gave him a jolt. Tilting the bottle upside down, he was able to press one finger against a corner of the paper and pull it out. Though French wine could be poured by anyone, he was not surprised as he opened the creased paper to see the script in his own language. The man taking first steps inside Mexico's border now worried that the landed message might be a futile plea for help or a last will and testament. He did not wish, from his first day in the new world, to be haunted by yet more sorrows.

"*Le 15 octobre, 1676*," he marveled to himself. "Oh, let this not be the voice of despair." The sound of shovels came from down the beach, and he read again the date at the top of the document. "Fifty years ago," he murmured. "*Mon dieu, mon dieu.* Four weeks out from the port at le Havre, nearly half a century ago."

The Dove Shall Fly

~~~~~~~~~~~~~~~~~~~~

The 19th of August, in the year of our Lord, 1676, two fortnights out from the Le Havre, France, I Madame Trezevant, do bear witness from our ship La Colombe. Should it please heaven, may all souls aboard reach the Americas, and this humble message as well come to rest on a hopeful shore.

I write my married name for perhaps the last time and shall go by my christening name if I am so fortunate to arrive in the colonies, as I cannot predict the disposition of foreign territories toward the Huguenots, who know nothing but peril within the borders of France.

My husband grew fervent in his Calvinist habits, though I seek communion in any house of worship, having learned the catechisms early, then much later having come to love a man devoted to "direct supplication." My dear Monsieur Trezevant is surely conversing with angels now, for his fate was not to rejoin relatives across the narrow water in the English land of Protestants.

He was taken by force in the streets of Le Havre as our children and I waited aboard La Colombe. When word came of ten heretics put to the sword by royal guards in the public gardens, the captain said my husband was listed among the doomed. He said, as well, that he dared not now sail the shorter distance to reformist shores, but must needs embark on the great voyage planned across the Atlantique.

I have mourned for a month. I have consoled my children and told them that we should all feel at peace. Their father's soul is lightened of every burden. And now, on this beautiful morning of calm seas and splendid sun, my little ones fret most for the lone bird that flits from mast to mast as the shore behind us grows ever distant.

It is my nature, truth be told, to hope, and so I have said to my darling children that the bird will surely again find hospitable shores. We may be at sea for weeks to come but the fragile thing, I assure them, will survive in our company until it spies new land and welcoming trees. Shouldn't we give thanks, I say before our evening prayer, for such soaring creatures sent to lift the spirits of mortal wanderers?

We—Madame Trezevant and her children Gabrielle and Jean-Pierre and Mathilde—do put our names and marks below as witnesses to simple belief in better worlds. On this day in 1676, we release one bottle into the great watery creation called Atlantique. May our message eventually find its way to land, just as we will surely step ashore one day.

We offer thanks for our safe passage thus far. We ask that comfort reach every sorrowing heart.

A hundred and a hundred years from now, may the world find itself so perfectly at peace that tales of long-ago strife seem curious history indeed.

~~~~~~~~~~~~~~~~~~~~

The signature and marks were illegible, but the Frenchman stood transfixed. Slowly registering in his mind was the scent of fresh vegetation and the noise of gulls feasting not far away.

"We will soon be ready for you to speak your words, Monsieur Séguin." The fellow in charge of rowers and diggers took him by surprise. Both voyagers sweated in the sun.

"Your men are fast with their shovels."

"They are eager to row back. We are but a single sunset from the mainland now, and they are wanting to sleep some nights in a bed that does not rock."

"The glint was an old wine bottle," the Frenchman said. "There was a page of writing inside."

"Ah," said the shipmate, gazing at the document. "It is in your language, am I right?"

"Yes, written a half century ago, by a woman perhaps destined to reach the Carolinas."

"And what is this word near the top, monsieur?"

"*La Colombe*," he said, "the name of their ship. It means *The Dove*."

"A bird of good omen in our country, *mon camarade* Guillaume."

"Ours as well. You must call me *Guillermo* from now on, *por favor*."

"But of course, monsieur. We have traded phrases with one another these past weeks, have we not?"

"Si, si." The Frenchman looked back with a new perspective at the waiting vessel, and he couldn't erase from his thoughts the group recently taken onto shore in Hispaniola. "At the grave, I could read from the ending of this letter. I'll have time, don't you think?"

"My men were quick at their work, Guillermo Seguin. Si, we have the time."

"The last lines express good will. I don't believe I could speak a fairer sentiment."

"Fair words in a bottle, another good omen, *mi amigo*."

The two men turned and took steps in the direction of trees that had given the diggers shade. Seguin was noticing the loose sand more this time as an impediment to easy walking, but he still was thankful that his time on a lurching ship was about to end. He thought, no matter how his search for silver turned out, he would never willingly depart from land again.

"Fair words," he repeated to his traveling acquaintance, a man he would likely never see again after making port at Veracruz the following day. "And who, among us, *mon camarade*, has no need of benediction?"

Afterword

In the last decade, I've watched a small-seed idea of mine grow into a complex project. During my final years as a foreign language teacher, I'd take students to the French Legation in Austin, Texas. I started imagining what residents in the log cabins below in 1841 thought of the plantation structure built for the new republic's first foreign dignitary. Some seamstresses among Austin's citizenry might have hemmed linens for the grand residence, and my first notion of the Harper women took root.

Gradually, my limited understanding of the Texas Revolution impacted my direction. Every inhabitant of Austin at its inception in 1839 must have known someone lost at the Alamo, someone executed at Goliad, or someone giddy from the rout of Santa Anna's forces at San Jacinto.

Then my own family connection sank in. In the summer of 1960, I watched my grandfather search the memorial at Goliad for the name of *our ancestral uncle* and that uncle's first cousin, neither of whom returned from the Georgia Battalion's ill-fated expedition to Texas. If my Grandpa Hunt were sitting next to me right now, I would love to let him know what I eventually learned about Francis Marion Hunt's service among Fannin's volunteers in 1836. I'd have a harder time explaining why I assigned our Francis Hunt the unrelated last name "Gideon" in my first historical novel. Somehow, the fictional surname freed my writing hand in the earliest chapters of this trilogy.

I hope that First Sergeant Francis Marion Hunt and all members of the family living today will be at peace with this book's dedication page.

Let me express equal regard and thanks for Trezevant family members whose remembrance of James Peter Trezevant inspired one of the main historical figures in *The Dove Shall Fly*. In 2010, I didn't predict I'd write a second narrative set in nineteenth-century Texas, much less a third.

I started off with the intention of writing a single Texas Revolution novel, a work of fiction that would pay tribute to Francis Hunt, his cousin Joseph Stovall, and other Georgia Battalion volunteers who never returned to their families. After finishing *How Far Tomorrow*, though, I realized what other accounts needed telling, like the story of John Spillers, who miraculously made it home to his three children residing outside Macon, as well as the youngest company recruit and survivor Sam Hardaway. After *Those Bones at Goliad* went into production, I felt I'd finished my historical fiction undertaking.

But in the spring of 2015, I happened upon an engrossing website dedicated to James Peter Trezevant, who not only survived the battalion's worst catastrophes but went on with a handful of others to join up with Sam Houston's forces. This Georgia Battalion soldier quickly rose in rank after San Jacinto.

Words can't express my astonishment at learning that James Trezevant was in the very same Georgia Battalion *company* as my own ancestors. Several cornerstones of JPT's experience helped me visualize his likeliest role at San Jacinto—before speeding to join the battalion, he was enrolled at Columbia's elite university and active in its militia; family letters refer to his being wounded in April's decisive battle; soon after the victory, he is listed as a member of the Karnes Cavalry Spy Unit; he resigned from Texas duty in late 1836 at the rank of Brevet Major. In the Refugio battle earlier that spring, battalion commander William Ward was desperate to map an escape route out toward Victoria. I easily picture him trusting trained equestrians like James Trezevant to ride night scout as Mexican forces closed in. During San Jacinto in the following month, Captain Karnes surely learned of Trezevant's riding and military abilities.

Muster rolls and military history, moreover, show the experience that the Georgia Battalion volunteers shared. In December of 1835, Hunt and Stovall and Trezevant sailed from New Orleans to the coast of Texas on the same schooner. They marched together inland from Copano to Refugio, and trudged in the sleet together from Refugio to Goliad that winter. Our ancestors toiled together in their efforts to fortify Goliad for anticipated attack. For three days back in Refugio, they resisted attack from General Urrea's army. They wandered together toward Victoria in their effort to regain the upper-hand.

Somewhere in the perilous plains and swamps not far from Victoria, a few Georgia Battalion men under Lieutenant-Colonel William Ward succeeded in their escape, some were caught and put to work at shipbuilding, while most were captured and marched back to Goliad and to execution soon after.

It was not hard for me to imagine these American recruits working together, comforting and encouraging one another, supporting one another in what had to be a signal event in their lives. How unlikely, but reaffirming, that descendants of these Georgia Battalion members should befriend one another over a hundred and eighty years later.

Corresponding these last three years with Robert W. Trezevant, as well as his researcher cousin Richard Allen, has been an extraordinary pleasure. When Bob Trezevant visited Austin in 2017, his partner took a photo of us in front of the Joanna Troutman Memorial in the Texas State Cemetery. At this somber site, the two of us are smiling. Bob and I were overjoyed to find the Trezevant name and the Hunt name listed on the monument plaque—commitment and devotion carrying on well into a second century after the revolution.

I cannot leave these Afterword pages without commenting on the significance of the character Yarico, as well as the Native Americans I visualized.

Yarico Harper's addition to my cast of characters came after I had committed myself to depicting my ancestors and to imagining a family of women who travel to Texas just as revolution is erupting.

But how could I conscientiously portray soldiers marching under the banner "Liberty or Death" without facing the discrepancy between that American pledge and the institution of slavery? No scholar or layperson will dispute the acceptance of slavery as commonplace in the South during the first half of the nineteenth century, but details I came across in my research still haunt me. In the same 1836 Southern newspapers that call on volunteers to help Texas settlers win independence, front-page rewards are offered for escaped slaves and for "dangerous abolitionists." Wanting to depict the era as honestly as possible, I could not ignore these painful references.

The same jarring juxtapositions occurred to me as I imagined what battalion volunteers saw on their journey to Texas of native people being forcibly displaced. So, the Tonkawa character Walk Far, the Creek neighbor Apokta, and the orphaned Comanche Youruh sprang from my desire to suggest the era's struggles from more than one perspective.

I cannot predict how future generations will look back on and judge our lives in the 21st century. Our virtues and accomplishments, I hope will not be romanticized. I doubt our flaws and transgressions will be overlooked.

Judith Austin Mills

Though certain I've brought my story-telling about this era to a close—unless Yarico's childhood and years up North compel me—I feel uplifted by a rising interest among readers in historical fiction. So many writers are taking the time to spotlight hallmark eras with objectivity and detail. So many readers credit more than one historical novel as having sparked their drive to learn more of our shared heritage.

However imperfect my depiction of our ancestors, I know that the extended Hunt family will continue their admiration for First Sergeant Francis Marion Hunt. May we all find new appreciation of the risks Colonel Juan Seguin took in championing an independent republic. Whether or not my imaginings of James Peter Trezevant fall short, his descendants are sure to lovingly maintain their records and recollections of his accomplishment—the college student who joined the Texas cause as a private and achieved officer ranks in less than a year.

While writing historical novels, I still think of two Thomas Grey lines as a kind of creed. A quotation from his "Elegy Written in a Country Churchyard" still seems a fitting close:

Perhaps in this neglected spot is laid

Some heart once pregnant with celestial fire.

Sources

Books and Periodicals

Bradle, William R. *Goliad, the Other Alamo*. Gretna, Louisiana: Pelican Publishing Company, 2007.

Brands, H. W. *Lone Star Nation*. New York: Random House, 2005.

De la Teja, Jesús. *A Revolution Remembered: The Memoirs and Selected Correspondence of Juan Seguin*. Austin: Texas State Historical Association, 2002.

Fehrenbach, T.R. *Lone Star: A History of Texas and the Texans*. New York: MacMillan Publishing, 1968.

Kerr, Jeffrey Stuart. *Seat of Empire*, Lubbock, TX: Texas Tech University Press, 2013.

Lamar, Howard R. *Texas Crossings: The Lone Star State and the American Far West, 1836—1986*. Austin: The University of Texas Press, 1991.

Moore, Stephen L. *Savage Frontier: Volume 1, 1835-1837*. Denton, TX: University of North Texas Press, 2002.

Newell, Rev. Chester. *Newell's History of the Texas Revolution*. Michelle M. Hass. Ed. Ingleside, TX: Copano Bay Press, 2015.

Scarborough, Jewel Davis. "The Georgia Battalion in the Texas Revolution: A Critical Study." *The Southwestern Historical Quarterly*, Vol. 63, No.4 (Apr., 1960). Austin: Texas State Historical Association, pp.511-532.

Online Sources

Davenport, Harbert. Notes from an Unfinished Study of Fannin and His Men, 1936. H. David Maxey, Editor. Web. 2011-2017.
https://tsaonline.207.200.58.4/supsites/fannin/hd_abou_htm/

Handbook of Texas Online. Web. 2011-2014.
https://www.tsha.utexas.edu/handbook/online/articles/

Index to Military Rolls of the Republic of Texas 1835-1845. Web. 2011-2017.
https://tshaonline.org/supsites/military

Lively, Garland. Colonel James Walker Fannin's Regiment at Goliad. Web. 2011-2017.
https://militaryhistoryonline.com

Macon Telegraph Archive (Georgia Historical Newspapers: Macon Telegraph). Web. 2011-2017.
https://www.galileo.usg.edu

San Jacinto Museum of History. The Battle/ The Monument. Web. 2015-2018.
https://sanjacinto-museum.org

Sons of Dewitt Colony. Web. 2011-2017.
https://tamu.edu/ccbn/dewitt/dewitt.htm

Trezevant, Robert (webmaster, researcher) and Richard Allen (researcher). The Georgia Battalion Project. Web. 2015-2018.
https://georgiabattalion.com

Trezevant, Robert W. Trezevant Family Project. Web. 2015-2018.
https://trezevantfamilyproject.com

About the Author

Judith Austin Mills Moved to Texas from up north when she was ten. The absence of distinct seasons and the spare, sprawling landscape in her adopted state may have been what taught her to look closely for signs of change. Her writing, both fiction and poetry, portrays awakenings. Since 2010, the complex shifts brought on by the Texas Revolution have fascinated her.

In 1989 at the University of Texas, the author earned her M.A. in English with a concentration in Creative Writing. Stories from her collection, *Lost Autumn Blues*, have appeared in literary journals. One piece from her poetry book *Accidental Joy* received a Pushcart nomination in 2015. The novel manuscript *Tripping Home* won the Writers' League of Texas mainstream competition in 2001.

Since retiring from the French classroom and from Austin Community College as an Adjunct, Associate Professor of English, Judith Austin Mills devotes her time to writing and to family. She is more and more convinced that hopeful change springs from a careful look at history.

Websites: judithaustinmills.wordpress.com and jaustinmills.info

The Dove Shall Fly

Monument to Joanna Troutman. Photo by author.

On a 2017 trip to Austin, Robert Trezevant visited the Texas State Cemetery. Here, he and the author of this book stand before the Joanna Troutman Memorial, where the names of their Texas Revolution ancestors appear—Trezevant and Hunt. Thanks to Jerry Ehernberger for taking a photo of these two family history enthusiasts, now friends.

www.ingramcontent.com/pod-product-compliance
Lightning Source LLC
Chambersburg PA
CBHW070049080526
44586CB00013B/981